| AUTHOR | CLASS No. |
|--------|-----------|
| | 510·7 |
| TITLE Mathematical reflections | BOOK No. |
| | 97245787 |

D0475716

# MATHEMATICAL REFLECTIONS

# MATHEMATICAL REFLECTIONS

*Contributions to mathematical thought and teaching, written in memory of*

## A. G. SILLITTO

*Edited by members of the*

## ASSOCIATION OF TEACHERS OF MATHEMATICS

CAMBRIDGE

AT THE UNIVERSITY PRESS, 1970

Published by the Syndics of the Cambridge University Press
Bentley House, 200 Euston Road, London N.W.1
American Branch: 32 East 57th Street, New York, N.Y.10022

© Cambridge University Press 1970

Library of Congress Catalogue Card Number: 72–85710

Standard Book Number: 521 07260 3 (cloth)
521 09582 4 (paper)

Printed in Great Britain
at the University Printing House, Cambridge
(Brooke Crutchley, University Printer)

# CONTENTS

# ACKNOWLEDGEMENTS

Thanks are due to the following for the permission to reproduce copyright material for this book: The Collection, The Museum of Modern Art, New York, for the 'Spiral Theme', 1941 by Naum Gobo; Percy Lund Humphries for '1932: Tragedy' from Paul Klee's *The Thinking Eye*; The Oriental Institute, University of Chicago for the photographs of The head of the statue of the god Abu, and A human-headed bull capital; Carl Strüwe, for the photograph of the bone structure of the human; Ullstein Bilderdienst, for the photograph of the eye of the cayman, and Dr Wolff and Trirshler O. H. G., for the photograph of the eye of the human, and finally Henry Moore, for photographs of the Two-piece reclining fig. No. 1, 1959.

# PREFACE

A. G. Sillitto died in August 1966. After his death those who were working with him had perforce to reconcile the cessation of community with the discussions, correspondence, debate, co-operation, inspiration in which they had been, and were, involved. That there was much to consider reveals Geoff Sillitto's range of activity even though actual published work is not extensive. Because of the vigour of his part in any dialogue we thought that the production of a collection of writings would stimulate exchanges in forms in which others could participate. Thus the major part of the contributions reflect this concern.

Sillitto was principally active in Scotland in a great variety of ways. Elsewhere he became a familiar figure in the Association of Teachers of Mathematics, with the School Mathematics Project and in international groups. The contributions are from those who knew him in these different, yet connected, fields. Only in the first three pieces has a more deliberately personal emphasis been introduced. An appreciation of his influence in Scottish schools is followed by his own hitherto unpublished 'Introduction to Trigonometry'. The nature of those personal relationships which develop in a creative atmosphere had a particular force for those who met him and in 'Idoneities' we find an echo of K. C. Hammer's aphorism that the most neglected existence theorem in mathematics is the existence of people.

So, though Sillitto's death was the impulse to produce this book, we anticipate that the contributions look forward to vigorous work and discussion. To help this the proceeds from the sale will go into a charitable fund established to further some purpose in mathematical education. This is expected to be in the form of encouragement and assistance of an individual, chosen from time to time, in forwarding work that he has chosen to do.

W.M.B.

1968

# A. G. SILLITTO'S INFLUENCE IN MATHEMATICS REFORM IN SCOTTISH SCHOOLS

## by A. G. ROBERTSON

It is no exaggeration to say that A. G. Sillitto was the mainspring in the movement during the past decade to revise the nature and the content of school courses in mathematics in Scotland. Conferences and courses arranged by Jordanhill College of Education, Glasgow, where he was principal lecturer in mathematics, encouraged and directed the rethinking that was evident in the late 1950s and early 1960s, and lectures and discussions in which he took part stimulated many students and teachers to look again at the mathematics they were learning and teaching.

In April 1963 the Scottish Education Department set up the Mathematics Syllabus Committee in order to review the school mathematics syllabuses; this committee consisted of fifteen principal teachers of mathematics in secondary schools, two College of Education lecturers, and four members of H.M. Inspectorate, and was later joined by four University lecturers. The Committee worked as a unit for the purpose of overall planning and policy making, but was divided into separate groups for detailed planning and writing. It was natural that A. G. Sillitto should have been given the task of directing the geometry development and writing team; his interest in new thinking and development in the content and teaching of mathematics in general and geometry in particular had long been apparent and his attitude to a new approach to school geometry had become clear, as the following extract from one of his early papers to the committee indicates:

The school approach to geometry should begin with events and objects in the real world. The sun, coins, clock faces, bicycle wheels illustrate the importance of the circle, and proclaim its essential properties; compasses bring the concept explicitly under control. Journeys which traverse the sea, deserts, open country, or even stretches of road free from 'bends', exhibit displacements and their composition; so also do wall paper or carpet or parquetry patterns: the transformation of 'translation' is an abstraction from such situations. A wheel on a shaft may be turned into any desired position, so that a boy can get the valve of the wheel of his upended bicycle into some convenient place; to every separate point of the plane the mental operation of 'rotation' about a point in the plane makes correspond one distinct image point. A 'figure', eventually, is a set of points—'reflection' a point by point mapping—but not in the first instance: we must first move some solids. Euclid wrote his book when he had reached the end of his geometry.

The principles here enunciated (naturally, without proof) apply as much to algebra and arithmetic as to geometry. There will come a time when our pupils will perform a mapping of $N$ into $R$, or $R$ into $N$, because they have come to like doing it; but in the first instance the exercise had better be about something other than itself—the magnitude of the interior angle of a regular $n$-gon, or the postage on letters of different weights.

The line of advance in geometry then will surely be from activities involving real things to the abstractions they suggest, coherent physical behaviour contributing to coherence of ideas, thinking in the early stages being 'thought-experiment' (Mach's word), 'interiorising' (Piaget's word) potential action. Thinking about 'figures' will usually be thinking in terms of potential operations on thought models, symbolising or representing the 'figures'.

At suitable times the geometrical forms of attention will be, not the figures, but the mental operations to which they are subjected (the transformations). This is one aspect of the stress on 'structure': the transformations are worth examining, because, few though they are, they describe all the geometry we do and unify our thinking about it.

Progress in mathematics is not merely a progress from easy exercises to complicated exercises, from short theorems to long ones. It should be a progress from the concrete to the abstract, from the particular to the general, from diversity (many little patterns) to unity (fewer, large patterns), from the comparatively unstructured to the comparatively structured.

Sillitto's interests and abilities ranged in considerable breadth and depth over a wide field of mathematics, so that his influence on the reshaping of school courses has been felt at every point. The mid 1960s were years of intense activity by members of the Syllabus Committee, with regular formal meetings, and irregular informal meetings in schools, houses, motor cars and railway sleeping cars. Helping to direct all this activity were Sillitto's enthusiastic drive, perceptive comments and criticisms, compelling arguments and boyish shafts of humour; at times his views were controversial, always they were sincerely held and clearly expressed.

The ideas and thinking and discussion and writing were crystallised in the *Alternative Ordinary grade syllabus* (*1965*) and *Higher grade syllabus* (*1967*) in mathematics, issued by the Scottish Certificate of Education Examination Board, and in the series of nine textbooks *Modern Mathematics for Schools* (presently being published by Blackie–Chambers) based on experimental material and methods tried out with a sample of 7000 Scottish pupils. But syllabus and textbook are merely the vehicles to take to pupil and teacher the kind of mathematics that must be brought to life in every classroom in a way that is indeed happening all over Scotland and in other countries where the Sillitto influence is helping to revive and revise the teaching and the learning of the subject. Sillitto's untimely death coincided with the infusion of new life which his immense, untiring efforts helped to give to mathematics in Scottish schools.

The section that follows is an *Introduction to Trigonometry* for pupils aged 14–15 years, a first, untouched draft he wrote for the Scottish project, but which was too late to be included in the general writing; it clearly illustrates his distinctive methods and approach.

# AN INTRODUCTION TO TRIGONOMETRY

*A draft chapter by* A. G. SILLITTO

## I PATTERN AND PERIODIC CHANGE

[*Outline only. Presentation mainly through diagrams. Introduce 'period'*]

*Patterns that recur in space:* wall papers; linear patterns (cf. 'Reflection') friezes, also on vases, in architecture; finite patterns especially cyclical—swastika, Isle of Man symbol; standing wave (wave on canal).

*Patterns that recur in time:* passage of trains on Milngavie–Springburn suburban railway line (especially on Sundays); phases of moon; positions of hour (minute, second) hand of clock; school time-table; basic dance figures (waltz, polka, military two-step, Highland Schottische, etc.); poem stanzas (Gray's *Elegy*, Burns' stanza); hoof-beats of cantering horse; drum (or double-bass) 'backing' of bagpipe (or pop) tune; water level—tidal.

*Patterns in space constructed to simulate or represent patterns in time:* Milngavie–Springburn distance-time graph; school time-table; 'length of daylight' graph; tide (or wave) level graph.

*Mental patterns* (especially mathematical):
   Squares (mod 10) 01496569410149...; cubes (mod 5) 01324013240...
   Squares (mod 3) 011011011... (cf. waltz); cubes (mod 3) 012012012...
   Digits in recurring decimals, e.g. $\frac{4}{333}$ (cf. cubes mod 3), $\frac{4}{11}, \frac{1}{7}$.
   Powers of 4 (mod 10) 464646...; powers of 3 (mod 10) 39713971...

## 2 A MODEL OF AN IMPORTANT KIND OF PERIODIC CHANGE

Some of the patterns we looked at in section 1 are so important, in everyday life and in mathematics, that we are going to examine them more closely. Look again at the length of daylight graph, and the tide-level graph; and at the 'standing wave' situation. This pattern occurs in a wide variety of different contexts.

   We shall construct a model to enable us to study its structure.

5

*Stage 1.* Set up a vertical rod near the edge of a record-player turntable. (Alternatively, mount a bicycle wheel horizontally and fix a vertical rod to the rim.) From some distance away, observe the changes in the *apparent* distance of the rod from the central pin; note the recurring sequence of events.

What we observe here is not the actual distance of rod from pin (which of course is constant) but how far to left or right of the pin it is: this distance is called the 'resolved part' or 'component' of the actual distance on this sideways direction.

*Stage 2.* Now we make a desk or drawing board or blackboard model of the stage 1 situation (see fig. 1).

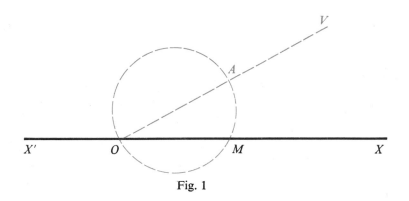

Fig. 1

*X'OX* is drawn on paper. A sheet of tracing paper or cellulose acetate pinned at *O* has drawn on it a long line *OV*; *OA* is a suitable unit of length; a circle with *OA* as diameter is drawn on the acetate.

Initially *OV* coincides with *OX*. In all positions (except one) of the tracing, *X'X* cuts the circumference at a second point (not named on the model) whose tracing name is *M*. (*M*, like *A*, is a variable, taking an infinity of positions with respect to the paper.)

## *Exercise 1*

1 Rotate the tracing round *O*; observe the succession of positions of the point *M*. Describe the locus of *M*.

2 Discuss the relationship between the locus of *M*, and the observed behaviour of the rod on the turntable in stage 1.

Note that the model serves as a *plan* of the turntable; *O* corresponds to the pin, *A* to the rod. The observer of the turntable is away in the direction of *AM* produced. The line *X′X* is the 'direction of sideways movement' of the rod.

Since *OA* is a diameter of the circle, angle *AMO* is a right angle.

We want to consider the length of *OM*, which is the 'projection' of the segment *OA* on the line *X′X*, or the 'component', in the *X′X* direction, of the vector represented by **OA**.

With the rod on the turntable, we noticed 'distance to right' and 'distance to left'. Here, then, we want to consider *OM* as a *directed* line segment. For example, when the length of *OM* is 0·8, and *M* is on the *X* side of *O*, we may agree to say 'measure of *OM* = +0·8'; for a point *N* 0·6 from *O* on the *X′* side, the measure of *ON* = −0·6.

## Exercise 2

1 In fig. 2, name carefully the directed line segment which is the projection of *OA* (or: which represents the component of *OA*) on *X′X*. In each case say whether the measure of the projection is positive or negative, on the assumption that *OX* is the 'positive half' of the number line *X′X*.

2 See fig. 1, where *OA* is of unit length. Consider the line segment *OA* to make a complete revolution, anti-clockwise, about *O*, from *OX* round to *OX*. Copy and complete this table:

| As *OA* rotates through | the measure of *OM* is positive/ negative, and increases/decreases from 1 to |
|---|---|
| (i)   the first 90° | |
| (ii)  the next 90° | |
| (iii) the third 90° | |
| (iv)  the last 90° | |

3 From the illustrations in section 1, pick out one or more graphs or diagrams which seem to indicate the same *kind* of sequence of events as you have reported in question 2.

4 Draw a graph to illustrate more accurately the way in which the measure of *OM* depends on the magnitude of the *angle* through which *OA* has rotated from *OX*. (Draw a line *X′OX*. Take 2·5 inches as unit length for *OA*. Insert lines at 30° intervals to indicate a sequence of positions of *OA*. Measure off in inches correct to two decimal places, and multiply by 0·4 to convert to scale.)

Draw a smooth curve and compare it with some of these in section 1.

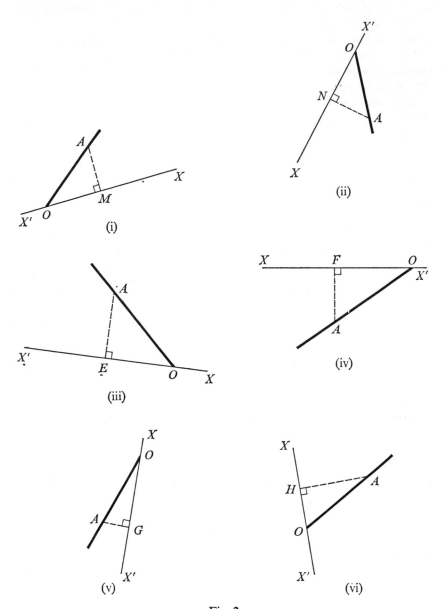

Fig. 2

## 3  COSINE: AN IMPORTANT PERIODIC FUNCTION

In section 1, the 'hours of daylight' graph was restricted to a single year. Obviously, the same sequence or cycle will be very closely repeated the following year and each succeeding year; and indeed it will have occurred in the preceding years as well. What would the graph for a large number of years look like? What is the 'period' of this pattern?

In the same way, the graph of section 2 can easily be extended. Again, suppose $OA$ begins rotating from $OX$, and continues to rotate beyond the 360° position, passing through positions corresponding to rotations of 390°, 420°, 450°, 480°, 510°, 540° 570°, 600°, 630°, 660°, 690°, 720°, 750°, .... Refer to the diagram and table of section 2, question 2, and extend the table to include the measures of $OM$ for these angles.

And we can extend the graph to the left, to include negative angles, if we start with $OA$ on $OX$ and let it rotate *clockwise*, passing through positions corresponding to rotations of $-30°$, $-60°$, $-90°$, ..., $-360°$, $-390°$, ...; each time noting the measure of $OM$.

An extended graph is shown in fig. 3.

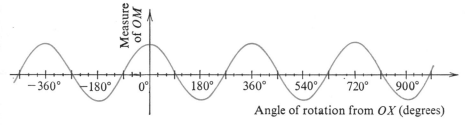

Fig. 3

## Exercise 3

1  What is the 'period' of the cycle of changes in the measure of $OM$?

2  Discuss how the extended graph is related to the movement of the vertical rod on the turntable.

3  Suppose the measure of $OM$, after a rotation of 116°, is $+0.9$. What will it be, after rotations of 476°, 836°, $-244°$?

4  Suppose you had lost your copy of the extended graph, but had a tracing of that part of it for angles of rotation between 28° and 388°. Explain how, with the help of a piece of carbon paper, you could reproduce as much of the graph as you wanted.

   Name some other 'angle-intervals' that would have served your purpose as well as the interval from 28° to 388°.

5 In question 4 you were really investigating some of the 'translations' that conserve the pattern of the graph.

(a) The graph is also conserved by reflection in certain lines. Locate half a dozen lines that are axes of bilateral symmetry of the (infinite) graph.

(b) The graph is also conserved by halfturns about certain points. Locate half a dozen points that are centres of symmetry of the infinite graph.

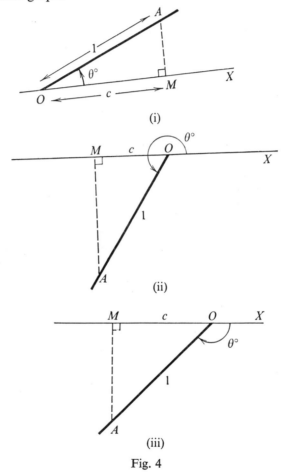

Fig. 4

We have seen that graphs of the type we have been looking at arise in situations quite different from the models or diagrams on which our graph was based. What is common to all these situations is that there is a 'first number' (the degree-measure of an angle of rotation; the date on the calendar) and a certain 'second number' (the measure of a line-segment; the duration of daylight) which is 'uniquely determined' by the first.

In our case, we can talk of a *function* which maps 'degree-measure of angle *XOA*' on to 'measure of segment *OM*'. The name of this function is 'cosine' (abbreviated to cos).

In fig. 4, with $OA = 1$ as before, $OM = c$, and measure of $\angle XOA$ equal to $\theta°$, we would write 'cos $\theta = c$'.

(*Note:* in (i) $\theta$ and $c$ are both positive numbers; in (ii) $\theta$ is positive, $c$ is negative; in (iii) $\theta$ and $c$ are both negative.)

Values of the cosine function, for angles from 0 to 90°, are tabulated in your book of tables, correct to three or four decimal places.

## *Exercise 4*

1 Read off from your tables:

cos 0°; cos 90°; cos 60°; cos 30°; cos 30·5°; cos 30·8°.

Check that your graph gives answers in fair agreement with these.

2 Read off from your tables the value of $\theta$ for which

$$\cos \theta° = 0·906; \qquad \cos \theta° = 0·910; \qquad \cos \theta° = 0·911;$$
$$\cos \theta° = 0·5; \qquad \cos \theta° = 0·05; \qquad \cos \theta° = 0·005.$$

3 Using the fact that cos is a periodic function, with period 360, write down two more angles (one positive, one negative) which would have the same cosine-values as those listed in question 1.

4 Using the fact that cos is a periodic function with period 360, write down two more angle-sizes (one positive, one negative) for which cos $\theta°$ would take the values given in question 2.

5 See fig. 5. $OA_1$, $OA_2$, $OA_3$, $OA_4$ are of unit length; $X'OX$ is an axis of symmetry. Assuming that cos 35° = 0·766, write down cos $(-35°)$,

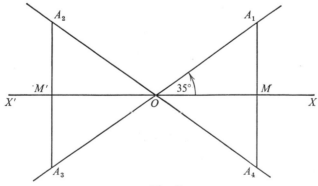

Fig. 5

cos 215°, cos 145°, cos 325°, cos (−145°), cos (−215°). Check by looking at, or sketching, an appropriate graph.

6 Use tables and a sketch like fig. 5 to obtain values for cos 70°, cos 110°, cos 250°, cos 290°, cos (−70°), cos (−250°), cos (−110°), cos (−290°).

7 Find as many angles as you can, between −360° and +360°, for which (i) cos $\theta° = 0.966$, (ii) cos $\theta° = -0.743$.

## 4  SOME POLAR GRAPHS

We have seen that, instead of using cartesian co-ordinates $(x, y)$ to specify the position of a point on the plane, we could use 'polar co-ordinates' $[r, \theta]$.

Thus the points $P[2, 40°]$ and $Q[1.5, 160°]$ are indicated in fig. 6 in which $OP = 2$, $\angle XOP = 40°$ and $OQ = 1.5$, $\angle XOQ = 160°$.

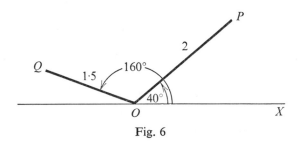

Fig. 6

## Exercise 5

1 (a) Which of the following co-ordinate-pairs indicate the point $Q$ of fig. 6? (i) [1.5, 520°], (ii) [1.5, −200°], (iii) [1.5, −20°].
   (b) Which of the following co-ordinate-pairs indicate the point $P$ of fig. 6? (i) [2, 320°], (ii) [2, −320°], (iii) [2, 400°].

2 Make a reasonable copy of fig. 6. Produce $PO$ to $P'$, making $OP'$ equal in length to $OP$; and produce $QO$ to $Q'$, making $OQ'$ equal in length to $OQ$.
   Write down three polar co-ordinate-pairs for $P'$, and three for $Q'$.

3 It is agreed that [2, 40°] refers to the point $P$, and that [−2, 40°] refers to $P'$ (because it indicates a rotation of +40° from $OX$, then a step of 2 units, not from $O$ to $P$, but in the opposite direction).
   Check that [+2, 220°] refers to $P'$, and hence [−2, 220°] refers to $P$. Write down, with negative $r$, co-ordinate-pairs for $Q$ and $Q'$.
   Just as an equation in $x$ and $y$ defines a set of points (or locus) in the cartesian plane, so an equation in $r$ and $\theta$ defines a locus in polar co-ordinates.

4   Copy and complete the following table, which refers to the equation $r = \frac{1}{90}\theta$.

| $\theta$ | 0 | 45 | 90 | 135 | 180 | 225 | 270 | 315 | 360 |
|---|---|---|---|---|---|---|---|---|---|
| $r$ | 0 | 0·5 | | | | | | | 4·0 |

Draw the polar graph corresponding to the equation, by plotting the number pairs in the table as polar co-ordinates, and joining the points by a smooth curve to obtain a 'spiral'. (Place $O$ in the centre and take $OX$ in the direction of the *length* of the page. Take 1 inch as the unit for $r$.)

5   With $r = \frac{1}{90}\theta$ again, extend the table thus:

| $\theta$ | 0 | $-45$ | $-90$ | — | — | — | — | $-360$ |
|---|---|---|---|---|---|---|---|---|
| $r$ | 0 | $-0·5$ | | | | | | |

Plot these points on the same page as for question 4. (As a check on correct plotting, note that these points are the images of those of question 4, in the line $\theta = 90$.) Complete the graph.

6   Draw the polar graph of the equation $r = 2\cos\theta°$ using a table thus:

| $\theta$ | 0 | 30 | 60 | 90 | 120 | 150 | 180 | 210 | 240 | — | — | 360 |
|---|---|---|---|---|---|---|---|---|---|---|---|---|
| $r$ | 2 | | | 0 | | $-1·73$ | | $-1·73$ | | | | |

Take 1 inch as the unit for $r$.

In plotting the points, note particularly what happens with $\theta > 180$. Consider also what would happen (i) for negative $\theta$, (ii) for $\theta > 360$. Why must the locus be a circle?

7   Draw the polar graph of the equation $r = 2\cos 2\theta°$, taking $\theta$ at intervals of $22\frac{1}{2}$ from 0 to 360. Include a $2\theta$ line in your table. Scale for $r$: 1 inch $\leftrightarrow$ 1 unit. (Your graph will be 'cruciform', like the arrangement of the petals of a wallflower.)

8   Draw the polar graph of the equation $r = 2\cos 3\theta°$, taking $\theta$ at intervals of 15 from 0 to 180. (Your graph this time will be a 'flower' with three petals. If you want the common five-petal arrangement, try $r = 2\cos 5\theta°$, at intervals of 9°. Could you obtain six petals?)

13

## 5 COS $\theta°$ AS MULTIPLIER: CALCULATIONS

Fig. 7 shows the basic diagram of section 2 subjected to a process of 'enlargement'. $PQ$ is perpendicular to $OX$. The measures of $OA$ and $OP$ are $l$ and $r$ respectively.

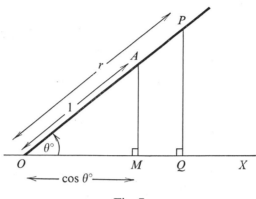

Fig. 7

From similar triangles, $\dfrac{OQ}{OM} = \dfrac{OP}{OA}$; hence the measure of $OQ$ is $r\cos\theta°$; and, in general, the component in the $OX$ direction of the vector represented by **OA** has measure $r\cos\theta°$.

Again, in fig. 8, $PQ$ is a directed line segment of length $r$, representing a vector **PQ**, making an angle $\theta°$ with $OX$; and $LM$ is its projection on $OX$. In each case, the measure of the projection $LM$ is $r\cos\theta°$.

*Example 1:* Fig. 9 represents the track of an aircraft which flies from $O$ to $A$, a distance of 120 miles, on a bearing of 330°; then from $A$ to $B$, 250 miles, on a bearing of 130°. Find how far east $B$ is from $O$; also how far south $B$ is from $O$.

*Easting:* $OA$ makes 60° with the westward direction, so the projection of $OA$ on the line $OE$ is $120\cos 60°$ miles westwards; and $AB$ makes 40° with the eastward direction, so the projection of $AB$ on the line $OE$ is $250\cos 40°$ miles eastwards.

Hence the total easting is

$$250\cos 40° - 120\cos 60° \text{ miles} = 250 \times 0\cdot766 - 120 \times 0\cdot500 \text{ miles}$$

$$= 130 \text{ miles approximately.}$$

14

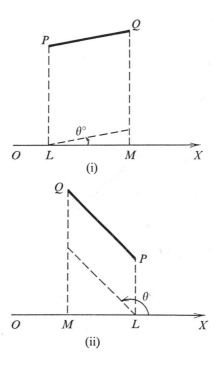

(i)

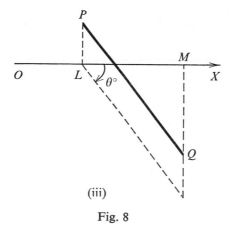

(ii)

(iii)

Fig. 8

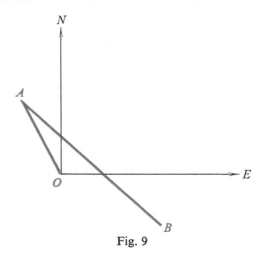

Fig. 9

*Northing:* The projection of *OA* on *ON* gives a northing of 120 cos 30° miles, and the projection of *AB* gives a southing of 250 cos 50° miles.

Hence the total southing is

$$250 \cos 50° - 120 \cos 30° \text{ miles} = 250 \times 0\cdot643 - 120 \times 0\cdot866 \text{ miles}$$
$$= 57 \text{ miles approximately.}$$

*Note:* This example will be repeated in section 7.

## Exercise 6

1   Work out, correct to two significant figures the easting and the northing of each of the following displacements:
  (i)   72 miles, 043°;   (ii)   72 miles, 137°;
  (iii)   72 miles, 223°;   (iv)   72 miles, 317°;
  (v)   100 miles, 100°;   (vi)   200 miles, 200°;
  (vii)   300 miles, 300°.

2   A large public clock, in which the hour hand is 10 inches long and the minute hand 15 inches long, has stopped in the 'four o'clock' position. Calculate the *length* of the projection of each hand on (i) a horizontal line, (ii) a vertical line, (iii) the '10 o'clock, 4 o'clock' line, (iv) the '12 o'clock , 6 o'clock' line, (v) the '11 o'clock, 5 o'clock' line.

3   Work out, correct to two significant figures, the easting and northing resulting from each of the following pairs of displacements:
  (i)   70 miles, 310°, followed by 100 miles, 080°;
  (ii)   70 miles, 130°, followed by 100 miles, 010°;
  (iii)   160 yards, 200°, followed by 800 yards, 320°.

16

Until now, our calculations in right-angled triangles have been restricted to finding the length of the third side by means of Pythagoras' Theorem. Using a table of cosines, we can solve problems involving angles which formerly we could only tackle by scale drawing. See fig. 10. Considering the length of the projection of $AB$ on $AC$ and on $BC$, we have, in (i) $b = \cos A$ and $a = \cos B$; and, in (ii) $b = c\cos A$ and $a = c\cos B$.

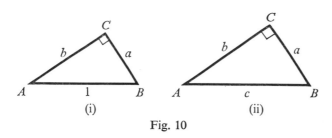

(i)                    (ii)

Fig. 10

*Example 2 (a):* In fig. 10 (ii), suppose $c = 12$, and angle $BAC = 28°$. Calculate $b$ and $a$.

$b = c\cos A = 12\cos 28°$, etc.; and $a = 12\cos 62°$, etc.

(*Note.* Knowing $c$ and $b$, we could obtain $a$ by Pythagoras' Theorem; but that would be more laborious.)

*Example 2 (b):* In fig. 10 (ii), suppose $c = 19$, $b = 15$. Calculate the size of $\angle ABC$, and hence find $a$.

Knowing $b$ and $c$, we first find $BAC$.

$b = c\cos A$, hence $15 = 19\cos A$ and $\cos A = \frac{15}{19} = 0\cdot789$, and $A = 37\cdot9°$. Hence $B = 52\cdot1°$, and $a = c\cos B = 19 \times 0\cdot614 = 11\cdot7$

*Example 2 (c):* In fig. 10 (ii), suppose $b = 8\cdot4$, $B = 20\frac{1}{2}°$. Calculate $c$ and $a$.

Knowing $b$, we use $b = c\cos A$; and $A = 69\frac{1}{2}°$.

Hence $8\cdot4 = c \times 0\cdot350$ and $c = \dfrac{8\cdot4}{0\cdot35} = 24$ approximately. Hence $a = c\cos B = 24 \times 0\cdot937 = 22\cdot5$ approximately.

## Exercise 7

1  Find the sizes of the acute angles in the right-angled triangles whose sides measure: (i) 3, 4, 5; (ii) 5, 12, 13; (iii) 8, 15, 17; (iv) 20, 21, 29.

2  A ladder 20 feet long leans against a wall, and makes an angle of 55° with the ground. How far is the foot of the ladder from the wall, and how far up the wall does it reach?

3  The diameter $PQ$ of a circle measures 4 inches. $PR$ is a chord, and angle $RPQ$ measures 42°. Calculate the length of $PR$ and $QR$.

4  A tangent $AT$ is drawn to a circle with centre $O$ and diameter 3·6 inches, from a point $A$ 4 inches from $O$. Calculate the size of $\angle OAT$ and the length of $AT$.

## 6  SINE: ANOTHER PERIODIC FUNCTION

We shall require again the model of section 2, but this time the traced circle rotates over a pair of perpendicular lines $X'OX$, $Y'OY$, as illustrated in fig. 11.

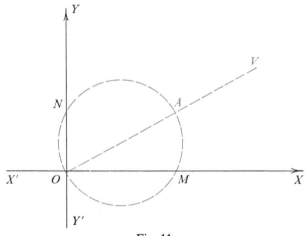

Fig. 11

As before, $OA$ is of unit length.

Rotate the tracing anticlockwise about $O$, and observe as before the periodic variation in position of the intersection $M$ of the circumference and the line $X'X$.

Observe also the point $N$, the intersection of the circumference and $Y'Y$.

## Exercise 8

1  (i)  Where is $N$ when $M$ is as far as possible from $O$?
   (ii)  Where may $N$ be when $M$ coincides with $O$?

2  Complete the following sentences. (Anticlockwise rotation assumed.)
   (i)  As $M$ recedes from $O$ towards the right, $N$ ... from below.
   (ii)  As $M$ approaches $O$ from the right, $N$ ...
   (iii)  As $M$ recedes from $O$ towards the left, $N$ ...
   (iv)  As $M$ approaches $O$ from the left, $N$ ...

18

3 For what positions of the line *OV* will *M* and *N* be equally far from *O*? Make a general statement about their directions of motion, as *OV* passes through these positions.

*Note:* In section 2, we described the directed line segment *OM* as the *projection* of *OA* on *X'X*, or the *component*, in the *X'X* direction, of the vector represented by **OA**.

In the same way, the directed line segment *ON* is the *projection* of *OA* on *Y'Y*, or the component, in the *Y'Y* direction, of the vector represented by **OA**.

As usual, the measure of *ON* will be taken as positive when *N* is on the *Y* side of *O*, and negative when *N* is on the *Y'* side of *O*.

4 Consider the line segment *OA* to make a complete revolution, anticlockwise, about *O*, from *OX* round to *OX*. Copy and complete this table:

| As *OA* rotates through | the measure of *ON* is positive/ negative, and increases/decreases from 0 to |
|---|---|
| (i)   the first 90° | |
| (ii)  the next 90° | |
| (iii) the third 90° | |
| (iv)  the last 90° | |

5 Discuss how the graph of the measure of *ON*, against angle of rotation of *OA* from *OX*, will resemble, and how it will differ from, the graphs drawn in sections 2 and 3.

6 Draw, with the same axes, graphs showing how the measure of *OM* *and* of *ON* depend on the angle of rotation of *OA*, from 0 to 360°.

7 The graph for *ON*, like that for *OM* in section 3 can be extended indefinitely in both directions.
   (*a*) Verify that the *ON* graph is a pattern of period 360, i.e. the pattern is conserved by translations along the 'angle' axis, whose magnitudes are integral multiples of 360.
   (*b*) Locate half-a-dozen lines that are axes of bilateral symmetry of the (infinite) *ON* graph.
   (*c*) Locate half-a-dozen points that are centres of symmetry of the infinite graph.

*Note:* In section 3, we named 'cosine' the function which maps 'degree measure of angle *XOA*' on to 'measure of segment *OM*'. In the same way, we name 'sine' the function which maps 'degree measure of angle *XOA*' on to measure of segment *ON*. 'Sine' is often abbreviated to 'sin'.

19

In fig. 12, where the measures of $OA$, $OM$, $ON$ and $\angle XOA$ are 1, $c$, $s$ and $\theta$ respectively, we would write

$$\cos\theta° = c \quad \text{and} \quad \sin\theta° = s.$$

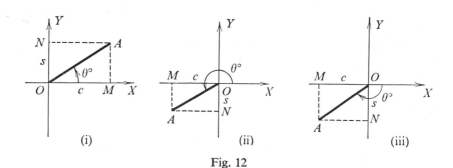

Fig. 12

(In (i), $\theta$, $c$ and $s$ are all positive; in (ii), $\theta$ is positive, $c$ and $s$ are negative; in (iii), all three are negative.)

## Exercise 9

1 Read off from your tables:

$\sin 0°$; $\sin 90°$; $\sin 30°$; $\sin 60°$; $\sin 59°$; $\sin 59·5°$; $\sin 59·2°$.

Compare your answers with the answers to exercise 4, question 1.

2 Read off from your tables the value of $\theta$ for which

$$\sin\theta° = 0·906; \quad \sin\theta° = 0·910; \quad \sin\theta° = 0·911;$$
$$\sin\theta° = 0·5; \quad \sin\theta° = 0·05; \quad \sin\theta° = 0·005.$$

Compare your answers with those for exercise 4, question 2.

3 Using the fact that sin is a periodic function with period 360, write down two more angles (one positive, one negative) which would have the same sine-values as those listed in question 1.

4 Using the fact that sin is a periodic function with period 360, write down two more angle-sizes (one positive, one negative) for which $\sin\theta°$ would take the values given in question 2.

5 See fig. 13. $OA_1$, $OA_2$, $OA_3$, $OA_4$ are of unit length.

$XOX'$ and $YOY'$ are axes of symmetry.

Assuming that $\sin 35° = 0·574$, write down $\sin(-35°)$, $\sin 215°$, $\sin 145°$, $\sin 325°$, $\sin(-145°)$, $\sin(-215°)$.

Check by looking at, or sketching, an appropriate graph.

6  Use tables, and a sketch like fig. 13, to obtain values for $\sin 70°$, $\sin 110°$, $\sin 250°$, $\sin 290°$, $\sin(-70°)$, $\sin(-250°)$, $\sin(-110°)$, $\sin(-290°)$.

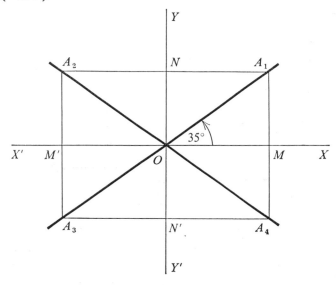

**Fig. 13**

7  Find as many angles as you can, between $-360°$ and $+360°$, for which (i) $\sin\theta = 0.966$; (ii) $\sin\theta° = -0.743$.

8  Draw the polar graph of the equation $r = 2\sin\theta°$, taking $\theta$ at intervals of 30 from 0 to 360.

Why must the locus be a circle?

9  Draw the polar graph of the equation $r = 2\sin 2\theta°$, taking $\theta$ at intervals of 45 from 0 to 360.

10  Draw the polar graph of the equation $r = 2\sin 3\theta°$, taking $\theta$ at intervals of 15 from 0 to 180.

## 7  SIN $\theta°$ AS MULTIPLIER: CALCULATIONS

Fig. 14 shows the line segment $OA$, of unit length, projected on to $OX$ and $OY$, so that the measures of $OM$ and $ON$ are $\cos\theta°$ and $\sin\theta°$.

This part of the figure has been 'enlarged', so that $OP$ measures $r$ units, and the diagram contains two pairs of similar triangles.

We saw in section 5 that the measure of $OQ$ is $r\cos\theta°$.

Also, since $\dfrac{OR}{ON} = \dfrac{OP}{OA}$, the measure of $OR$ is $r\sin\theta°$.

21

These important formulae give the measure of the projections on the axes $OX$ and $OY$ of a line segment of length $r$ which makes an angle $\theta°$ with $OX$.

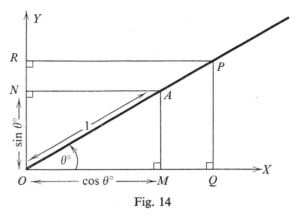

Fig. 14

*Example 1* (from section 5): Fig. 15 represents the track of an aircraft which flies from $O$ to $A$, a distance of 120 miles, on a bearing of 330°; then from $A$ to $B$, 250 miles, on a bearing of 130°.

Find how far east, and how far south, $B$ is from $O$.

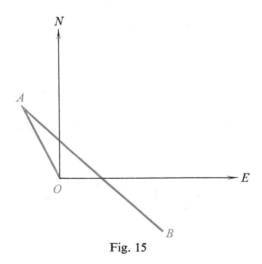

Fig. 15

In section 5, we calculated both easting and northing by using cosines. Here is another way. We use only the angles $OA$ and $AB$ make with the west–east line, using cosines for 'easting' and sines for 'northing'. To see whether steps are to be added or subtracted, we refer to the diagram.

22

*Working:* $OA$ makes $60°$ with the westward direction, giving a 'westing' of $120° \cos 60°$ miles and a northing of $120 \sin 60°$ miles.

$AB$ makes $40°$ with the eastward direction, giving an easting of $250 \cos 40°$ and a southing of $250 \sin 40°$ miles.

Hence total easting $= 250 \cos 40° - 120 \cos 60°$ miles
and total southing $= 250 \sin 40° - 120 \sin 60°$ miles.

*Another method:* We begin by noting that $OA$ makes an angle $+120°$ with $OE$, and $AB$ makes an angle of $-40°$, (or $+320°$), with $OE$. Having got this right, we need not look at the figure again.

Total *easting* $= 120 \cos 120° + 250 \cos(-40°)$ miles
and total *northing* $= 120 \sin 120° + 250 \sin(-40°)$ miles.

## Exercise 10

1  Rework question 1 of exercise 6, using cosines for easting and sines for northing.
2  Rework question 3 of exercise 6, setting out the solution as in the 'working' above.
3  Complete the working for the 'other method' shown above, using sketches like that of exercise 9, question 5, in order to replace the angles $120°$ and $-40°$ by angles between $0°$ and $90°$.
4  Rework exercise 6, question 4, by the 'other method'.
5  Check that, in fig. 16 (i),

$$b = \cos A, \quad a = \cos B$$

and
$$b = \sin B, \quad a = \sin A.$$

Check that, in fig. 16 (ii), $b = c \cos A$ and also $b = c \sin B$; and write write down two corresponding expressions for $a$.

In either figure, prove that $(\sin A)^2 + (\cos A)^2 = 1$.

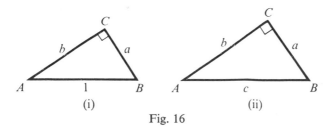

Fig. 16

6  Use the table of sines to find the sizes of the acute angles in the right-angled triangles whose sides measure: (i) 3, 4, 5; (ii) 5, 12, 13; (iii) 8, 15, 17; (iv) 20, 21, 29.

7  Rework exercise 7, question 2, using the table of sines.

8  Rework exercise 7, question 3, using the table of sines.

9  Rework exercise 7, question 4, using the table of sines.

10 In figure 17, $A = 60°$, $B = 70°$, $C = 50°$.

    (i)  Using sine or cosine tables in triangle $ABD$, calculate $x$ and $h$.

    (ii) Using sine or cosine tables in triangle $ACD$, calculate $y$ and $b$. Hence find $a$.

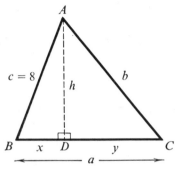

Fig. 17

11 Redraw the triangle of question 10, but this time draw the altitude from $B$, not $A$. By methods similar to those of question 10, calculate $b$ and $a$.

12 A triangle $ABC$ has $A = 48°$, $B = 75°$, $C = 57°$, $a = 12$. Draw an altitude and calculate $b$ and $c$.

13 Rework question 12, using a different altitude.

## 8  THE TANGENT FUNCTION

[Summary.  (i)   Introduce $\tan\theta$ as $\sin\theta/\cos\theta$.

        (ii)  Illustration via the traced-circle model.

        (iii) Graph, periodicity, symmetries.

        (iv)  Calculations leading up to solving an acute-angled triangle, given two sides and the included angle.]

# IDONEITIES

by D. G. TAHTA

I first met Geoff Sillitto in 1962, when a group of about twenty A.T.M. members met at Leicester to write the book, *Some Lessons in Mathematics*. It was hoped to produce a joint book rather than a collection of individual pieces but there was little or no precedent to help twenty individuals, some of them meeting for the first time, to do this. The being together while we were writing was in itself an exploration in communication. If anything was achieved in this exploration it was surely in those curiously intimate groups that met towards the end of the week to discuss, to tear to pieces and reconstruct, the first drafts. Out of a kaleidoscopic medley of memories I recall most vividly a group that discussed some material on vectors. I was making some tired phrases, about the need to realise the vector space notion in some other framework than that of things with magnitude and direction, when I became strongly aware that the quiet Scotsman, with the pawky manner and twinkling eyes, nestling incongruously in an old leather armchair, was listening to me very carefully. It can be very disconcerting to be listened to, for it makes you listen to yourself. Most people merely hear, but Geoff Sillitto always listened. Perhaps this is why he had so much to say for anyone who could listen in turn. How could I continue repeating stale thoughts about vector spaces in the presence of a man who, I suddenly realised, knew intimately things that the rest of us in the group were just beginning to explore. Yet it was not like that. If in the middle of the arm-waving he had pointed, it was with patience—and, yes, with love. There had to be dialogue so that we could all learn. And Geoff was a modest and humble learner; in the discussion on vector spaces we were all teaching each other and ourselves.

Geoff was a quiet catalyst for many during the writing week. In turn, he himself was stimulated to produce some of his best work. His written contributions to the book can now be seen as an important part of his whole contribution to geometry teaching. Of all his published work, a section from *Some Lessons in Mathematics* is still for me the most illuminating. In a lesson on the symmetries of the rectangle there is a discussion of where different corners go, when a rectangle is replaced in some way into the space it originally occupied. 'Where is corner *X* now? In corner *H*. *And it fits*. And corner *H*? In corner *X*. *And it fits*.' The notion of 'fit' was

25

2-2

the subject of other dialogues I was fortunate to have with him after Leicester. I was not, therefore, surprised to find that it is a central idea in the work of Gonseth, an author who, those who were at the A.T.M. Winchester conference in 1964 will know, had influenced Geoff's thinking considerably. I cannot state my meaning, let alone his, explicitly. And that fits—according to the following story translated from Gonseth.

A man called in some workmen. 'Build me without delay the house of my dreams', he said and left without another word. The workmen consulted amongst themselves and one of them went after the man. 'We have to have a plan of the house you want. Without this plan and without someone to tell us what material to order and how to dispose it we cannot undertake the work you require.'

The man was persuaded. He went to find an architect. 'I want to build the house of my dreams. But without a plan my workers don't know how to start. Would you make one without delay?' And he left without saying more. The architect prepared a plan of some sort. What else could he do? The man returned to inquire about his plan. 'Someone very ordinary could use this perhaps, but it is not the plan of my dreams,' he said and left. The architect thought—he needs a metaphysical house. With much trouble he drew up a plan determined, in whole and in part, by absolute rules like the golden section. The client was recalled. 'It is a coffin for a dead dream,' he said, 'I doubt whether anyone would want to house his life's dream in that.' The architect was vexed. 'How could I imagine a plan to correspond to your dream if you neglect to tell it me. And besides, can your dream be realised?'

'Calm yourself', said the man whom experience had made wise, 'I don't mind telling you my wants. I don't even expect you to realise them absolutely.'

They agreed then to a way of confronting the dream with reality. Together they examined the available material, together they thought up the way it should be assembled. After lots of attempts, the man declared, 'This last plan will do. I cannot wait indefinitely for a better.' The architect directed the work without hesitation. He knew in advance what were the *suitable* materials to use, what were the *fitting* ways of putting them together. He knew the means and ends of his activity. But how could he have known them to begin with?

*Moral*: a preliminary assumption does not justify itself during preliminaries. It proves its *idoneity* by its applications and its consequences.[1]

We met again at Birmingham at the A.T.M. annual conference in 1964. Again I choose some single snaps from a wide selection. The memories jostle and suddenly still. A small group is waiting for the evening meal. Someone is talking about line-reflections. He is making the image of a point in a line by drawing a perpendicular. Geoff leans over and suggests marking the equal distances along another line through the point. 'You

---

[1] F. Gonseth: *La géométrie et la problème de l'espace*, vol. 1, p. 56, Neuchatel, 1945. The original French uses the word 'idoine'. An entry in the shorter O.E.D. reads: Idoneous. Now rare. 1615. Apt, fit, suitable...idoneity.

can't do that,' says someone. 'Why not?', asks Geoff and there is genuine inquiry in his voice. The group discusses the notion of symmetry. There seem to be many more possibilities than we thought. (Cf. fig. 11, facing p. 32.) Again the feeling that Geoff is engaged in the exploration as a partner. It is important to emphasize this. After a group of people have achieved some insight it is easy to wonder at the difficulties that seemed to have been in the way at the start. Yet real anxieties are aroused when horizons are extended. Geoff was often the one who said 'you can't do that', and it needs to be said as part of the dialogue that releases the 'why not?'.

A further stimulus to extend my thinking arose from the fact that Geoff was on the platform as chairman when I gave a lecture to the conference. Trying to say something about the actuality of mathematics I quoted the comments of a seven-year-old girl to whom I had shown a circle with some lines, red ones intersecting the circle and green ones not doing so.

'What could you say about the red lines?'
'Well, they are fighting—sort of cutting up the circle.'
'And the green lines?'
'They are protecting—yes, they are guarding.'
I had then drawn a tangent in pencil and asked what colour it might be given. There was a pause. Then:
'It's green escaping from red.' A brief pause. 'Or red escaping from green.' Another pause. 'Oh dear, it's a helpless man.'

I had been at the blackboard drawing the lines as I told this story; as I walked back to my notes I suddenly realised that there was Geoff Sillitto in the chair and that he was—damn it—listening. And I felt his interest. The comments of the girl were quoted as an introduction to some remarks I had wanted to make about the notion of space. I don't think that what I said was particularly clear or useful but at any rate for me a further exploration had commenced. A single act of attention prompted me to extend my notion of space.

Spengler claimed that mathematics was an actualization of our feelings about space. What sort of space? Spaces? Let's see.

See? Seeing is not always used to mean looking with our eyes. The double meaning reminds us that when we use our eyes we often see what we have already foreseen. We look at objects and see them in a perspective that we have learned to impose on our view. It has taken the experiments of modern artists, and the study by psychologists of the child's view of the world, to remind us that it is possible to see in many other ways. The achievements of the Renaissance painters had a dominating effect for a very long time.[1] They felt they had achieved a certain objectivity and this view is reflected in some philosophies of perception. But,

> Locke sank into a swoon
> the garden died,
> God took the spinning jenny
> out of his side.

It has been suggested by McLuhan that the garden is here the interplay of all the senses in haptic harmony and that the special domination of a certain way of seeing has had a blinkering effect on our culture as a whole. Yeats' garden cannot be described in a phrase, but I find my memories of dialogue with Geoff Sillitto useful when trying to think of seeing as a dynamic interchange between the perceiver and the perceived.[2]

We have imposed our ways of looking on our ways of seeing, in the sense of structuring, our experience. Thus 'in our culture the line is so basic that we take it for granted—as given in reality. We see it in visible nature, between material points and we see it between metaphorical points such as days or acts.' Anthropologists have emphasized recently that we may gravely misinterpret if we impose our sense of physical linearity when observing the layout of huts in a Trobriander village or if we impose our sense of temporal linearity when interpreting Hopi culture.[3] But our spatial concepts invade our whole way of thinking.

[1] 'Even those who questioned the norm still accepted the categories to which it had given rise.' E. H. Gombrich: *Norm and form*, Phaidon Press, 1966.

[2] It was in following up a reference given to me by Geoff that I found this comment on Coleridge: 'The mind, he now teaches, works actively in the mere act of perception. It knows its object not by passive reception but by its own energy and under its own necessary forms. Indeed, it knows not mere objects as such, but is itself the object.' B. Willey: *Nineteenth century studies*, Chatto and Windus, 1947. I have drawn on Marshall McLuhan in these paragraphs, in particular from *The Gutenberg galaxy*, Routledge, 1962. His famous slogan, 'the medium is the message', seems to me to be relevant to the general theme. Moreover it has encouraged me to ignore the technical content of discussions with Geoff. In general there is an important issue at stake. If the value of mathematics in education lies in process rather than product, then we have to revise radically many notions of what is important in school mathematics.

[3] The quotation about the role of the line in our culture and a discussion of Malinowski's observations of the Trobrianders can be found in an essay by Dorothy Lee in M. McLuhan and E. S. Carpenter (ed.): *Explorations in communication*, Boston: Beacon Press, 1960.

The Hopi Indians do not have verb tense in their language. They do not need to—or cannot—use terms that refer to space or time as such. Cf. B. Whorf: *Language, thought and reality*, New York, 1950, p. 64. Recent work in linguistics has raised general questions about the relation between language and experience. Whorf is particularly insistent on the linguistic relativity of experience. 'We dissect nature along lines laid down by our natural languages. The categories and types that we isolate from the world of phenomena, we do not find there because they stare every observer in the face; on the contrary, the world is presented in a kaleidoscopic flux of impressions which has to be organised by our minds—and this means largely by the linguistic system in our minds.'

We use geometric metaphors to express our feelings and attitudes towards other people. We say that our friends are close to us; some people we keep at distance, at arms length. We place someone on a pedestal because they may fulfil our highest ideals. We look up to, as well as down on, people. A broad-minded person is not expected to have narrow views, an honest person is said to be straight. A flat voice may be recounting a low joke; in current idiom, the speaker may be a square...[1]

Reciprocally, our whole way of thinking determines what spatial concepts we form. We can think of our friends being close to us and then revise our notions of proximity so that we see space in a different way.[2]

It all depends on what we bring to bear when we perceive. Primitive organisms feel, smell and taste the space they see. It has been suggested that primitive man employed all his senses in a similar way.[3] Yeats' garden might seem like Rousseau's paradise at this stage, but despite our rejection of Rousseau's romantic attitude to savages we do, it seems, have something to learn from them after all. Certainly we have learned more respect for the other natural inhabitant of the garden—the child.

Space now becomes a convenient context word to indicate that a certain discussion is taking place. As an example of the relative nature of the space we choose to see I recall an occasion when I was helping my six-year-old son to tidy up his toy soldiers. He objected to the way I was grouping them. With ill-concealed adult impatience, I was sorting the American cavalry, the cowboys and the Indians into one pile, the mediaeval knights into another, and the grenadier guards into a third. A monstrous caveman, brandishing a club, defeated me. I would have liked to hide it away. It didn't *fit*. And whose classification was that? Certainly not my son's, though I was unable to understand his patient explanation.

Impatient with our perceptions we surrender love to premature unification.[4]

My own understanding of some of Geoff's ideas was considerably enhanced by a discussion that took place the evening before his lecture at the A.T.M. summer conference at Winchester in 1964. (Or was it the evening after? It doesn't matter, for the events I am trying to recall took place out of

[1] A.T.M., *Notes on mathematics in primary schools*, Cambridge University Press, 1967.
[2] Cf. Peter Caldwell: *Neighbourhoods, open sets and continuity*, A.T.M. Supplement No. 1 (1965).
[3] Levi-Strauss, in *The savage mind*, London, 1966, has indicated the totality and richness of primitive experience. The savage mind intransigently refuses, he claims, 'to allow anything human (or even living) to remain alien to it.'
[4] Adapted from Mary Boole. It is ironic to compare her writings on mathematical education and on the ideas of her husband, George Boole, with our present concerns with the theory of sets. The sorting of toy soldiers is currently being recommended as an introductory activity for infants.

time—or rather they took place in private and not in public time.) Someone had opened a discussion about infinity by recalling the image of the cocoa-tin with a picture of a cook holding a cocoa-tin with a picture of a cook holding... Various people remembered similar experiences from their childhood. The intensity of recaptured epiphany became too strong for us. There was a silence. The discussion was taken up gently by Caleb Gattegno who talked at one stage about the notion of indifference and about choice. I did not understand clearly at the time, but the themes that were introduced were to be developed, in various ways by various people, over the next few days.

Geoff introduced the notion of indifference in his lecture on symmetry in a delicate way. But there was a stirring depth of feeling in his references to Gonseth's discussion of indifference and the image of the surface of a perfectly calm lake. I found later that this came from a Swiss geometer, Louis Bertrand, who is quoted by Gonseth. 'Once upon a time,' wrote Bertrand, 'a hunter killed a deer...'

Once upon a time a hunter killed a deer in the plain with an arrow. He wanted to know at what distance he had shot his prey. To find out, he placed his bow successively along the distance and found the length he was after in the number of times he had to place the bow. He reflected that when placing his bow on the ground he had been particularly careful to keep it pointing exclusively in a certain direction. This direction, he thought, is what is called a straight line. I have such a clear idea of this; if someone asked me what it was and what distinguishes it from other lines, how would I reply? Would I say that it is the direction of an arrow fired from a bow, or of a thread bearing a weight at one end, or better still that of a ray of light penetrating the dark?

But not one of these images would clarify completely the properties which distinguish a straight line from all others. These properties must be seen clearly and sharply distinguished. Might the required picture be the path of string stretched along the plain? The plain is given bounds. Would the string not divide it into two equal parts without veering towards one more than the other? Could this notion become more like an abstract intellectual idea by substituting for the plain the surface of a perfectly calm lake and for the cord the straight edge that imagination subtly traces on the surface of the lake. And again would not this surface, called a plane, divide space into two equal parts without veering towards one rather than the other? And would not this be its distinguishing characteristic?...

...One can conceive space divided into two equal parts by a boundary, all or any part of which relates to the half of space on one side in the same way as to the half on the other side. It is this boundary, continuously indifferent to its two partitions of space, that the hunter calls a plane or plane surface. As space is infinite and homogeneous even so is the plane. It is infinite since it equally divides the infinite space; it is homogeneous since it is continuously indifferent to its two partitions of the homogeneous space.

The hunter goes on to say that the plane, being infinite and homogeneous like space, can—like space—also be divided into two equal parts by a boundary, all or any part of which relates to the half of the plane on its right in the same way as to the half of the plane on its left. It is this boundary, continuously indifferent to its two partitions of the plane, that the hunter calls a straight line. He then observes that it is, like the plane, infinite and homogeneous. Infinite since it equally divides the infinite plane; homogeneous since it is continuously indifferent to its partition of the homogeneous plane.[1]

When it was my turn to lecture, I found myself trying to take into account some of the ideas that had been around. I had been interested in Papy's treatment of infinite sets[2] and what I had interpreted as an intuitionist position with regard to the axiom of choice. The formation of the 'ribambelle' involved a succession of choices. The symmetry of the straight line lay in a particular choice out of infinitely many taken at each moment as the line was traced. Position and extension involved choice—mental acts— and in each configuration lay the shadow configurations that might have been or were to come. What is can also be otherwise.

A few days after the conference, I had a postcard from Geoff with an extract from a poem:

> How could they penetrate that perilous maze
> backwards again, climb backwards down the scree
> from the wrong side, slither among the dead?
> Yet as they travelled on for many days
> these words rang in their ears as if they said,
> 'there was another road you did not see.'[3]

I think mathematics—and life—was for Geoff a matter of the right choice. I would have liked to know how far he related this to Gonseth's notion of idoneity or best fit.

Gonseth distinguishes three aspects of geometry which might roughly be described as primary intuition, immediate perception and theoretical study. These are aspects, not stages. The primary intuition is not something childish that you grow out of when you start doing proper geometry. The three aspects are equally valid, equally and simultaneously necessary. Geometry must involve all three in a totality of experience. There may, however, be conflicting tendencies in the development of geometry, e.g. a theoretical need for formal rigour can conflict with the prompting of intuition. At any time, the state of geometry is seen as 'a precarious and transitory equilibrium, based on an estimate of what is convenient in a

---

[1] Louis Bertrand, 'géomètre genevois' (?–1791), wrote an extensive account of elementary mathematics. The geometry section was republished in 1812 and its opening pages, which are translated here, are quoted by Gonseth, *op. cit.*, vol. 11, p. 141.
[2] G. Papy: *Mathématique moderne*, vol. 1, ch. 16, Brussels, 1963.
[3] From *The road*, by Edwin Muir.

given situation.'[1] And the idoneity of the given situation is eventually a matter of choice.

*The mathematics is in the activity.*
*Is?*[2]
*I do not want to tie up loose ends...* '*The truth I am trying to grasp is the grasp that is trying to grasp it*'.[3]
*How shall I end? I shall tell a story and show some pictures. I choose a particular story for Geoff Sillitto. Because he was a teacher.*

Time and again, Nasrudin passed from Persia to Greece on donkey-back. Each time he had two panniers of straw and trudged back without them. Every time the guard searched him for contraband, they never found any.

'What are you carrying, Nasrudin?'

'I am a smuggler.'

Years later, more and more prosperous in appearance, Nasrudin moved to Egypt. One of the customs men met him there.

'Tell me, now that you are out of the jurisdiction of Greece and Persia, living here in such luxury—what was it that you were smuggling when we could never catch you?'

'Donkeys.'[4]

*And it fits.*

---

[1] The quotation is from an account of Gonseth and similar thinkers by Beth in *The development of mathematics*, McGraw-Hill, 1954.

Gonseth's views are in fact here criticised as running into the danger of 'divesting science of its indispensable stability.'

[2] In Spanish there are two forms of the verb 'to be'. One expresses permanence, the other implies a temporary state. Soy enfermo. I am an invalid. Estoy enfermo. I am unwell.          '...as a Chinese jar still
moves perpetually in its stillness.'

[3] R. D. Laing, *The politics of experience and the bird of paradise*, Penguin Books, 1967.

[4] From I. Shah and R. Williams, *The exploits of the incomparable Mulla Nasrudin*, Cape, 1966.

The Sufi masters are said to have used such stories as a vehicle for their teaching.

---

Fig. 1. The Gokstadskibet ship, Fig. 2. Head of the god Abu, Fig. 3. Head from the tripylon at Persepolis, Fig. 4. A cayman eye and a human eye, Fig. 5. The bone structure of man, Fig. 6. Naum Gobo's 'Spiral Theme', 1941, Figs. 7–10. Children's drawings, Fig. 11. Symmetry....

GOKSTADSKIBET

Fig. 2

Fig. 3

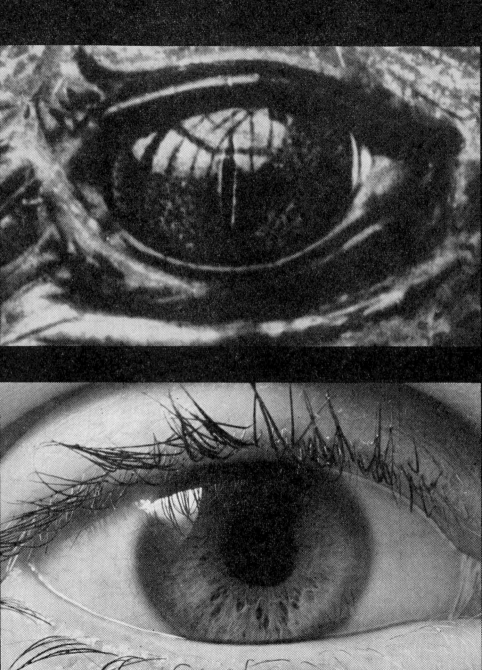

Fig. 4

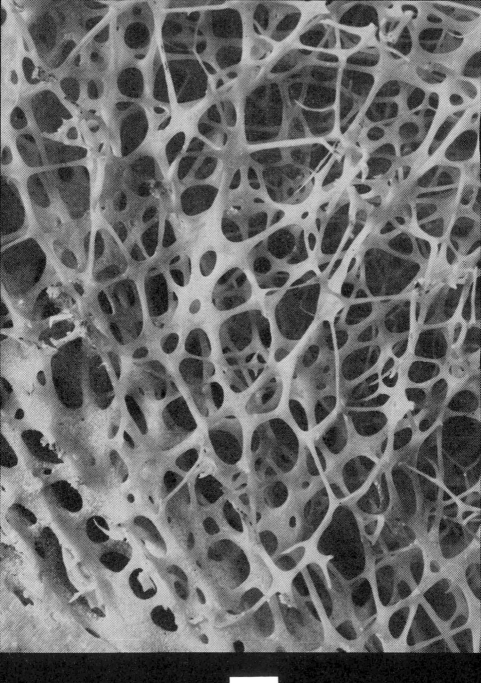

Fig. 5

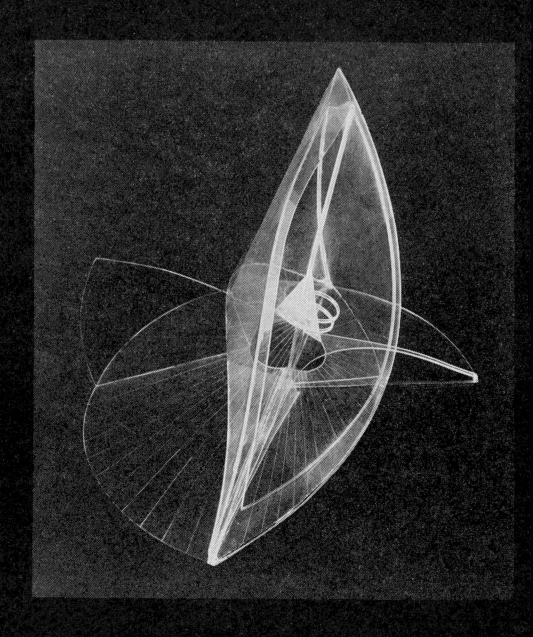

Fig. 6

Fig. 7

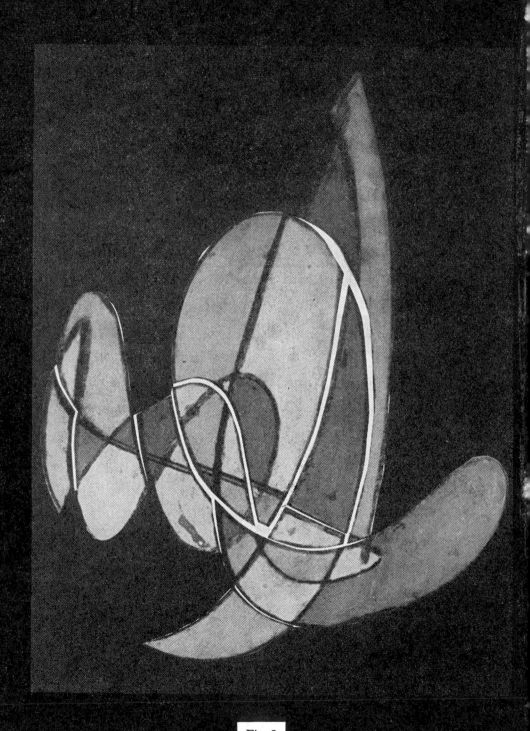

Fig. 8

Fig. 11

# TESSELLATIONS OF POLYOMINOES

*by* A. W. BELL

The problem of tessellating various polyominoes has been arousing some interest, and a recent number of *Mathematics Teaching* featured on its cover the tessellation of *Fs* shown in fig. 1, said to have been found by a primary schoolboy. This tessellation uses half-turns to repeat the *F*, but, of course, some polyominoes can be tessellated by translations alone. Two examples of this are shown. It is a simple matter to find, by direct trial, whether a given polyomino will tessellate in this way.

A colleague pointed out that a tessellation using half-turns can be made of every polyomino that is a 'distorted quadrilateral' or *quadriside*—a four-sided figure in which each side need not be straight but must have half-turn symmetry about its mid-point. In the examples shown in fig. 2 it is worth noting that the tetromino can be obtained from the quadrilateral by distorting two of its four sides. It is clear that the vertices of the quadriside do not need to be at corners of the polyomino, or even on its boundary.

In these diagrams a dot indicates a vertex of the quadriside, a cross a mid-point; the tessellation is built up by successive half-turns about the mid-points.

The reader may like, at this point, to try to find some tessellations for himself. (There are at least two further ones for the pentomino of fig. 2.)

The question which arises from these observations is whether we have here a general method of finding all possible tessellations of a given polyomino. Are there any restrictions on the positions of the vertices of the quadriside, so that we may know when we have exhausted all the possibilities? And does the quadrilateral method deal with all possible types of tessellation? This is the problem from which this piece of work starts. The results include a set of rules of procedure for seeking tessellations of a given polyomino which, without entirely eliminating the need for 'trial and error', provide clear limits within which to operate. Examples will be given of the use of the rules, leading to the discovery of nineteen different tessellations of the *L*-shaped tetromino of fig. 2, and four of the *F*.

The first comment is that every plane pattern must belong to one of the seventeen plane symmetry groups. These are described in the pamphlet

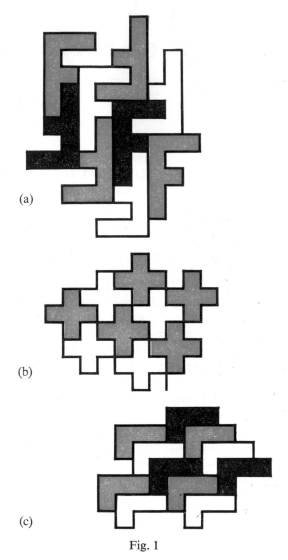

(a)

(b)

(c)

Fig. 1

Symmetry Groups, by Bell and Fletcher,[1] from which fig. 3 is taken; and sets of generators for each group are given in Coxeter's *Introduction to Geometry* (p. 413).[2] A pattern having no symmetry other than the two translations necessary to spread the unit over the plane belongs to the group called Type 1 or $p1$. Fig. 1(c) is an example of this but fig. 1(b) is

[1] Bell, A. W. and T. J. Fletcher, *Symmetry Groups*. A.T.M., Nelson, Lancs. 1964.
[2] Coxeter, H. S. M., *Introduction to Geometry*. Wiley, 1961.

44

not since it has other symmetries—for example quarter-turns about certain points. The patterns of fig. 2, having half-turn symmetries as well as translations, belong to the group *p*2. Thus the two methods suggested above for

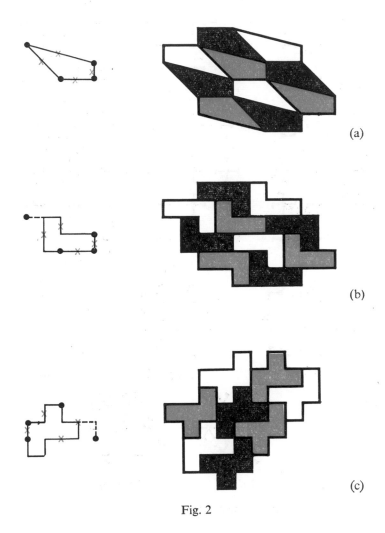

(a)

(b)

(c)

Fig. 2

seeking tessellations cover, at best, only two of the seventeen symmetry groups. What we need to do is to consider each of the groups in turn, and find what conditions must be satisfied by a polymino if it is to have a tessellation belonging to that group.

Five of the seventeen can be excluded immediately, since they have three- or six-fold rotational symmetry, which is not possible for a pattern of polyominoes (though they would come into their own with patterns made with units formed from triangles or hexagons). We take the remain-

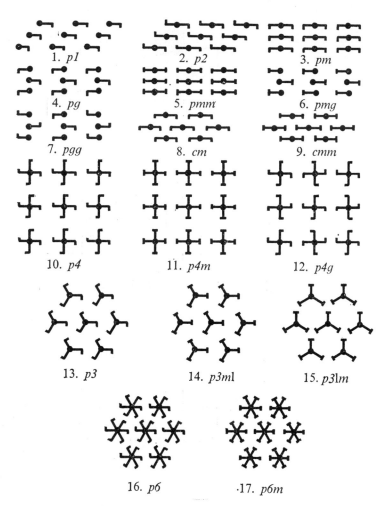

Fig. 3   The seventeen plane groups

ing twelve in turn. There is no further comment to be made about $p1$. The one possible tessellation of our $L$ of this type is shown in fig. 1($c$). The group $p2$ can be used to explain the standard procedure. Working from the appropriate diagram of fig. 3, we first mark all the symmetries of the pattern, then pick out a smallest possible 'fundamental region' which, when transformed by a suitable minimum set of the symmetries, will generate the whole pattern. (One such fundamental region will be associated with each hook of the diagram.) Fig. 4 shows the symmetries and three possible fundamental regions for the *p*2 diagram of fig. 3. (Only two translations are shown.) The reader is invited to verify that each of these regions can be repeated to cover the plane, using the three generating rotations.

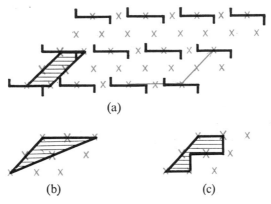

(a)

(b)　　　　　　(c)

Fig. 4　Symmetries and possible fundamental regions for *p* 2

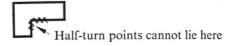

Half-turn points cannot lie here

Fig. 5

It is clear that although the fundamental region may have different shapes its area is fixed; this is half the area of the translatable parallelogram or, what is more important at present, four times the area of the triangle formed by three adjacent half-turn points. So if we are looking for a way of making a given polyomino the fundamental region for a tessellation of this type, we must try to fit a parallelogram lattice of half-turn points on to the polyomino (*a*) in such a way that the half-turn symmetry remains possible, and (*b*) so that the area of the triangle formed by adjacent half-turn points is one quarter of the area of the polyomino.

Taking the *L*-shaped tetromino, condition (*a*) means that the half-turn points cannot be on the part of the boundary marked in fig. 5, since, if they were, the performance of the half-turn would destroy the original figure. Nor can they lie inside this or any other figure which does not possess half-turn symmetry of itself. Condition (*b*) implies a triangle of area one.

47

Some possibilities are shown in fig. 6, but before studying this the reader may like to investigate for himself. The tessellation arising from fig. 6(e) is the one shown in fig. 2. Fig. 6(f) shows a fitting of a lattice of half-turn points on to the tetromino which satisfies the conditions (a) and (b) but does not produce a tessellation since the translation which is the result of performing successively a pair of the closer half-turns does not move the tetromino clear of its original position. So although the two conditions are necessary they are not sufficient; we need to enlarge condition (a) to

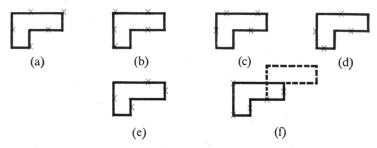

Fig. 6   Fitting a lattice of half-turns on to the tetronimo

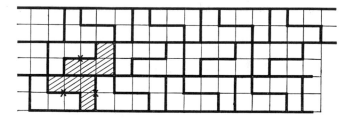

Fig. 7   A tessellation generated by two tetronimoes

require that all the symmetries, both the generating half-turns and the compositions of them, are possible. So far, then, we have found that the L-shaped tetromino has one tessellation with symmetry group $p1$ and five with group $p2$. The reader may like to sketch some of the ones which are not illustrated.

It may be of interest at this point to draw attention to fig. 7, which is a tessellation of the tetromino which one might arrive at by first fitting two together to form a rectangle, and then fitting the rectangles together in different ways. This is, in fact, not a tetromino tessellation in the sense that we are using, since its fundamental region is not a single tetromino but a pair, as shown; or in other words the pattern cannot be generated from the tetromino by the use of the symmetry transformations.

48

We consider next the third symmetry group of fig. 3, the group *pm*. As before, we begin by making a diagram showing all the symmetries of the group, and also a fundamental region and set of generating symmetries (fig. 8).

In this figure the shape of the fundamental region has been chosen to show what kind of variation from the obvious rectangle is possible. The

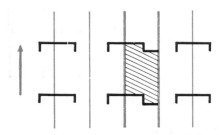

Fig. 8 Symmetries and a possible fundamental region for *pm*
(The symmetries shown in bold form a generating set.)

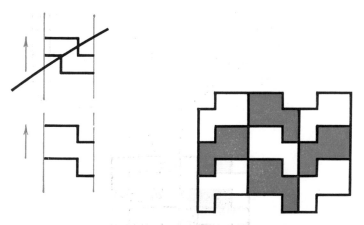

Fig. 9 A polyomino tessellation with group *pm*

left- and right-hand boundaries must remain along the mirrors or the performing of the reflection will leave a gap; but the upper and lower boundaries may be of any shape as long as they translate into each other. These requirements limit severely the number of polyominoes which will tessellate with this symmetry group. Neither the *L* or the *F* will do so; fig. 9 shows another which will not, and one which will, with its tessellation.

The next symmetry group to be considered is *pg*: the fourth in fig. 3. In fig. 10 we show its symmetries, a generating subset of them and a fundamental region. (The half-headed arrows indicate glides; these are

49

combinations of a reflection with a translation parallel to the mirror.) With the generating glides of 'length' 3 and distance 2 apart, the fundamental region is of area 12. So if we are to tessellate a tetromino in this way,

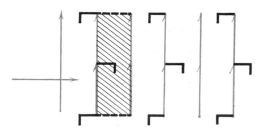

Fig. 10   Symmetries, generators and a fundamental region for *pg*

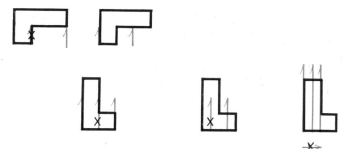

Fig. 11   Trying the *pg* symmetries on the *L*

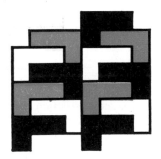

Fig. 12   A tessellation of the *L* of group *pg*

the glides must be either (*a*) of length 1, distance 2 apart, or (*b*) of length 2, distance 1 apart, or (*c*) of length 4, distance $\frac{1}{2}$ apart. These possibilities are tried out in various ways on the *L* in fig. 11; where the *L* is not compatible with the symmetries this is indicated. Fig. 12 shows the one tessellation of this type which we find.

50

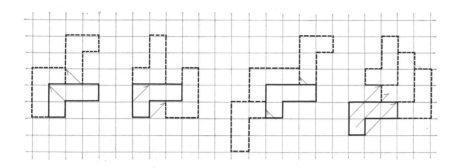

Fig. 13 Fitting the *L* to diagonal *pg* symmetries

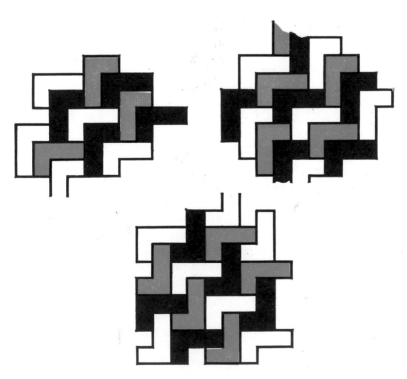

Fig. 14 Three of the four tessellations found in fig. 13

However, there is another kind of possibility for *pg* here; the polyominoes can be consistent with glide symmetries at 45° to the square grid. For the tetromino, glides of length $\sqrt{2}$ and distance $\sqrt{2}$ apart, or length $\frac{1}{2}\sqrt{2}$ and distance $2\sqrt{2}$ apart, or length $2\sqrt{2}$ and distance $\frac{1}{2}\sqrt{2}$ apart seem possible initially. Experiment similar to that illustrated in fig. 11 produces the four arrangements shown in fig. 13, three of which are shown as tessellations in fig. 14. Altogether we have found five *pg* tessellations of the *L*.

The *F*, an octomino, also has a tessellation of group *pg* which is shown in fig. 15. The analysis is left to the reader.

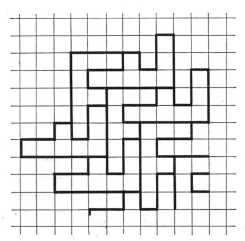

Fig. 15 : A tessellation of *F* with group *pg*

The remainder of this investigation will be presented more briefly, stating the results and giving sufficient notes to enable the reader to do the working for himself.

The fifth group of fig. 3, *pmm*, has reflections in two perpendicular directions and its fundamental region can only be a rectangle (compare *pm*).

The sixth group, *pmg*, is generated by a reflection and two half-turns, and for a fundamental region of area 4 the rectangle formed by two adjacent half-turns and the mirror has area 2. The *L* has a tessellation of this type.

The seventh group, *pgg*, has glides in two perpendicular directions and half-turns about the centres of the rectangles formed by the glide axes. The *L* has three tessellations of this type (not illustrated) and, more remarkably, the *F* has two. We give some diagrams here. Note that the area of the fundamental region is equal to that of the rectangles formed by the glides, so that for area 8, $4 \times 2$, $2\sqrt{2} \times 2\sqrt{2}$, $4\sqrt{2} \times \sqrt{2}$ are the only possibilities which ensure sufficient translation (= 2 × glide distance) for the *F* to be clear of its original position. The fitting of what is possible from these is shown in fig. 17 and the corresponding tessellations in fig. 18.

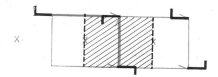

Fig. 16   Symmetries, generators and fundamental regions for *pgg*

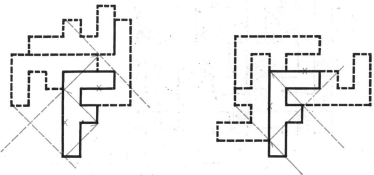

Fig. 17   Fitting *pgg* symmetries to the *F*

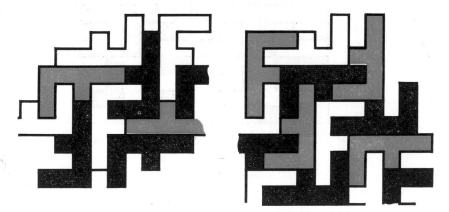

Fig. 18   Two tessellations of the *F* with symmetry *pgg*

Groups 8 and 9 of fig. 3, *cm* and *cmm* are left for the reader's own enjoyment; we have found one tessellation of the *L* of each type. There remain the three groups containing quarter-turns, *p*4, *p*4*m* and *p*4*g*. Of these, *p*4*m* has a fundamental region in the shape of a 45° right-angled triangle and symmetries of reflection in its sides, which makes it impossible to tessellate any asymmetric polyomino in this way. The other two groups have fundamental regions which are a quarter of the square formed by four adjacent lattice points—and so must have areas which are a quarter of a perfect square; 4 is possible, 8 is not (what about 9 . . . ?). The *L* has a tessellation of each of these types and we give the tessellations only for these, leaving the reader to supply the analysis.

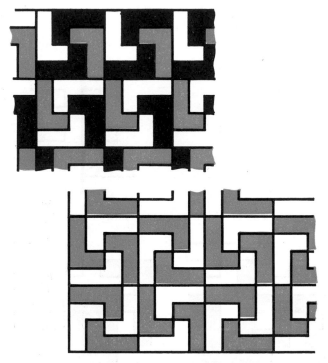

Fig. 19   Tessellations of the *L*, with groups *p*4 and *p*4*g*

We have concentrated attention here on two particular polyominoes and have found a total of nineteen different tessellations of the *L*, and four for the *F*. The reader may like to consider the symmetry group of fig. 1(*b*); or to try one of the asymmetrical hexominoes; or to get some isometric paper and consider figures made not of squares, but of triangles or hexagons. . .

And, by the way, why is it possible to print all these diagrams with only three colours?

# MAGNITUDES, MEASUREMENT AND CHILDREN

### *by* W. M. BROOKES

We are as teachers in a paradoxical situation. The thoughts and energies of mathematicians past and present have taken up old issues, reclothed them, seen them in new lights, developed ways of speaking that outstrip the ancients in the control of situations. Yet in our movement from immediate perceptions to the creative world of the mathematician there are many traps. 'One cannot re-tread 2000 years of history...it is the teacher's task to short circuit.' It is an appealing metaphor but is it a valid one? It is the teacher's task to recognise the history and to recommend actions in the experiencing of which the pupil will grow under his own power into a world with which he can deal.

This simultaneously arrogant and naive cliché is too often used to justify a glossing over of problems in which the young mind, if given the opportunity, will revel and grow. If it is arrogant it is because it carries the assumption that all the problems of the past have been solved and what is more that the solutions are available to all teachers. Usually it is a naive statement because it appears that the briefest acquaintance with some of the techniques of differential calculus, algebra of numbers, geometry, trigonometry, set theory, gives the justifier an impression of having more at his finger tips than, say, the Greeks. But the knowing of techniques does not endow wisdom: the problems of the Greeks are still with us, though couched in different terms. The issues Plato appears to have considered sufficiently difficult and testing for prospective Guardians are matters still open to us. The solutions offered for one purpose at one time merely shift the emphasis. The invention of symbol systems, of new ways of talking, have not really released us from the sources that make the study of mathematics essentially one that always expands. They may obscure the issues. In the assumptions we make about young children learning mathematics we tend to think of simplified systems; and though this is reasonable, it is not reasonable to expect the growth of thought to proceed consequently in a rational manner.

It is too common that elementary courses devised to help children and young people meet the problems of mathematics accept that learning is a rational procedure. We become obsessed with what are called 'basic skills' with no distinction made between those blind skills operationally handled to achieve limited goals and those other skills essential if the conscious investigation of a mathematical situation is to be accomplished at all. One of these latter basic skills is to learn how to ask questions. When we recognise that they are often best asked at inconvenient times some measure of the problem can be felt.

I propose to look at some questions which arise in this context concerning magnitude, quantity and number, which appears to be an area fraught with traps. We expect children to measure, we accept that the idea has surrounded them from birth. We feed them with notions of number allied with the lengths of straight segments. And they can enjoy this. The early Greeks did, too. But shadows fell on the Pythagoreans and so they do on our budding thinkers.

The word magnitude conjures up for us size and, if asked what the magnitude is, we would tend to answer in terms of measurements. Measurement is part of the world-history of children brought up *now*. It is associated essentially with instruments. Rarely will children learn about measurement as comparison except casually, since so many measuring instruments are available for their use. To find a length we use a ruler; to weigh we have a spring balance, and so on. We shall eventually see what skins may be drawn over our eyes by these facilities. The world in which we grow up is one of operational measuring—not of the casual comparison where each craftsman had his own mode of communicating with his fellows. How long was it before trade insisted that common measures must be established? How many children think that tables of common measure refer to tables in ordinary everyday use, not realising the 'sharing' implied by the word 'common'? These tables embody the historical attempts of commerce to reconcile the difficulties arising from the seemingly arbitrary choice of modes of measurement made by individual crafts. But now we exist in a 'measurement medium' where too often a question will be, 'Can you measure it?', without meaningfully referring to comparison.

Forgetting for a moment the impositions of such forms by the powerful technological developments in society conceived by commerce, with science as midwife, which have produced intra-structures, disturbing and unifying at the same time, we can look at the folk use of measures.

In cereal agriculture in modern England the bushel is very much a live notion relative to the farm worker's appreciation of his land's productivity. Conscious as he is of variation in water content, density of different grains, much of this garnered wisdom is embodied in his use of concepts of measure which appear to give him the best guide for action. We can observe such traditional practices not with the eye of the modern reforming rationaliser but with the sensitive eye of the onlooker recognising the unity between the practice and the means of practising. An observer may note carefully that a particular practice seems to be obsolescent; dying in such sense that it no longer appears connected with the necessary actions associated with its use. The observer may then also expect to see an explicit rejection by the user. Too ready an acceptance of over-rationalisation may well lead to steps which may show, in the outcome, disadvantages arising out of ignoring the ways in which adaptatory processes have produced optimum methods. The ease with which a craftsman can estimate halves gives rise essentially to that aspect of our measuring based on a binary process: $\frac{1}{2}, \frac{1}{4}, \frac{1}{8}, \frac{1}{16}, \frac{1}{32}$ inches. The existence of 1, 2, 4, 8, 16 ounce weights as part of a folk tradition suggests a nice evolution to the most efficient set of weights for the estimating of any weight in ounces less than a certain one. Compare with 100, 50, 20, 20, 10, 5, 2, 2, 1 gram weights one is expected to use in the metric system. What theories of measure have developed from similar folk uses? Magnitudes are amounts which can be compared. Measurement comes later.

Simple awareness of folk activity has developed into the study called anthropology. Though the anthropology of mathematics is growing (see, for instance, Levi-Strauss[1]) I should like to invent a simple story. Consider two pots, the one produced in kilns of a certain tribe and the other a product of a different tribe. How can there be trade between these tribes using these pots? The first attempt is to ask how many of the smaller pots fill the larger? Immediately our modern state asserts itself and we shall make such statements as 'nearly three', 'two and two-thirds', '2·7', as we use our modern techniques to estimate. But in doing this we have not really felt the social problem of the exchange of valuable commodities through the medium of the pots and it is easy to dismiss the situation without seeing the implications.

Consider the care that the exchangers wish to bring to their transaction. They can count. How long will it be before their solution is phrased thus: How many of one pot fill how many of the other?

When the larger pot is first filled by a sequence of pourings from the smaller it is likely that there will be liquid left in the smaller pot when, during that particular pouring, the bigger one was estimated full. To empty the larger one and to continue pouring with the smaller is to broach the problem and thence to solve it.

Though to do this requires a decision as to whether the little pot is empty. This sounds trivial until the final moment at which a simultaneous pair of decisions must be made: that the large pot is full and that the smaller one is empty. This is not trivial for it implies an order in the assessment of fullness of the big pot on each occasion.

[1] Levi-Strauss, C. *The Savage Mind*, London, 1966.

With agreements as to fullness and emptiness, we shall arrive at

$$m(p) \lozenge n(P),$$

where (i) $\lozenge$ indicates 'social agreement as to equality',

(ii) $m(p)$ symbolically represents the number $m$ of replications of the repeatable magnitude $(p)$. Similarly with $n(P)$.

Note that we have no other control over the 'actual quantity' than the operation described so far. No measures, no standards, nothing, and here the matter may rest as we have certainly solved, in one sense, a practical problem.

The writings on matters related to this are extensive and one of the difficult matters to sort out is whether numbers should be considered as magnitudes.

The difficulty arises here in two ways. As soon as extensible matter could be handled by means of number, the ability to control the real world concentrated man's thought on the properties of numbers and how they were apparently manifest in extensible matter through the establishment of these notions of measure. But the handling of extensible matter depended on 'social agreement as to equality' and the numbers only appeared after this agreement.

Notice that from the relation between $(p)$ and $(P)$, that we have shown:

$$m(p) \lozenge n(P).$$

So $\qquad 1/n \text{ of } (m(p)) \lozenge (P)$

and $\qquad 1/m \text{ of } (n(P)) \lozenge (p).$

Hence $\qquad 1/m \text{ of } (1/n \text{ of } (m(p)))$

and $\qquad 1/n \text{ of } (1/m \text{ of } (n(P)))$

may both represent a common magnitude $(k)$. Note that these are conclusions drawn in terms of the 'social agreement as to equality'.

Thus $\qquad (p) \lozenge n(k), \quad (P) \lozenge m(k)$

and this is always possible for arbitrary comparable magnitudes. Again the matter may rest here with some practical procedure but of a more sophisticated form. This time the numbers $n$ and $m$ can be used in the transaction rather than the actual pouring operations, or the equivalent, which produced socially agreeable results in the past.

It is also possible that other situations requiring similar comparisons also led to pairs of numbers being associated with paired magnitudes, for example, length, weight, angles, but always the equality would be an agreed one.

# Magnitudes, measurement and children

*Example:* Mark an arbitrary length *a* on a straight edge of paper. Draw a line on a sheet of paper and mark a different arbitrary segment *b*. Lay *a* off along *b* allowing the left hand ends to coincide *as well as you may estimate.* If *a* is less than *b* mark a point on *b* where *a* terminates. Lay off *a* again and repeat until *a*, when laid off, extends beyond the end of *b*, in which case mark on *a* a point where *b* terminates. Making this latter point on *a* coincide as before with the left-hand end of *b*, lay off once more making marks on *b* and *a* appropriately. The diagram shows the length *a* about to be laid off after the first three layings off when marks 1, 2, 3 were made on *b* and 1 on *a*. 4 is about to be made.

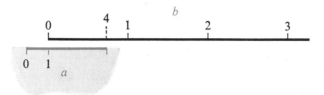

Fig. 1

The whole procedure finishes when a decision is made that the two right-hand ends of *a* and *b* coincide. This is equivalent, in the case of the pots, to the one being empty simultaneously with the one being full. Because of the nature of the magnitude, length, we may not only notice that we have ended the length *a* 10 times and the length *b* 3 times, thus $10a \bigcirc 3b$, but also that there is apparent a length *k* such that

$$a \bigcirc 3k, \quad b \bigcirc 10k.$$

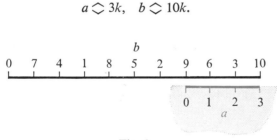

Fig. 2

It is easy to see how the use of number to control these activities became paramount after this kind of experience. The decision as to equality is necessary perceptively, but in abstraction becomes perceptively unimportant until the next breakthrough.

If our perception of the unit, by sight or by any other sense, is quite unambiguous, then it provides no more stimulus to seek for truth than did our perception of a finger. But if it is always combined with the perception of its opposite, and seems to involve plurality as much as unity, then it calls for the exercise of judgement and forces the mind into a quandary in which it must stir itself to think, and ask what unity in its absolute sense means; . . .[1]

With the establishment of numbers as the abstract guides to action we can use number properties and there are two distinct problems: one is the generation of magnitudes from a given magnitude and the other is the comparison of two unknown but like (i.e., comparable) magnitudes. We have seen that given the possibility of counting—replication of unity leading to what the Greeks referred to as 'multitude'—then, through social agreement as to equality, a model for dealing with magnitudes can be arrived at. This is not a 'deriving' but an 'arriving'.

For multitude and magnitude seem to refer, the one to replication of indivisible unities and the second to the abstraction involved in the notion of *extension* and implicitly of *intension*.

The use of number for exchange and this kind of common measure led to Euclid being able to include in Book VII[2] a full theory where he unhesitatingly used line segments and number as interchangeable. This typically antedates the Pythagorean discovery of line segments that were not so 'expressible' and the arguments are hence much simpler than those adduced by Eudoxus in his treatment represented in Book V[3] of Euclid's work.

There was a time in our schools when a technique for finding a highest common factor was taught which was explicitly the Euclidean algorithm for finding a common measure of two line segments. Always it must be remembered that his algorithm was an abstraction from the perceptive world of comparing to a point of agreement. It could not be absolute.

Using whole numbers $a$ and $b$ the theory rests on the postulate that if $a$ and $b$ have a common measure then their difference will also have this common measure. Heath refers to this as an unexpressed assumption in his note in Book VII on Definition 22 of a perfect number.[4]

This provides good material for children's investigation when it is seen to be associated with arbitrary jugs, weights, lengths and so on. The process known as antanairesis is involved: subtracting one from the other. For example, take $a = 258$ and $b = 96$:

[1] Plato, *The Republic*, Transl. H. D. P. Lee, Penguin, p. 291.
[2] Heath, T. L. (Ed.). *Euclid's Elements*, Book VII, Vol. II, p. 277. New York, 1956. Hereafter referred to as *Euclid's Elements*.
[3] *Euclid's Elements*, Book V, Vol. II, p. 112.
[4] *Euclid's Elements*, Book VII. Bol. II. p. 294.

| Algebraic equivalent | | Stages | | | Algebraic equivalent |
|---|---|---|---|---|---|
| $a$ | 258 | | | 96 | $b$ |
| $2b$ | 192 | 1 | 3 | 66 | $a- 2b$ |
| $a-2b$ | 66 | 2 | 4 | 30 | $-a+ 3b$ |
| $-2a+6b$ | 60 | 5 | 7 | 30 | $15a-40b$ |
| $3a-8b$ | 6 | 6 (i) | | 0 | $-16a+43b$ (ii) |

Conclusion: (i) $3a-8b = 6$;

           (ii) $16a = 43b$.

If the numbers had been relatively prime then an expression of the form $pa-qb = 1$ would have resulted for conclusion (i). For example,

$$a \quad 743 \qquad\qquad 521 \quad b$$

gives $\quad 115a-164b = 1 \quad$ for (i).

For these relatively prime numbers conclusion (ii) is $521a = 743b$.

It is a pity that the bath water, muddied by the destructive teaching of a blind technique, obscured the baby that was thrown out when this technique ceased to be taught in schools. It is the experience of most students of mathematics to meet this algorithm only in its more abstract form when dealing with algebraic expressions.

Let us now look at this algorithm with respect to magnitudes in an attempt to identify a measure acceptable in a bargaining procedure, using our concept of 'social agreement as to equality' again. In the case of lengths it can be seen by subtraction to lead to a point when a socially agreed measure may be established (p. 58). But for those magnitudes, such as liquids, not so susceptible to ease of operation the following model is appropriate.

Given that $\qquad\qquad (p) \gtrless n(k)$

$\qquad\qquad\qquad (P) \gtrless m(k) \quad$ (see p. 58),

we know that numbers $a$, $b$ can be found so that

$$an \sim bm = 1 \quad \sim : \text{difference.}$$

So $\qquad\qquad\quad a(p) \sim b(P)$

$\qquad\qquad\quad \Rightarrow a.n(k) \sim b.m(k) \quad$ (i)

$\qquad\qquad\quad \Rightarrow (an \sim bm).(k) \qquad$ (ii)

$\qquad\qquad\quad \Rightarrow 1(k).$

61

Note: (i) assumes the 'detachability' of $n$, $m$ (*not* 'associativity' which is linked with binary operations), (ii) assumes the distribution of the magnitude over the numbers.

In this way we demonstrate how a common measure may be identified, given social agreement as to equality.

If with the pots we used previously it had been discovered that 13 little pots filled 5 big pots thus

$$(p) \lessgtr 5(k) \quad \text{and} \quad (P) \gtrless 13(k).$$

We know that there are numbers $a$, $b$, where

$$5a \sim 13b = 1,$$

so that

$$a(p) \sim b(P)$$

will give a socially acceptable common measure which will be $1(k)$.

For example,

$$a = 5; \quad b = 2,$$

and hence

$$5(p) \sim 2(P) = 1(k).$$

This gives instructions to fill the little pot five times using two big pots. The remaining amount will be the common magnitude $(k)$. A pot can even be made to take this amount, to within the usual agreement!

The relevance for us at this time of the foregoing remarks is seen in the fact that most introductions to elementary mathematics allow the concepts, first of integers and then of rational numbers, to become too solid and certain a foundation for measurement. It means that young children surrounded as they are by practical measuring acts find their belief in the certainty of measure supported by the over-use of exact numbers to match their operational measuring activity.

Infants are often introduced to measuring by being encouraged to give exact numerical answers when estimations between numbers would be a different activity. We see the consequences in many examples.

'Go and find how many pints there are in a gallon.'

Six year old goes off to the tap with pint and gallon 'measures'.

He comes back.

'Thirteen.'

'Go and try again.'

On his next return—

'Twelve.'

Teacher asks himself, 'What can he be doing?' He doesn't find an answer except to say 'Do it more carefully'. Eventually he may show the boy that 'there are eight'.

Suppose the teacher thinks more carefully over what the boy has done and suppose instead of, 'Do it more carefully', he recognises that the boy has counted the number of pourings that he had performed! What will the question, 'Fill the big one with the little one with as small a number of pourings as you can', or words to that effect, produce?

In any case what we have here is the tension between a child and an activity and the teacher with his 'exact' knowledge. A study of the act of filling and pouring will allow the child to attend to the meaning of a 'full measure'.

Still another child may not even see that he can repeat his use of one milk bottle to fill a larger, saying that he has only two little bottles and needs more...[1]

At a later stage teachers in Primary School have shown worry at the suggestion that an area of a rectangle can be estimated from the following data:

Length of one side is between 11 and 12 inches.

Length of the other side is between 8 and 9 inches.

Hence area is between 88 and 108 square inches.

Their comments were to the effect that such activity would lead to carelessness and a lack of concern for the precision necessary in dealing with numbers!

Still later most books recommend a 'counting squares' method for finding the area of an irregular figure. But the method mainly used is of drawing the figure on a piece of graph paper, counting the *whole* squares contained and then counting bits and combining them so that a number of whole squares is reached.

The graph paper actually allows the effective use of the maximum of the internal square polygons as a greatest lower bound and the minimum of the external square polygons as a least upper bound with a consequent trapping of the 'area' between two exactly countable 'areas'.

So someone will say...'Oh! But for practical purposes we can use a number'. Of course, but that does not mean that we use this as an excuse to arrive at a number every time. There is need to educate judgement, to know which number model is appropriate to which practical situation. If at an early stage we do damage, as I believe we do, to the child's potential understanding of the many different ways of seeing numbers in action then we must look at the ways in which this can be avoided.

It was suggested earlier by implication that we pay only lip-service to 2000 years of mathematical history when we deliberately, though unwit-

[1] Association of Teachers of Mathematics, *The Development of Mathematical Activity in Children*, p. 69, 1966.

tingly, train our young to be early Greeks. We engender in them a delight in the exactitude of number and by drawing on so-called concrete exemplifications convince them from a very early age that number, and in particular the integers, holds sway over a measurable world. Even when introduced to the problems of extension, real numbers and continuity, operational solutions of a kind which imply certain universal agreement are not sought for. The frequent reference as a standard of clear truth to 2 and 2 making 4 does not help. Of more help is the growing articulacy of those who attack the 'doctrine of the uniqueness of mathematical reality or intersubjective intuition; of its accessibility in principle; of its unambiguous and exhaustive reflection in conceptual or linguistic formulations'.[1]

By making the essentially negative original definition of incommensurable magnitudes positive, obscurity developed where light was in the process of being shed.

Heath's translation of Euclid's Definition 1 in Book X reads, 'Those magnitudes are said to be commensurable which are measured by the same measure, and those incommensurable which cannot have any common measure'.[2]

This may appear as a simple dichotomous definition, but note how the first part allows of the construction of commensurable lengths, implicitly by replication, while the second part refers to a theoretical method of construction which will show positively that for two lengths no such common measure would exist. In fact we have here no more than a distinct and straightforward statement of the two fundamental issues raised by the perception of magnitudes (p. 60). In elementary work it is generally supposed that arbitrary magnitudes are of two classes: commensurable and incommensurable. This is clearly false, for given two such *a*, *b* then without more ado using antanairesis we can safely 'lay them off' (as they are comparable) so that the successive remainder is always less than a finite magnitude. It is this false classification that is at the root of much misunderstanding. One can see how far this went when one recognises Heath's own declaration, after Aristotle, in an introductory note to Euclid, Book V: 'It could not have escaped him (Euclid) that numbers fall under the conception of magnitude. Aristotle had plainly indicated that magnitudes may be numbers when he observed that you cannot adapt the arithmetical method of proof to the properties of magnitudes if the magnitudes are not numbers'.[3]

[1] Körner, S. 'Some relations between philosophical and scientific theories', *Brit. J. Phil. Sci.* **17**, 4, 265–78. 1966.
[2] *Euclid's Elements*, Book X, Vol. III, p. 10.
[3] *Euclid's Elements*, Book V, Vol. II, p. 113.

# Magnitudes, measurement and children

Here Heath is concerned by Euclid's double treatment of proportion in Book V (Eudoxus) and in Book VII (integers only), which I shall refer to later. Though Van de Waerden[1] quotes Aristotle in more direct support of Heath than Heath's own interpretation, this remains obscure. It should be seen from the non-rigorous treatment I have given to magnitudes above how one has to avoid applying 'arithmetic' rules to magnitudes. What is assumed in the traditional treatment? There are tautological traps here. De Morgan draws our attention to this confusion when he extols the virtues of indicating 'simple algebraic expressions of magnitudes by large letters and of numerical multipliers by small ones',[2] in facilitating the demonstration of ratios and proportion.

Certainly it is the case that a modern approach has been to treat magnitudes in terms of 'double structures'. Grassman's calculus of extension seems to be the first formulation of 'extensive magnitudes' as objects which can be linearly expressed in terms of others of the same kind. This appears to be an extension of the number modelling we found in the primitive exchange of pots. We can see it in the further general development of the notion of a vector space and linear transformations in general, and by the eventual disappearance from pure mathematical language of the term *magnitude*.[3] But for our purposes here it appears that magnitude need only, but must, satisfy a discrete additive law. In the 'coming together' of two like magnitudes there is no 'absorption'. Some may refer tautologically to this as 'conservation'.

So long as arbitrary magnitudes in this sense are being compared we have no commensurability. The notion of commensurability belongs to the deliberate act of making units replicable as precisely as possible (in terms of social agreement?) and by thus using the consequential 'measuring' instruments to construct magnitudes apparently 'commensurable'. It means no more than that the counting number model is usable to compare the replications. It is a useful tautology but a tautology nevertheless.

Any counting of repeatable acts will serve so that a child can work out by toe-to-heel action a distance 20. He can also estimate a length which has not been made by a similar process. Note that all he is doing on the second occasion is to find a number that he can attach to the 'length'.

[1] Van der Waerden, B. L. *Science Awakening*, Holland, 1954.
[2] De Morgan, A. Article on 'Proportion', *Penny Cyclopaedia*, Vols. 19, 20, pp. 49–53. 1841.
[3] Manheim refers to 'the conceptual difficulties associated with the word *limit* derived from attempts to define it in terms of magnitude rather than aggregation' (Manheim, J. H. *The Genesis of Point Set Topology*. p. 26, Pergamon, 1964) and this may well give the hint as to the reason for the disappearance.

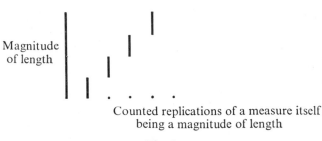

Magnitude
of length

Counted replications of a measure itself
being a magnitude of length

Fig. 3

This 'graph' is rough as it is only an image...one may ponder on it and picture the relation between counting and extension. Perhaps, as Poincaré has pointed out 'perceived equality is not transitive' and we may look with some doubt on the small vertical lines—they may overlap!

Some 6 to 7-year old children were measuring a corridor from the door at one end, to the end wall. They had used sticks of a 'certain length' and then were faced with a gap at the end less than the length of a stick. (Certainly they could not lay a stick beyond the end of the corridor and to lay it as $A$ would not have been 'natural', see fig. 4.)

Fig. 4

The job continued by their finding a sequence of magnitudes of length such that at each time the new length went into the gap left. Note that they were choosing in this way—that the length would go into the gap...not that it would fill the gap.

A similar problem arises in the economics of building, dress-making, etc., where it is impossible to forecast exactly the requirements for the job to be done but where it is imperative that the material available must always be *more* than is required. He who is able to estimate accurately a least amount that is more than is required, and then defend his judgement, will be the most successful quantity surveyor.

The exact relations we can obtain between numbers and the use we can make of them in the construction of artificial structures is basic to much of our control of the environment. But where the control is required over non-artificial structures, variable and, in a definite technical sense, 'non-parametric', then the pervasive notions of the first kind will not help us with the second kind. Thus the formulae that the quantity surveyor uses for areas of shapes and so on, are only trivially involved with the logistic assessment of the least quantity of material required.

This notion seems to point precisely to the failure of the consequences of the analysis attributed to Eudoxus in Book V of Euclid. Here we find that in Definition 5 he comes to terms with the important issue of ratio[1], for without ratio there is no control of the replication of a unit and hence no commensurability.

But here is the biggest defect of all in the approach to learning mathematics in the nineteenth and twentieth century through a study of Euclid, even in the emasculated forms due to the reformists of the late nineteenth and early twentieth centuries. It is apparent that Euclid's geometry is that which investigates the space delineated by the axioms (even though these were found wanting). In his notes on Postulate 3, Book I: 'that a circle of any centre and any distance can be drawn', Heath observes that thus the space is delineated, saying also: 'The Postulate has the effect of removing any restriction upon the size of the circle. It may be indefinitely small, and this implies that space is *continuous*, not discrete, with an irreducible minimum distance between contiguous points in it.'[2]

Euclid's work is hence an attempt to set up a watertight theory of incommensurable magnitudes *ab initio*. Hence the straight edge and compass. The work was set in a background whose power had derived from the tautological equalities of number controlled replicated magnitudes. But for the newer theories the 'marked ruler' had to be rejected. Intriguingly the reformers seem to ignore this. But having accepted certain 'intuitive' proofs without making these logical distinctions, the approach to ratio and proportion confined them to commensurables. They turned their backs on Eudoxus and De Morgan, Dedekind, Hamilton, Weierstrass and Cantor and a host of others and committed their charges to the trials of the early Greeks.

So we have it. When a child of eleven is annoyed with the task of proving equal what we can well measure as equal, he is failing to distinguish between lengths as identified discretely through the existence of a basic unit (measurable) and lengths which are not so. But does his teacher note the distinction and if not can the child be blamed for being puzzled? Notice how after chastising him for this annoyance, we later sell the pass by introducing 'commensurability only' proofs for similarity properties.

So the history of the movement away from Euclid is a history of recog-

---

[1] *Euclid's Elements*, Book V, Vol. II, p. 114.
[2] *Euclid's Elements*, Book I, Vol. I, p. 199.

nising the power of the countable set as the source of reasonable operations in space. Unfortunately those who led us away do not appear to have seen it in this light; so that though we can explore and create a geometry based on unit segments, co-ordinates, vectors, etc., the step to the geometry of the real plane has still not been taken except by a kind of sleight of hand.

The definition referred to above (Book V, 5) attempts to pin down the ratio of magnitudes in order to justify the inclusion of what we call the 'real plane'. We have seen already that arbitrary magnitudes of a comparable kind are essentially incommensurable. The proof that the diagonal

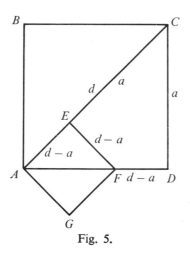

Given a square $ABCD$ of side magnitude $a$ and diagonal $d$. Lay off $a$ on $d$ then the remainder $AE$ is $d-a$. Construct a square $AEFG$ on this segment as side then $EF = FD = AE = d-a$ and $AF = a-(d-a) = 2a-d$. $a$ and $d$ are comparable magnitudes and linear combinations are comparable magnitudes. The repeatable construction shows that $a$ and $d$ are necessarily arbitrarily related and hence incommensurable.

Fig. 5.

of a square is incommensurable with the side is on the whole irrelevant—in the sense that the only lengths that can be commensurable are those that are constructed to be so. The problem probably arose because it had been discovered that an unlimited sequence of sets of three commensurable magnitudes would make right-angled triangles; so that the power of numbers suggested that an arbitrary right-angled triangle could be linked with one of the Pythagorean triads.

The discovery of some such process as is suggested by Chrystal and reported by Heath[1] to show that the diagonal of a square is essentially incommensurable with the side did no more than show the foregoing statement about all right-angled triangles to be a false hypothesis. Thus commensurable right-angled triangles can be constructed (obviously) but the incommensurability of arbitrary magnitudes implies anyhow that arbitrary right-angled triangles are incommensurable. Having said this we

[1] *Euclid's Elements*, Book V, Vol. III, p. 19.

are still faced with difficult problems of, on the one hand, how we meet practical situations and, on the other, how we use contemporary mathematical language to discuss events of the past. For example:

(i) Pythagorean triads of integers are such that given an arbitrary right-angled triangle a set of three can be formed such that the proportion of the three is as near as we could decide with the instruments at our disposal (social agreement once more?).

(ii) The usual proof that $\sqrt{n}$, where $n \neq k^2$, $k$ integral, is irrational, using modern algebraic symbolism, is irrelevant to past endeavours.

If we are to recognise the present state of mathematical education as requiring a more enlightened view of continuity then we must look at how we deal with equality. One may observe simultaneously the power of equality and the difficulty in defining it. The recent development of the notion of equivalence relation opens up the prospects enormously so that it is possible to see much more light in this confused issue than hitherto.

If, as I have stated, Euclid's work is unequivocally a systematisation of the geometry of extensive magnitudes, then in modern parlance we can recognise the efforts of Eudoxus, represented in Book V, to produce equivalence classes of ratios.

The failure of Eudoxus was in the confused attempt to deal simultaneously with ratios which could be equal in terms of commensurability and those which could never be. The modern concept of 'equivalence class' helps greatly in the distinguishing between different kinds of equality. It allows control with respect to defined sets of aggregates of elements in the distinguishing which is necessary, dependent on the transformations which are allowable both within and between sets. Definition 5 of Book V runs as follows: 'Magnitudes are said to be in the same ratio, the first to the second and the third to the fourth, when, if any equimultiples whatever be taken of the first and third, and any equimultiples whatever of the second and fourth, the former equimultiples alike exceed, are alike equal to, or alike fall short of, the latter equimultiples respectively taken in corresponding order.'[1] This is re-stated in terms of De Morgan's two sets of letters thus: 'Four magnitudes, $A$ and $B$ of one kind, and $C$ and $D$ of the same or another kind, are proportional when all the multiples of $A$ can be distributed among the multiples of $B$ in the same intervals as the corresponding multiples of $C$ among those of $D$.'[2] He gives this after he has shown, given four magnitudes $A$, $B$, $C$, $D$ and $m$ and $n$ which are any two numbers whatsoever, that $mA \gtreqless nB$ according as $mC \gtreqless nD$, or $mA - nB$

---

[1] *Euclid's Elements*, Book V, Vol. II, p. 114.
[2] De Morgan, A. Article on 'Proportion', *Penny Cyclopaedia*, Vols. 19, 20, pp. 49–53. 1841.

always having the same sign as $mC-nD$, for all integral $m$, $n$, gives a definition of proportion for the magnitudes $A$, $B$, $C$, $D$.

It will be observed that by replicating magnitude $A$ alongside replicated $B$, an order of occurrence of end-points will be established.

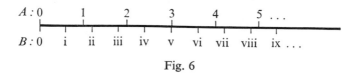

$A:0 \quad 1 \quad 2 \quad 3 \quad 4 \quad 5 \ldots$

$B:0 \quad i \quad ii \quad iii \quad iv \quad v \quad vi \quad vii \quad viii \quad ix \ldots$

Fig. 6

thus: 0 i 1 ii iii 2 iv v 3 vi 4 vii viii 5 ix ...

It is this order of distribution which must be the same for $C$ and $D$ so that they are in the same proportion as $A$ and $B$.

There are three things possible:

(i) that we have chosen $A$ and $B$ knowingly to be commensurable, that is, they are constructed out of a common unit;

(ii) that having chosen $A$ and $B$ arbitrarily we are prepared to accept a social agreement as to coincidence;

(iii) that $A$ and $B$ are identifiably arbitrary and logically no question arises about practical agreements.

Effectively the Greeks failed to provide an operational calculus that corresponded to this third category and as it seems they were not sure what the theory was trying to do they relied on its interpretation applied to commensurables to provide the calculus necessary for incommensurables. This has caused quite a lot of trouble usually obscured under what are called 'approximations' and 'errors'.

It was not until Dedekind[1] formulated his theory of the cut ('schnitt') that the misconception had a chance of being removed. As far as school mathematics is concerned we are still a long way from doing this. Dedekind was at considerable pains to claim to be the first to investigate the notion of 'cut' 'in its logical purity without any notion of measurable quantities'. He objected strongly to suggestions that his work was anticipated saying that although he depended on Euclid, Book V, Definition 5, all other work that he had seen either ignored the problem[2] or used the notion of approximation.[3]

The formulation given by De Morgan can be used to relate the distribu-

[1] Dedekind, R. *Essays on the Theory of Numbers*, Dover, 1963. However, as Manheim points out many statements were being made within the same period, involving Hamilton, Weierstrauss, Cantor, Bolzano and others.

[2] Legendre, according to de Morgan.      [3] Bertrand, Dedekind's own reference.

tion of the replicated magnitudes to Dedekind's notion of a cut. Given two like magnitudes $\alpha$, $\beta$ and pairs of integers $p$, $q$, $m$, $n$, such that $p\alpha < q\beta$ and $m\alpha > n\beta$, then by arguments similar to previous ones

$$n p\alpha < nq\beta \quad \text{and} \quad qm\alpha > qn\beta.$$

Thus
$$qm\alpha > np\alpha, \quad qm > np, \quad \frac{m}{n} > \frac{p}{q}.$$

It should be noted that the magnitudes involved here are not put in ratios directly. This happens only to the numbers which operate on them. By showing how two separate sets of ratios may be formed satisfying Dedekind's cut requirements, the way is paved for defining explicitly the new entity when there is no question of *equality* in the older sense. The equality aspect of Euclid's Definition 5, even in De Morgan's formulation, is irrelevant to the equivalence classes of ratios formed out of the inequality relations linking an arbitrary pair of magnitudes through arbitrary pairs of integers.

Children brought up in the pre-Dedekind mode believe in the existence of the square root of five, say, and produce rational numbers which are 'approximations'. Until we have an adequate calculus linked with the explicit recognition of the real number as a separate entity, much of the work done in elementary mathematics courses is tantamount to trickery. Thus one can hardly point to any elementary English textbook of the differential calculus which, depending on a continuity axiom, rarely states or even hints at, one. What is found instead is a reliance on an intuition linked with the ability to draw a line with a pencil.

So much of so-called 'modern' mathematics, and by this I mean the misnamed newer topics being injected into secondary school courses, miss the point that we face a really radical challenge from real modern mathematics. The present changes are often no more than a reshuffling of some interesting Victorian mathematical notions laced with a set theoretic language which appears to give respectability. The main challenge still lies, as it did with the Greeks, in the dichotomy between discrete finite and infinite concepts on the one hand and problems of continuity on the other. We must guard against procedures which obscure this dichotomy, for example, the traditional approach to Euclidean geometry with the confusions described above; or the casual invoking of the continuity of the rationals in work on measurement when the only operational calculus available is of the integers, that is, calculation with decimal fractions obscures the step that has been taken because the operational calculus involved is essentially integral.

The guarding that is necessary is a protection of one of the main virtues of a mathematical education—the sustenance of honesty in the experiencing of perception and intellectual construction. In hard mathematical terms this can come to the issue that the development of point set theory in the last hundred years has been the basis of the study of continuity. There is a considerable lack of coherence in any theoretical structure of choice in mathematical curricula and that sets are introduced into mathematical activity in order to deal with problems of continuity will appear to many teachers as an odd paradox.

Unless we develop a philosophy of the choice that is made in mathematical educational terms within a curriculum context, the teaching of mathematics will continue its accidental way relying mainly for success on the cunning use of the Hawthorn effect. That is, novelty produces an increase in output, and while resourceful teachers continue to find ways of interesting pupils this will guarantee a steady supply of mathematicians. But this is Machiavellian rather than mathematical. The implicit honesty of real mathematics is missing.

# 'I THOUGHT YOU WERE GOING TO TELL US ABOUT AUTOMORPHISMS'

*by* A. P. K. CALDWELL

'And how will your night dances
Lose themselves. In mathematics?'
Sylvia Plath

A: I thought you were going to tell us about automorphisms.

B: And it turned out to be about aesthetics. Yes; I know.

A: What do you mean by an automorphism anyway?

B: A mapping of a map on itself which leaves some relations unaltered?

A: I know you can say something like that, but that doesn't tell us what automorphisms are about.

B: Symmetries.

A: How do you mean 'symmetries'? Geometrical symmetries?

B: Yes, those as well.
   But I really mean the most general idea of symmetry. Speaking metaphorically, looking at something from different viewpoints and saying that it is the *same* thing we are looking at.

A: You mean this is what is going on if I walk round a piece of sculpture, looking at it from different points of view?

B: Yes, perhaps, though I did say 'speaking metaphorically'. Really much more like looking at problems from different points of view.

A: I have heard that said before—the solution of a problem comes from identifying the symmetries in it. But coming back to the sculpture: you said 'Yes, perhaps'; is it the same sculpture we are seeing if we see it not only from different angles but against different backgrounds too?

B: If you like. It's up to you. Being able to call things the 'same' is the most powerful mental operation we know, and is, of course, the mainspring of mathematics. It is what enables us to act; and its validity in any particular case is a pragmatic one.
   For your sculpture it might be valid, so what? The real interest here is aesthetical not mathematical. Although the sculpture looks

73

different from different points of view, and is seen against different backgrounds, perhaps it might be fair to say that the basic structure of our feelings evoked by the sculpture remains essentially the same as we move round it.

A:  Yes, I think I'd expect that.

It occurred to me that in this mathematical preparation for action, calling things the same, this is one thing that words themselves do, by their nature.

B:  Like 'table', to be philosophical!

A:  Of course! Or 'two', to be mathematical. When 'words fail us' though, it is a question of differentiating feelings. A word like 'love', doing duty for an infinite variety, is miserably inadequate.

B:  And this is what aesthetics is about, conveying significant differences.

A:  Go on.

B:  We need the structuration of symmetries to tell us when things are the 'same'; but we need to be able to respond to differences when the symmetries are broken. It is often impossible to describe adequately subtle differences which may be significant.

A:  Yes, that's the point; as we say doing so-and-so 'is an art', meaning that to do it successfully, to do it well, you must be responsive to fine differences in ways that are difficult or impossible to describe or prescribe: 'It's an art', we say; and 'he has the art of—' doing something or other.

B:  Doing mathematics is an art!

A:  I rather had the idea that aesthetics was a precious preoccupation of dilettante art-lovers.

B:  No, no. Aesthetics is to do with the expression of human thoughts and feelings in general.

There are the media of expression: movement which may be dance, sound which may be music, words written and spoken, paint, clay, stone, and so on. Within the media we allow ourselves different resources; the gestures of a polite social interchange are restricted compared with those of a dance drama, you can paint in black and white or use a rainbow palette. Using these resources, we may give our thoughts and feelings embodiment in more or less complex expressive forms: we may use a simple song or a whole opera, a sonatina or a symphony, a stroll in step with someone or a dance of courtship. Often we use expressive forms which have another purpose, like preparing a meal, designing a car, making a garden or building a boat. Either way, we sometimes say 'that was a work of art'; and sometimes a work of art endures.

The essence of a work of art is its particularity; especially in its detail, it is an expression different from all others. We recognise artistry by the skill and subtlety of the differentiation; and it is an artist's concern that we shall perceive and understand differences.

Though particularity is of its essence, a work of art necessarily has a structure embedded in it. The structure of a work of art is what gives it its coherence, and gives generality to the particular expression of human thoughts and feelings that it is. Its structure is what allows it to stand up on its own. A work of art in its particularity is concrete; its structure is abstract. Generally speaking, structures are abstractions from our experience we make in order to act. A work of art is a by-product of a dialectic between experience and action.

Structures are patterns, symmetries, discerned when we ignore some parts of experience, when we ignore differences. They may be patterns of ideas or feelings; and they may or may not be connected with patterns in physical space or time. Metaphorically (and here we use the pattern of a pattern) we can use the notion of a space to cover realms of experience, of ideas and of emotions, and think of these as different spaces.

We move from one space to another by making maps, mapping one space into another. An artist maps from domains of ideas and emotions into ranges of experience, using the patterns of his experience which he has mapped into his own mental and emotional spaces.[1] It is his choice and use of a particular range of experience in which to express himself that is the aesthetic praxis. In the most general sense every theory is mathematical. I am trying to sketch a theory of aesthetics for you.

And whether you like a piece of mathematics or not is a matter of aesthetics.

[1] 'It's what I try in my sculpture. It's a metaphor of the human relationship with the earth, with mountains and landscape. Like in poetry you can say that the mountains skipped like rams. The sculpture itself is a metaphor like the poem.'—Henry Moore.

*Legend to figures appearing on* pp. 76, 77, 78.

Two-piece reclining figure no. 1, 1959. (Pp. 99, 98, 17, 101 in *Henry Moore* by David Sylvester, The Arts Council of Great Britain.)

# THE CONCEPT OF FUNCTION IN THE TEACHING OF ELEMENTARY MATHEMATICS

*by* LUCIENNE FÉLIX

'Do you give the lesson this way because you know you can do it well and you enjoy it, or because it is really effective for your pupils?'     A. G. Sillitto

The school teacher's art lies in effacing himself, merely stimulating the growth of ideas in his pupil's minds until the day when another teacher, with the ground well-prepared, is able to present the grand climax. When a topic is thought difficult to teach, it is rarely because the concepts are truly complex and beyond reach. Nearly always the fault lies in our teaching. The acquired habits and strict adherence to learned rules paralyse the activities of children's minds already mature enough to react to a new situation.

So children of four or five will respond to playing with the problems of Tom Thumb[1] while their older brothers and sisters who come to school will remain unresponsive because the teacher 'hasn't done that yet.'

Among the topics often thought of as difficult are those concerning functions. Several years ago a teacher at the Technical Institute in Moscow asked me, 'How do you deal with this? My students haven't mastered the idea of a function. They know all the functions in the programme—quadratic and homographic functions, for examples—but that hardly helps at all!'

I replied by telling him of a recent event.

One morning, an extremely black cloud rapidly covered the Paris sky; it happened so suddenly that it frightened some of the pupils. In my class of 11-year-olds I had to stop the work they had begun and I suggested, to calm them down, that they should show on the blackboard the behaviour of the phenomenon which had produced the effect.

We quickly agreed to draw a horizontal axis of time and we discussed how to make a 'graph' (I gave them the word) like one which shows, for example, the temperature of an invalid.

[1] *Les cent problèmes du Petit Poucet*, Editions Blanchard: 9, rue de Médicis, Paris (6ème).

79

Some pupils chose to show the spread of darkness and others the change of light. Without my having to say anything, except to encourage them to explain, they compared the graphs they had drawn.

I was now sure of the extent of the children's knowledge and of its potentialities: they had a good intuitive grasp of how to represent change of state; of continuity; of the connection between the speeds at which the conditions changed (which later on becomes the derivative); and of the slope of the curve (which becomes that of the tangent), as well as the variations in curvature.

The discussion, in fact, centred on the instruments which would be needed to make measurements, and not on the concept of a function and its representation which seemed self-evident to the children.

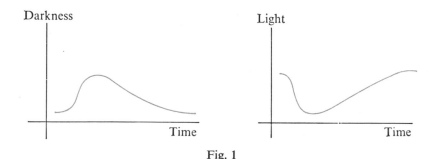

Fig. 1

Does this mean that the ideas were securely established, solid enough to be a beginning for a deductive structure? Certainly not! But the experience shows what children not spoiled by dogmatic teaching can do. Instead of ignoring the rich experience gained by a child from his daily life, we should assist these still unconscious resources and so hasten the day when we know that systematisation is now appropriate.

Teaching an essential concept at primary or secondary level (not to speak of the university!) should be the building, the axiomatisation of mathematical structures which are already familiar through use, though they may be poorly co-ordinated, vague and only partly realised. Then a certain amount of dogmatism becomes inevitable; it is necessary to impose a logical sequence, to make rules, even if the pupil does not immediately see the need for them. At any rate the pupils will mostly be meeting again, put more clearly, those things they already possess. We help them to build up and take apart a machine-tool which is more complex and subtle than they thought possible, but which they can comprehend and use, so that they can move to a higher level of understanding without sacrificing their earlier intuitions.

I am not going to describe here a topic called 'Functions' which suddenly erupts into the classroom without anyone quite knowing why. My suggestion is rather that we look at the track of this concept across the mathematical experience of the pupils, and how it gives them occasions to see something of its fundamental aspects. This is possible for us now that the language of sets and relations has given unity and continuity to our thinking and expression.

Mathematicians, and mathematics courses in particular, have, until the present century, confined their attention to numerical functions and their analytic expression. Here we shall use the word 'function' in a much wider sense and we shall not talk about numerical functions first, although we can and must introduce functions as soon as schooling begins.

We will describe three paths in the study of functions; they will be followed simultaneously by the pupils until they begin to converge (at about 15 years old, for example, in French lycées). A coherent and definitive study can then be undertaken at any chosen level after this.

## I  WHAT IS THE NATURE OF A FUNCTION?

As the dictionary indicates, the concept of *function* is bound up with the notion of *action*. We sometimes use the model of a machine like a coffee-grinder: an element $a$ is inserted through one aperture, the handle is turned, and an element $b$ is ejected through another hole. There must be, in fact, a starting-set $A$ from which $a$ is selected, a finishing-set $B$ to which $b$ belongs, and the machine must operate deterministically: that is, $b$ must

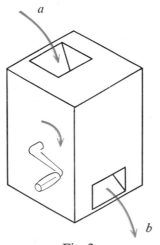

Fig. 2

81

be completely determined once *a* is chosen. The function in this example is the grinder (or the act of grinding, if you like) and not the set of coffee beans or the set of blobs of powder leaving the machine. Notice that the machine can reject beans which are too large or too hard! Lastly, we will distinguish the starting-set *A* and its subset *X* for which the function is defined, the finishing-set *B* to which the transformed elements belong (the *images* of the starting-elements), and the function *f*, represented by an arrow. More than one arrow can point to the same finishing-element, but only one arrow can start from an element *a*.

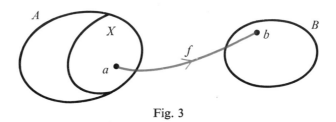

Fig. 3

## First path

*Example 1:* (here is the first contact with a study of functions for 6 or 7-year-old children).

The material comprises four kinds of objects. For ease of drawing, we will take them to be white squares, black squares, white triangles and black triangles. We will bring into action two kinds of machine: one which

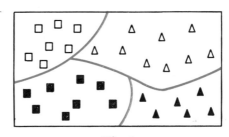

Fig. 4

changes the colour and the other which changes the shape. The role of the machines will be played by the children, of course. We will agree to use the symbols ⓒ for those which change colour, and ⓢ for those which change shape. One factory submits an object to the action of several machines in succession. To be able to replace a factory by a single machine, two other types of machine have to be imagined: one which changes both colour and shape, which will be written (cs), and a strange machine which does nothing, the neutral machine n.

We pass over the details of the game[1] and the children's reactions, and look at the conclusions which emerge for us, the teachers.

1   Each machine respects the partition into equivalence classes, so that the starting-set is in reality the set of the four classes.

2   The finishing-set is the same as the starting-set (the functions are permutations). We see this in diagrams like the following, which shows the behaviour of the function (s).

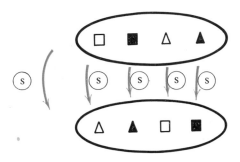

Fig. 5

3   We have introduced the *product by composition*, but that forces us to make an *extension* of the set of functions. This product of functions is clearly an operation in the set of functions since the product does not depend on the starting-element.

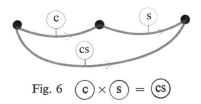

Fig. 6   (c) × (s) = (cs)

This holds *for every* starting-element (the universal quantifier appears already).

4   Each function is its own inverse.

$$(c) \times (c) = (n), \quad (s) \times (s) = (n), \quad (cs) \times (cs) = (n).$$

[1] See the account of the experiences of Mme Picard, published by the Institut National de Pédagogie de Paris.

So we have, surprisingly,

$$\forall k, \forall h, \quad \textcircled{k} \times \textcircled{x} = \textcircled{h} \Leftrightarrow \textcircled{x} = \textcircled{k} \times \textcircled{h}.$$

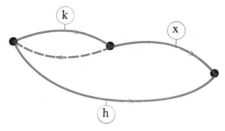

Fig. 7

5   The product by composition is associative by nature, as the diagram indicates.

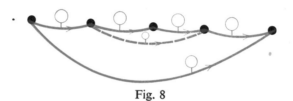

Fig. 8

6   Moreover it is commutative.
(All this emerges from studying the machines in action.)
7   A table readily summarises the information once and for all.

|  | n | c | s | cs |
|---|---|---|---|---|
| n | n | c | s | cs |
| c | c | n | cs | s |
| s | s | cs | n | c |
| cs | cs | s | c | n |

Fig. 9

8   Without needing to return to the initial situation, we know how to simplify every possible product, and solve equations in one unknown. In short, we have achieved *the algebraic study of this set of functions* under the operation of product by composition. This set has the structure of the commutative group with four elements (Klein's group).

What does the child understand about this structure? What is the purpose of the game? We know of other games which show the same or analogous structures. The pupils of Mme Picard made up a game with letters which they immediately recognised as being 'the same'.

As further examples of the same structure, here are two examples which we can use later on in this chapter.

*Dolls*: The starting-set is made up of four positions of a doll.

Fig. 10

The functions can be described as, for example,

|             |     |
|-------------|-----|
| 'turn round' | Ⓣ |
| 'fall over' | Ⓕ |
| 'turn upside down' | Ⓤ |

and the 'neutral' function   Ⓝ.

85

*Right angles:* The starting-set is

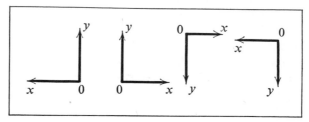

Fig. 11

and the functions are the same as for the dolls.

*Example 2:* The starting-set is the set of six positions of three objects. The set of functions is the set of permutations.

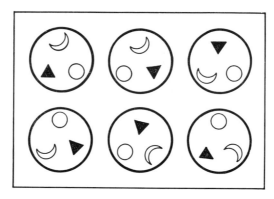

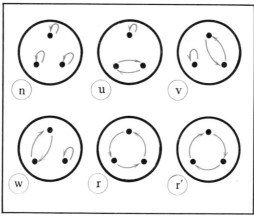

Fig. 12

A similar study to the one made in the previous example will show the *non-commutativity* of the product by composition.

It is a quick and enjoyable task for children of 10 to 12 years to write out the operations of the group in the form of a multiplication table, and it leads to instructive algebraic computations because of its non-commutativity. A particular point is the solution of equations by using inverse functions. $(\mathbf{n})$, $(\mathbf{u})$, $(\mathbf{v})$, $(\mathbf{w})$ are each self-inverse, while $(\mathbf{r})$ and $(\mathbf{r'})$ are each the inverse of the other.

*Example 3:* The last two-models have an obvious geometrical aspect. Can we move from them to the classical geometrical functions of symmetries and rotations?

But be careful! Let us look at the doll game. It is ideal for allowing us to study angles as ordered pairs of half-lines (the line of the body, the lines of the arms). This is a fruitful meaning for the word 'angle'; but can we really see rotations as functions? We know that we must be able to define (for those functions which are permutations) the product by composition. Now let us give the doll two of these 'rotations' and try to settle the matter of commutativity. (The dolls are held in the hand!) It is clear that the functions are not well enough defined to let us invert the order. What is rotation $b$ if I only have doll $P_1$?

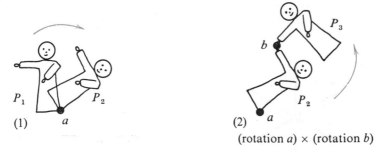

(1)     $a$          (2)   $a$

(rotation $a$) × (rotation $b$)

Fig. 13

This is an opportunity to describe a situation in very precise mathematical terms. The starting-set is the plane, a set $P$ of points, given a system of co-ordinates so that each particular point ($a$, for example) can be picked out, and so that a typical element $m$—a 'roving point'—can be made to coincide with *every* point of the starting-set. The function (rotation, for example) acts over an infinite set

$$\forall m, \quad m \in P, \quad m(f)m', \quad m' \in P.$$

This does not prevent the transformation of subsets of points (figures).

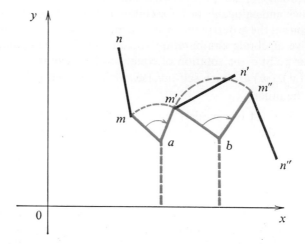

Fig. 14

Our Example 2, then, displays a set of three points. Making them the vertices of an equilateral triangle, we could think of three axial symmetries and two rotations of a third of a complete turn.

Example 1 suggests that we consider the vertices of a rhombus, two axial symmetries about perpendicular axes, and a central symmetry.

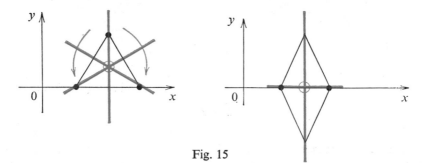

Fig. 15

## Second path

The principal feature here is to develop, by means of more precise examples, what we said before about the darkness incident; that is, to describe functions we meet which do not involve any systematic use of numbers, and where we certainly do not know the formulae which would tell us how to calculate the values of the images. It is for this reason that the teacher draws attention to the growth of a bean, or the inclination of the pointer of a balance. The object of the study, in short, is not a special figure or a particular case, but a set of figures or a category of situations.

*First example:* In geometry, we define perpendiculars and oblique lines. Let us put $\overline{Ob} = d$, $\overline{Om} = x$, $\overline{bm} = y$. We will consider the functions indicated by the diagram. By copying the distances with compasses, and without measurement, the children can construct point graphs of the function (f), or, better, the function (g).

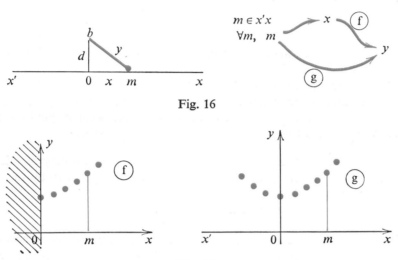

Fig. 16

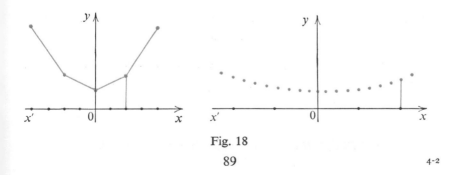

Fig. 17

The feeling of continuity awakens a need to join the points with lines; should they be straight or curved? The teacher does not legislate, but suggests that the scale be changed in order to make a detailed study of critical parts of the graph—near $x = 0$, for example.

Fig. 18

89

4-2

LUCIENNE FÉLIX

*Similar example:* (using angle measure).

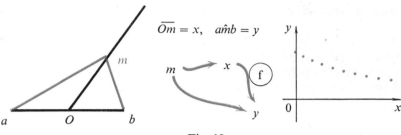

Fig. 19

(The results of this were used spontaneously by children when they came to deal with inscribed angles several months later.)

In these two examples, we perceive the preservation or inversion of the order relation (demonstrations are given only if the ability to argue deductively has not been reached). Numerous exercises can be put forward for optional work to give further rich and varied experience.

*Second example:* (for a higher level, after the fundamentals of affine geometry have been met.) Here we make the traditional study of the function

$$m \in \text{straight line } ab \ \forall m, \ m \leadsto y = \frac{\overline{mb}}{\overline{ma}}.$$

We will use the method which it is natural to adopt if one knows how to construct $m$ given $y$; that is, the construction which employs the inverse function.[1] We suppose that the point $s$ is fixed and consider the line $Q$ parallel to $as$ such that

$$y = \frac{\overline{mb}}{\overline{ma}} = \frac{\overline{bq}}{\overline{as}},$$

where $\overline{as}$ is constant.

To make the graph, we will take $\overline{as} = +1$ so that we need only copy $\overline{bq}$ with compasses.

We consider

$$m \in x'x \backslash \{a\}$$

$$\forall m, \ m \leadsto y$$

and, having chosen an origin $O$ of co-ordinates on $x'x$, putting $\overline{Oa} = k$, $\overline{Ob} = h$,

$$\forall x, x \in R \backslash \{k\}$$

$$x \leadsto y = \frac{x-h}{x-k}.$$

[1] Félix, L. *Géométrie, Classes de 4ème et 3ème*, Dunod.

$x$, $h$, $k$ being measured, $y$ can be calculated and compared with the measure of $bq$.

We will return later to the rich study that this example offers. We merely take note of the fact that the calculus which leads to the numerical functions can be made as precise as we like.

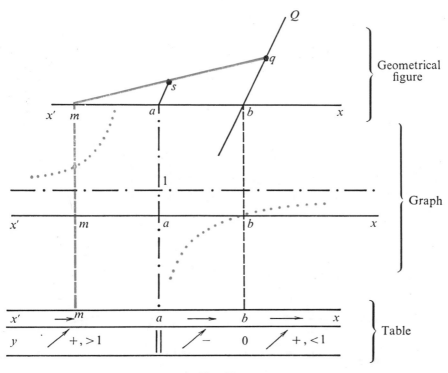

Fig. 20

## *Third path*

*Numerical functions:* As soon as the child knows the first four natural numbers, he can be introduced to the function 'add 2'. I have seen very young children at work, in Argentina, with grains of maize and squared paper. Some of them began to ask how to talk about and write the last results (see fig. 21).

Children who have played with 'machines' are able to write quite naturally...(see fig. 22).

The function 'multiply by' is basically very similar, since from the definition of multiplication, 'multiply by 3' changes each element into three elements (see fig. 23).

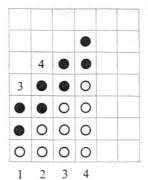

Fig. 21

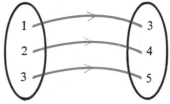

Fig. 22

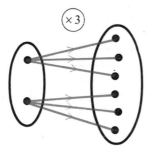 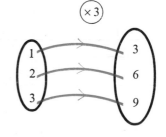

Fig. 23

A little later, the function 'multiply by $\frac{1}{4}$' or 'by $\frac{5}{4}$' introduces the idea of fractions.

Products by composition are only straightforward provided we do not mix up addition machines and multiplication machines.

We might then go on to consider all the functions that we commonly meet in problems (with only slight variations at the primary school level); then in the case of algebraic expressions we shall produce formulas of the kind $y = f(x)$ to be represented by means of point graphs—and create plenty of surprises for our pupils. The starting-set will be the richest one we know: $Q$ (the set of rational numbers) or $R$ (the set of real numbers). In this way, the systematic study of several simple functions can be approached.

## Conclusions

*What does the study of a function entail?* We must distinguish an algebraic study from a topological study. We will just point out, without making very much of it here, that not only can we define the product by composition in the set of numerical functions, but also a vector space structure and a ring structure.

*Consideration of the inverse of each function studied* forces us to distinguish (long before the technical words are available) injective, surjective and bijective functions. In the example of oblique lines, the non-injective function $(\mathbf{g})$ forces us to consider the pair of points $m$, reciprocal images for a chosen value of $y$.

## The search for different kinds of invariants

1 If there are *order relations in the starting-set and finishing set*, the preservation or inversion of the order is immediately recognised or examined. In the case of numerical functions, the state of the natural order relation is unfortunately called the 'growth of the function' as if the function were changing! (The historical reasons for the phrase are clear and respectable, though not the less regrettable for that. It is a source of errors in dealing with the product by composition, where the results are so evident when the term is avoided.)

2 Particularly noteworthy are the *invariant elements* for a function, apart from the neutral element (1 for a multiplicative function, the centre of a rotation, etc.).

3 A *relation may be preserved* between every pair of elements in the starting-set.

*Example:* The length or direction of an ordered pair under the 'translation function'.

$$x \, \textcircled{f} \, x + a \quad (a \text{ being given})$$

$$\forall x_1, \forall x_2, \quad f(x_2) - f(x_1) = x_2 - x_1.$$

4 *Preservation of a relation* (preservation of angle, parallelism, etc.). We must stress the fundamental importance of the *linear function: a* being given, $x \, \textcircled{f} \, ax.$

This preserves addition and multiplication by a constant, and hence all linear relations; for example,

$$(k_1 x_1 + k_2 x_2 + k_3 x_3) \, \textcircled{f} \, (k_1 f(x_1) + k_2 f(x_2) + k_3 f(x_3)).$$

If this is used from the beginning in applying numbers to the solution of problems, it shows the need to study reciprocals when dealing with functional equations in $Q$ or $R$.

$$\forall x_1, \forall x_2, \quad f(x_1+x_2) = f(x_1)+f(x_2)$$

and

$$\forall x_1, \forall k, \quad f(kx_1) = kf(x_1).$$

The comparison of the additive and multiplicative structures imposes the introduction of the function defined by

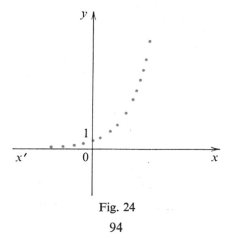

and of the inverse function. One can obviously only hope to find an isomorphism if the neutral elements are made to correspond: $0 \frown 1$.

To be free to move, we need another pair. In order to make the computations easy, children of 13 and 14 spontaneously choose $1 \frown 10$, from which other pairs can be obtained to fill out the table.

$$1 \frown 10$$
$$2 \frown 10^2 = 100$$
$$\tfrac{1}{2} \frown 10^{\frac{1}{2}} = \sqrt{10} \simeq 3 \cdot 162$$
$$-1 \frown 10^{-1} = \tfrac{1}{10} = 0 \cdot 1$$

This introduces the logarithmic and exponential functions in a natural way (together with the use of tables, and even the formula for changing the base)

Fig. 24

94

The problems that arise over the accuracy of approximations come because the multiplicative structure does not lend itself to the study of differences. The urgent need for a topological study emerges, but this crown of the algebraic study is prepared over a long period!

*Topology.* From the first calculations with small numbers, and the first measurements, approximations have to be introduced.

The important thing is to acquire the idea of *neighbourhood*: neighbourhoods of a number in a known set ($Q$ or its extensions); neighbourhoods of a point (on a line, in a plane, in space, on a curve): and also neighbourhoods of an element in the set of straight lines, or circles, or triangles, etc. We must know what we are doing when we verify a theorem or a calculation experimentally.

The need to consider *neighbourhoods in the set of functions* starts with the first graphs. Not only are the points we plot approximate, but we must decide how to join them. Where must we change the scale in order to improve the graph? The continuity of the phenomenon being graphed is

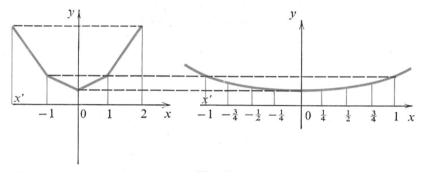

Fig. 25

too obvious to young children to give them reason to question it, but that which will later on be seen to be the continuity of the derivative comes up for discussion at an intuitive level early on.

The crucial examples come in the form of movements which are 'piecewise uniform'. The movement of a train is observed from the platform by noting the times when it passes some chosen positions. The graph, which is the union of several straight line segments, is a good approximation for certain purposes. The function is 'piecewise affine'; the speed is a 'step function' (see fig. 26).

But we have shown the movement as three jolts and a tremendous shock which sends the train backwards! We must smooth out the graph and make the speed continuous. This gives a good start to the idea of a derivative and of a primitive. We can surely see here a preparation for the calculation of areas using primitives, although I have never found this particular situation normally leads to any thought of area.

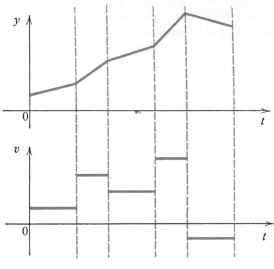

Fig. 26

## 2 CONTINUITY OF A FUNCTION AT A POINT. LIMIT. INFINITY

Fourteen-year-old children, trained to use graphs in the way we have described, understand and can use by themselves the strict analytical definitions without difficulty.

Let us recall what is necessary.

1 The image of a neighbourhood of $x_0$ is a neighbourhood of $y_0 = f(x_0)$, and the function preserves the inclusion of neighbourhoods.

Since we get from $w_1$ to $w_2$ by suppressing the images of the elements in $v_1 \backslash v_2$,
$$v_2 \subset v_1 \Rightarrow w_2 \subset w_1.$$

2 *Continuity* replies to the question: How can we make sure that $y \in w$, where $w$ is a neighbourhood of $y_0 = f(x_0)$?

If the question is asked by a physicist, we answer by looking for a neighbourhood $v$ of $x_0$ whose image is included in $w$. Every neighbourhood $v_1$ included in $v$ will work even better (we need a margin of security because of approximations in calculation).

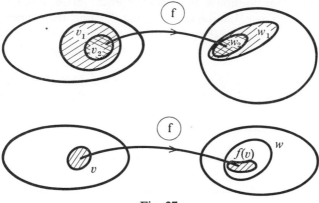

**Fig. 27**

Then the mathematician, to be sure that he has satisfied the physicist, demands the existence of $v$ so that for any given $w$

$$x_0 \rightarrow y_0 \; \forall w, \; \exists v : f(v) \subset w.$$

For our pupils, we replace 'there exists' by 'I can construct' or, in appropriate circumstances, by 'I can compute'.

The problems that occur with the graphs of functions which are defined geometrically (the example of the oblique lines, or the ratio $\overline{mb}/\overline{ma}$) interest the pupils and are readily resolved since the quantifier $\forall$ is very familiar.

In the case of the oblique lines, the answer is valid for every point $m$; but the investigation of $m \rightarrow y = \overline{mb}/\overline{ma}$ creates great involvement.

### 3   *Limit. Point at infinity*

We again consider the figure used to introduce $y = \overline{mb}/\overline{ma}$.

What should we say if we require $q$ to belong to a neighbourhood of $c$: that is to say, $y$ must belong to a neighbourhood of 1?

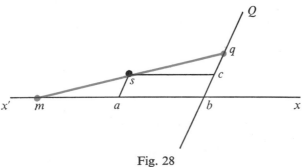

**Fig. 28**

For every other position $q_0$ of $q$, the reciprocal image of the neighbourhood of $q_0$ was a neighbourhood of $m_0$, but this time the reciprocal image of a neighbourhood of $c$ is the union of two half-lines. Examining the effect of the inclusion, we decide to call this union a neighbourhood of the *point at infinity*.

There is no difficulty about the image of a neighbourhood of $a$. Lastly we *adjoin the point at infinity* to the set of points of the straight line, and the *limit* 1 to the set of images $f(m)$.

The complete table is:

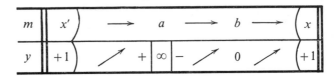

Fig. 29

At the end of the preceding geometrical study, the pupils prove to have no difficulty in writing down in mathematical symbols and enunciating precise definitions of the point at infinity and of a limit. It is apparent that the geometrical model, and the colours used when showing the various neighbourhoods, sustain their intuition, whilst words and calculations only serve to screen them from the ideas.

The calculations based on this situation are done afterwards, having chosen in various ways the position of the origin in order to define $m$. From these, various values of $h$ and $k$ can be substituted in $y = (x-h/x-k)$.

## 3   ANOTHER SITUATION

An example of a limit not involving infinity comes when we reach the idea of a tangent to a circle, where certain situations lead us to consider a line analogous to a secant, but having only one point in common with the circle.

Given a circle $\mathscr{C}(O, R)$ and $a \in \mathscr{C}$. Among the bundle $\mathscr{A}$ of lines passing through $a$, we distinguish the straight line $D$ perpendicular to $Oa$, and we know that

$$\mathscr{C} \cap D = \{a\}.$$

Let $m$ be an arbitrary point of $\mathscr{C}$ and write $M$ for the secant $am$. We study the function $m \underset{\longrightarrow}{\textcircled{f}} M$ defined over $\mathscr{C}\backslash\{a\}$. This function $\textcircled{f}$ is the product

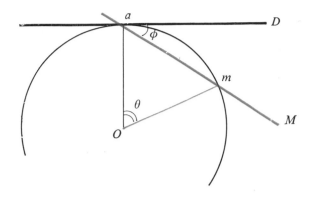

Fig. 30

by composition of

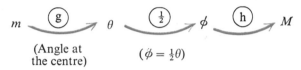

This product gives no problems when *m* is on *a*.

$$a . \quad \textcircled{g} \quad 0 \quad \textcircled{\tfrac{1}{2}} \quad 0 \quad \textcircled{h} \quad D$$

If we decide to complete the definition of ⓕ by putting $a \,\textcircled{f}\, D$, the function

ⓕ becomes defined and continuous (as the neighbourhoods show).
   *D* cannot be called a secant. We say it is 'the limit of the secant when *m* is at *a*' and give it the name *tangent to the circle at a*.
   Analysis at the level studied here has only served to clarify the work in geometry and algebra. It has not been studied for its own sake, and the results obtained have not been completely assimilated and sufficiently fixed to be usable.
   But at the end of this study, the pupils are ready for a systematic treatment of functions in the last stage of secondary education (15 to 18 years).
   We hope only that this preparation, which is quite feasible as our experience has shown, will be tackled perceptively and patiently by the teachers, and that the sixth form teacher who receives the pupils will first of all build on this foundation when he gives his formal exposition.

# DIRECTED NUMBERS

*by* BERYL FLETCHER

One way of developing a Stage A approach to the topic which has been nicknamed 'Directed numbers' is to consider the information given by statements of withdrawals and deposits into the bank accounts of shop-keepers, on two consecutive days. This information can be displayed in tabular form as in the following example:

Table 1

| | Record of transactions on 3rd May Total amount in £'s | | Record of transactions on 4th May Total amount in £'s | |
|---|---|---|---|---|
| | withdrawn | deposited | withdrawn | deposited |
| Mr Black | 17 | 14 | 12 | 18 |
| Mr Brown | 9 | 12 | 14 | 17 |
| Mr Dalton | 13 | 14 | 10 | 16 |
| Mr Green | 9 | 8 | 14 | 9 |
| Mr White | 16 | 10 | 7 | 6 |
| Mr Wood | 14 | 13 | 12 | 12 |

From this table, we can construct another table which shows the change in the balances of the shop-keepers' accounts due to these transactions as follows:

Table 2

| | Change in balance due to the transactions of 3rd May | Change in balance due to the transactions of 4th May |
|---|---|---|
| Mr Black | 3 | 6 |
| Mr Brown | 3 | 3 |
| Mr Dalton | 1 | 6 |
| Mr Green | 1 | 5 |
| Mr White | 6 | 1 |
| Mr Wood | 1 | No change |

Unfortunately, these entries in Table 2, do not indicate whether these changes in the balances were gains or losses. We can, however, improve these entries so that the kind of change is shown also, as follows:

Table 3

|  | Change in balance due to the transactions of 3rd May | Change in balance due to the transactions of 4th May |
|---|---|---|
| Mr Black | L3 | G6 |
| Mr Brown | G3 | G3 |
| Mr Dalton | G1 | G6 |
| Mr Green | L1 | L5 |
| Mr White | L6 | L1 |
| Mr Wood | L1 | 0 |

where G indicates that the change in the balance was a gain; L indicates that the change in the balance was a loss, and 0 indicates no change.

Similarly, if a lift in a large hotel makes successive stops at the following floors:

2nd;   6th;   3rd;   5th;   1st;   4th;   6th;   1st,

we could record the changes in position of the lift, between successive stops by

U4;   D3;   U2;   D4;   U3;   U2;   D5.

Here we are using U in front of the appropriate natural number to indicate that the change in position was up, and D in front of the appropriate natural number to indicate that the change in position was down. We could also use F6 to show that

(i) a soldier has taken six paces forwards,
(ii) we have turned on six pages in a book,

and B2 to show that

(i) a soldier has taken two paces backwards,
(ii) we have turned back two pages.

However, in all the situations that we have considered, we have been concerned with changes of two kinds. For example, changes in the balance of accounts are either gains or losses. The other situations concerned movements either up or down; forwards or backwards. In order to emphasize this similarity we will use the two symbols + and − to indicate which of the two possible ways the change between the quantities has taken, rather than G and L for balances; U and D for lifts, etc.

102

We are now using the familiar symbols + and − in a new way; they are to be regarded as much a part of the number as the digit(s) and to emphasize this we will write these symbols above and to the left of the appropriate digit(s). Thus we can now write the entries in Table 3, as follows:

Table 4

|  | Change in balance due to the transactions of 3rd May | Change in balance due to the transactions of 4th May |
|---|---|---|
| Mr Black | $^-3$ | $^+6$ |
| Mr Brown | $^+3$ | $^+3$ |
| Mr Dalton | $^+1$ | $^+6$ |
| Mr Green | $^-1$ | $^-5$ |
| Mr White | $^-6$ | $^-1$ |
| Mr Wood | $^-1$ | $0$ |

Numbers, such as $^+6$, which have a plus sign attached to them in this way, are called *positive* numbers and we read the symbols $^+6$ as 'positive six'.

Numbers, such as $^-4$, which have a minus sign attached to them in this way, are called *negative* numbers and we read the symbols $^-4$ as 'negative four'.

Positive and negative numbers, together with zero which indicates no change, form a set of numbers called the *integers*.

Each integer, in Table 4, has been derived from a pair of natural numbers. For example, we obtained the integer $^-3$ in the first row and first column of Table 4, from the natural numbers 17 and 14 which occurred in the first and second columns, respectively, of the first row of Table 1. Similarly, we obtained the integer $^+3$ in the second row and second column of Table 4, from the natural numbers 14 and 17 which occurred in the third and fourth columns, respectively, of the second row of Table 1. Thus $^-3$ has been derived from 17 and 14, and $^+3$ from 14 and 17. This emphasizes that the order of the pair of natural numbers indicates which of the possible ways the change between the quantities has taken. This, in turn, implies that we could have written the changes in balances, position and so on, as ordered pairs of natural numbers. For example, the change in the balance of Mr Green's account on 3rd May, can be denoted by the ordered pair of natural numbers (9, 8). Thus (9, 8) can be used to denote a loss of £1 or a movement downwards or backwards by one unit. Similarly, (10, 16) can be used to denote a gain of £6 or a movement upwards or forwards by six units.

However, (9, 8) is not the only ordered pair of natural numbers we can use to denote a loss of £1 and so on, for the ordered pairs (7, 6) and (14, 13) obtained from Table 1, also indicate a loss of £1 and can also be used to indicate a movement downwards or backwards by one unit, and so we write

$$(9, 8) \equiv (7, 6) \equiv (14, 13) \equiv (3, 2) \equiv \ldots$$

We can also illustrate that each of these ordered pairs represents a movement downwards or backwards by one unit, by directed line segments of unit length of a number line, as follows:

Similarly, the ordered pairs (9, 12), (10 13), (4, 7), (3, 6),...can be used to indicate a movement upwards or forwards by three units, that is,

$$(9, 12) \equiv (10, 13) \equiv (4, 7) \equiv (3, 6) \equiv \ldots$$

and these can be illustrated by directed line segments of length three units of a number line, as shown below:

A set of ordered pairs, such as

(i)  (9, 8), (7, 6), (14, 13), (3, 2),...
(ii)  (9, 12), (10, 13), (4, 7), (3, 6),...

which represent equivalent changes between two quantities in one of the two possible ways, is called a *set of equivalent pairs* or an *equivalence class*.

Thus (9, 8), (7, 6), (14, 13), (3, 2),...are members of the equivalence class {(1, 0)} where {(1, 0)} is the set of ordered pairs equivalent to (1, 0), and (9, 12), (10, 13), (4, 7), (3, 6),... are members of the equivalence class {(0, 3)} where {(0, 3)} is the set of ordered pairs equivalent to (0, 3). We can, in fact, denote the equivalence classes {(1, 0)} and {(0, 3)} by using { } around any member of the set of ordered pairs equivalent to (1, 0) and (0, 3) respectively.

Note also that the integer ⁻1, can be derived from any member of the equivalence class {(1, 0)} and that the integer ⁺3 can be derived from any member of the equivalence class {(0, 3)} and so we give the equivalence classes {(1, 0)} and {(0, 3)} the names 'negative one' and 'positive three' respectively, that is

$$-1 = \{(1, 0)\},$$
$$+3 = \{(0, 3)\}.$$

We can, therefore, now define the set of integers as a set of equivalence classes of ordered pairs of natural numbers.

If we plot the ordered pairs of negative one as the co-ordinates of points on a graph, as shown below

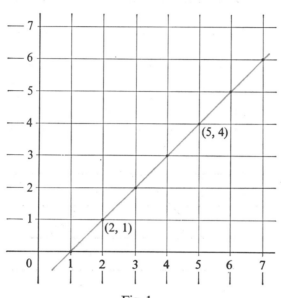

Fig. 1

we see that these ordered pairs lie on a straight line. Similarly, if we plot the ordered pairs of positive three as the co-ordinates of points on a graph, fig. 2, we see that these ordered pairs lie on a straight line which is parallel to the straight line on which the ordered pairs of negative one lie. In fact, if we plot the ordered pairs of any integer as the co-ordinates of points on a graph, we find that these ordered pairs lie on a straight line which is parallel to the straight lines we have already drawn. Thus each integer can be used to define a set of lattice points which lie on a member of a set of parallel lines (see figs. 3 and 4).

Any transversal of this set of parallel lines meets each member of this set of parallel lines in a unique point (fig. 5).

The members of an eqivalence class lie on a member of the set of parallel lines. This line maps all the members of its equivalence class onto a unique

105

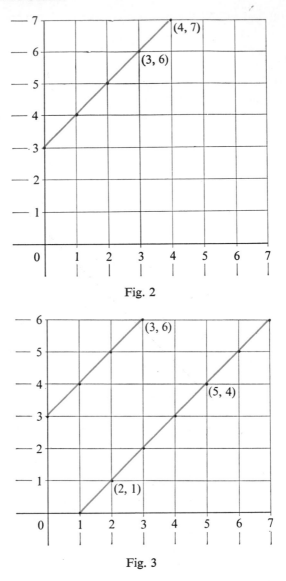

Fig. 2

Fig. 3

point of the transversal. This point can, therefore, be labelled by the name of the particular equivalence class which is mapped onto this point. For example, in fig. 6 the ordered pairs (1, 0), (2, 1), (3, 2), (4, 3),...are mapped onto the point $a$ of the transversal $T$, by the member of the set of parallel lines on which these ordered pairs, when used as co-ordinates of points, lie. Hence we label the point $a$, $^-1$. Similarly, the ordered pairs

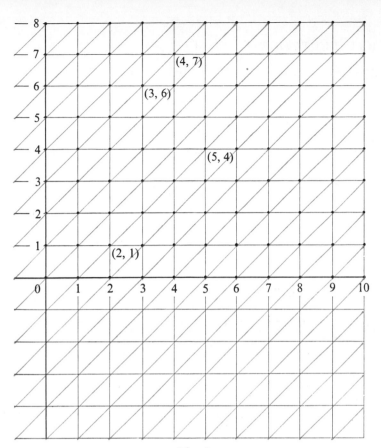

Fig. 4

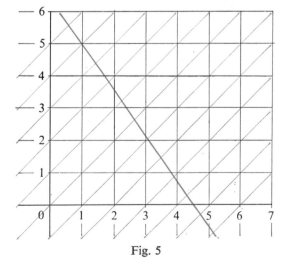

Fig. 5

107

(0, 3), (1, 4), (2, 5),...are mapped onto the point $b$ of the transversal $T$, by the member of the set of parallel lines on which these ordered pairs, when used as co-ordinates of points, lie. Hence, we label the point $b$, $^+3$.

In this way we can form an extended number line. The reference points of this number line however, will be labelled by integers (fig. 7).

By convention, we usually represent this extended number line as shown in the diagrams on p. 110, where the positive numbers are either to the right or above zero and the negative numbers are either to the left or below zero. Note also that for every integer to the right or above zero, there is a corresponding integer to the left or below zero, that is, for every positive number there is a corresponding negative number.

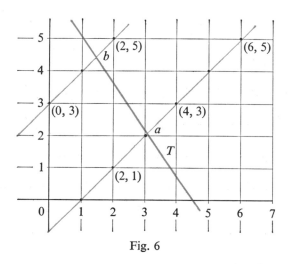

Fig. 6

This property enables us to use the extended number line as a scale of measure for situations where we apparently have things whose measures are less than zero, as in the following example. A boy has 10p and he wishes to buy a stamp from a friend which costs 12p. He can purchase the stamp if he is prepared to owe his friend 2p. If he decides to owe his friend 2p he is worse off than if he had nothing at all. A boy who owes money to somebody else, has, in a sense, less than nothing.

The integers are, therefore, used to describe situations in which a sense of above or below a chosen level, called the origin, is involved.

In many traditional approaches to 'Directed numbers' this use of the extended number line as a scale of measures for situations where we apparently have things whose measures are less than zero, was regarded as the starting point. This method of approach makes the physical interpretation of the operations of addition and multiplication of integers, rather artificial.

This also raises the question, how can we combine any two integers to form a third integer which corresponds to the resultant change between the quantities?

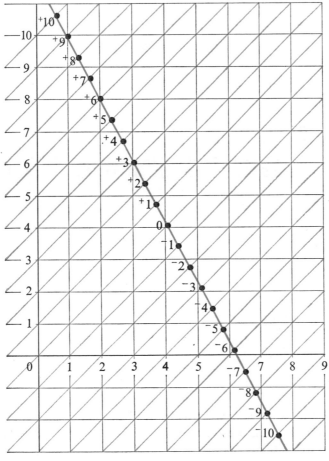

Fig. 7

Since each integer has been derived from an equivalence class of ordered pairs of natural numbers, we must first consider how we can combine any two ordered pairs to form a third ordered pair which is equivalent to the resultant change between the quantities, and then consider what happens when the two ordered pairs are replaced by other members of the equivalence classes to which they belong.

In using the ordered pair of natural numbers $(a, b)$ to denote the situation where a man in the course of a day, withdraws £$a$ from his bank account and pays in £$b$, and using the ordered pair of natural numbers $(c, d)$ to denote the situation where the man withdraws £$c$ and pays in £$d$ on the following day, as in our initial example, we can see that over the two days, the man has withdrawn £$(a+c)$ and paid in £$(b+d)$, which we can denote by $(a+c, b+d)$. We will thus take as our definition of 'addition' of ordered pairs of natural numbers, the relation

$$(a, b)+(c, d) = (a+c, b+d). \tag{1}$$

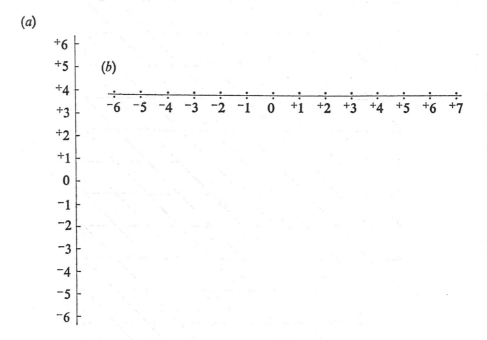

Now we must consider what happens when the terms on the left-hand side of equation (1), are replaced by other members of the equivalence classes to which they belong.

From our earlier discussion of ordered pairs which belong to the same equivalence class, we see that the ordered pairs of natural numbers $(p, q)$ and $(s, t)$ belong to the same equivalence class if

   (i)   $p-q = s-t$,   where $p > q$ and $s > t$,

   (ii)  $q-p = t-s$,   where $p < q$ and $s < t$,

that is, $(p, q)$ and $(s, t)$ belong to the same equivalence class if

$$p+t = q+s.$$

Thus if $(a, b)$ and $(a', b')$ are members of the same equivalence class, then

$$a+b' = a'+b$$

and if $(c, d)$ and $(c', d')$ are members of another equivalence class, then

$$c+d' = c'+d.$$

Hence $\qquad\qquad (a+b')+(c+d') = (a'+b)+(c'+d)$

that is $\qquad\qquad (a+c)+(b'+d') = (a'+c')+(b+d)$

since $a, b, c, d, a', b', c'$ and $d'$ are natural numbers which are commutative and associative with respect to addition. Thus the ordered pairs

$$(a+c, b+d) \quad \text{and} \quad (a'+c', b'+d')$$

are equivalent.

Thus we have shown that if the terms on the left-hand side of equation (1), are replaced by other terms in the same equivalence classes, the resulting terms on the right-hand side of equation (1), all belong to the same equivalence class. For example,

$$(5, 8)+(8, 7) = (13, 15),$$
$$(5, 8)+(3, 2) = (8, 10),$$
$$(1, 4)+(8, 7) = (9, 11),$$
$$(1, 4)+(3, 2) = (4, 6).$$

$(5, 8)$ and $(1, 4)$ belong to the equivalence class $\{(0, 3)\}$; $(8, 7)$ and $(3, 2)$ belong to the equivalence class $\{(1, 0)\}$ and $(13, 15)$, $(8, 10)$, $(9, 11)$ and $(4, 6)$ belong to the equivalence class $\{(0, 2)\}$. Thus we may define a new operation, the operation of addition of equivalence classes, and hence the operation of addition of integers, as

$$\{(a, b)\}+\{(c, d)\} = \{(a+c, b+d)\}. \qquad (2)$$

Hence

(i) $\quad \{(0, 3)\}+\{(1, 0)\} = \{(1, 3)\} = \{(0, 2)\}$

or $\qquad\qquad\qquad {}^+3+{}^-1 = {}^+2.$

(ii) $\quad \{(0, 3)\}+\{(0, 1)\} = \{(0, 4)\}$

or $\qquad\qquad\qquad {}^+3+{}^+1 = {}^+4.$

(iii) $\quad \{(3, 0)\}+\{(1, 0)\} = \{(4, 0)\}$

or $\qquad\qquad\qquad {}^-3+{}^-1 = {}^-4.$

(iv) $\quad \{(3, 0)\}+\{(0, 1)\} = \{(3, 1)\} = \{(2, 0)\}$

or $\qquad\qquad\qquad {}^-3+{}^+1 = {}^-2.$

etc.

111

The behaviour of ordered pairs and equivalence classes under the operations of addition as defined by equations (1) and (2), can be demonstrated geometrically by using the ordered pairs of natural numbers as co-ordinates of points. For example, by joining the points with co-ordinates (1, 4) and (6, 2) to the origin and completing the parallelogram which has these three points as vertices and the lines joining the origin to (1, 4) and (6, 2) as adjacent sides, we see that the fourth vertex of this parallelogram is the point with co-ordinates (7, 6).

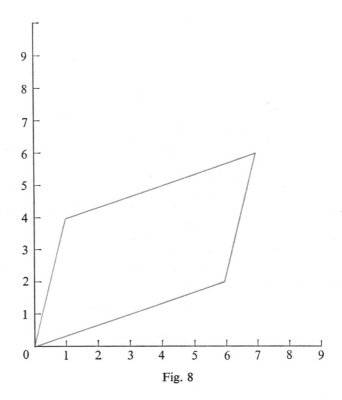

Fig. 8

Any parallelogram which has the origin, $(a, b)$ and $(c, d)$ as the co-ordinates of three vertices, will have $(a+c, b+d)$ as its fourth vertex, if the lines joining the origin to $(a, b)$ and $(c, d)$ are adjacent sides.

On replacing the ordered pair (1, 4) by other members of the equivalence class $\{(0, 3)\}$ namely, (0, 3), (2, 5), (3, 6), (4, 7),...and repeating the construction of the parallelogram which has the origin, (6, 2) and a member of $\{(0, 3)\}$ as the co-ordinates of three vertices, we form a family of parallelograms each of which has its fourth vertex at a point with co-ordinates which belong to the equivalence class {(1, 0)}.

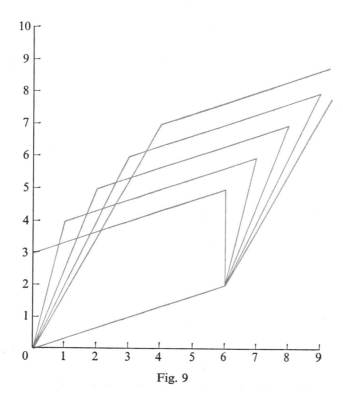

Fig. 9

Similarly, on replacing the ordered pair (6, 2) by other members of the equivalence class {(4, 0)} and repeating the construction of the parallelogram which has the origin, (1, 4) and a member of {(4, 0)} as the co-ordinates of three vertices, we form a family of parallelograms each of which has its fourth vertex at a point with co-ordinates which belong to the equivalence class {(1, 0)}, (fig. 10).

From these two results we conclude that on constructing any parallelogram which has the origin, a member of (0, 3) and a member of (4, 0) as the co-ordinates of three vertices, we always form a parallelogram which has its fourth vertex at a point with co-ordinates which belong to (1, 0). The ordered pairs (1, 4) and (6, 2) were arbitrarily chosen representatives of the equivalence classes on which the families of parallelograms were constructed.

113

This, in turn, implies that we can generalize still further and state that on constructing any parallelogram which has the origin, a member of $\{(a, b)\}$ and a member of $\{(c, d)\}$ as the co-ordinates of three vertices, we always form a parallelogram which has its fourth vertex at a point with co-ordinates which belong to $\{(a+c, b+d)\}$.

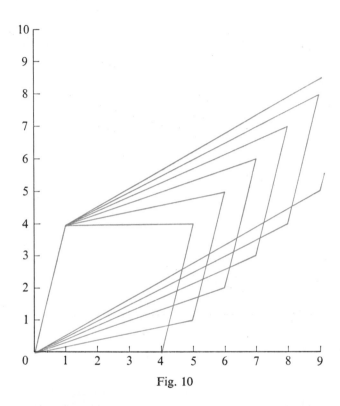

Fig. 10

Note also that this behaviour of ordered pairs and equivalence classes under the operation of addition as defined by equations (1) and (2), and illustrated above, is not fully developed by considering some of the other situations mentioned earlier. For example, in recording the changes in position of a lift by

$$^{+}4; \quad ^{-}3; \quad ^{+}2; \quad ^{-}4; \quad ^{+}3; \quad ^{+}2; \quad ^{-}5,$$

rather than U4; D3; U2;... we can interpret the symbols

$$^{+}2+^{-}4 = ^{-}2$$

at a Stage A level, as 'a lift moving up through two floors followed by the

114

lift moving down four floors has the same effect as the lift moving down two floors'. However, in using this and similar examples in this way, we are making statements about the operation of addition of integers which are not strictly justified by the situation we are considering, for, in fact, we can demonstrate only that we can combine ordered pairs such as (3, 5) and (5, 1), as follows:

$$(3, 5)+(5, 1) = (3, 1)$$

$$(4, 6)+(6, 2) = (4, 2)$$

etc.

These results can be illustrated by directed line segments as follows:

etc.

In other words, we are demonstrating that
(i) we can combine certain ordered pairs from two equivalence classes as follows:

$$(a, b)+(b, c) = (a+b, b+c) = (a, c);$$

(ii) if we take any member of the first equivalence class and a particular member of a second equivalence class, their sum is always in the third equivalence class.

The operation of addition of integers, as defined by equation (2), also has the following properties:
(i) it is commutative,

$$\{(a, b)\}+\{(c, d)\} = \{(c, d)\}+\{(a, b)\}$$

for

$$\{(a, b)\}+\{(c, d)\} = \{(a+c, b+d)\}$$

$$= \{(c+a, d+b)\}$$

$$= \{(c, d)\}+\{(a, b)\},$$

since $a$, $b$, $c$ and $d$ are natural numbers which are commutative with respect to addition;

115

(ii) it is associative,

$$\{(a, b)\} + [\{(c, d)\} + \{(e, f)\}] = [\{(a, b)\} + \{(c, d)\}] + \{(e, f)\}$$

for
$$\{(a, b)\} + [\{(c, d)\} + \{(e, f)\}] = \{(a, b)\} + \{(c+e, d+f)\}$$
$$= \{(a+c+e, b+d+f)\}$$
$$= \{(a+c, b+d)\} + \{(e, f)\}$$
$$= [\{(a, b)\} + \{(c, d)\}] + \{(e, f)\},$$

since $a, b, c, d, e$ and $f$ are natural numbers which are associative with respect to addition;

(iii) there is a unique identity element, for in the set of integers there exists $\{(0, 0)\}$ which contains the ordered pairs

$$(0, 0,) \quad (1, 1), \quad (2, 2), \quad \ldots, \quad (a, a), \quad (a+b, a+b), \quad \ldots$$

This integer has the property

$$\{(a, b)\} + \{(0, 0)\} = \{(a, b)\};$$

that is, there exists an element of the set of integers which when added to any element of the set leaves that element unaltered. Thus the set of integers has an identity element $\{(0, 0)\}$, and this identity element is unique, because if there exists $\{(c, d)\}$ such that

$$\{(a, b)\} + \{(c, d)\} = \{(a, b)\}$$

then
$$\{(a+c, b+d)\} = \{(a, b)\}.$$

For these integers to represent the same set of ordered pairs of natural numbers, we require

$$(a+c, b+d) \equiv (a, b)$$

for all $a$ and $b$, that is,
$$a+b+c = a+b+d$$

that is,
$$c = d \quad \text{or} \quad c+0 = d+0$$

but this is the condition for the ordered pairs $(c, d)$ and $(0, 0)$ to be equivalent, and so

$$\{(c, d)\} = \{(0, 0)\}$$

that is, the identity element of the set of integers is unique;

(iv) each element of the set of integers has a unique inverse element; for

$$\{(a, b)\} + \{(b, a)\} = \{(a+b, a+b)\} = \{(0, 0)\}$$

for all $a$ and $b$. This inverse element $\{(b, a)\}$ of $\{(a, b)\}$ is unique because if $(c, d)$ exists such that
$$\{(a, b)\} + \{(c, d)\} = \{(0, 0)\}$$

then
$$\{(b, a)\} + \{(a, b)\} + \{(c, d)\} = \{(b, a)\} + \{(0, 0)\},$$

that is
$$\{(c, d)\} = \{(b, a)\}.$$

Thus the inverse element $\{(b, a)\}$ of an element $\{(a, b)\}$ of the set of integers, is unique.

These four properties show that the set of integers form a commutative group with respect to the operation of addition of integers defined by the relation

$$\{(a, b)\} + \{(c, d)\} = \{(a+c, b+d)\}.$$

Also we can now define the operation inverse to the operation of addition of integers, namely, the operation of subtraction of integers, as

$$\{(a, b)\} - \{(c, d)\} = \{(a, b)\} + \{(d, c)\},$$

for if this new operation, denoted by $-$, is the inverse of the operation of addition, we require

$$\{(a, b)\} - \{(c, d)\} + \{(c, d)\} = \{(a, b)\}.$$

Thus $\quad \{(a, b)\} - \{(c, d)\} + \{(c, d)\} + \{(d, c)\} = \{(a, b)\} + \{(d, c)\}$

that is $\quad\quad\quad \{(a, b)\} - \{(c, d)\} = \{(a, b)\} + \{(d, c)\}.$

Hence

(i) $\{(0, 5)\} - \{(0, 2)\} = \{(0, 5)\} + \{(2, 0)\} = \{(2, 5)\} = \{(0, 3)\}$

or $\quad\quad\quad\quad\quad ^+5 - ^+2 = ^+5 + ^-2 = ^+3.$

(ii) $\{(0, 5)\} - \{(2, 0)\} = \{(0, 5)\} + \{(0, 2)\} = \{(0, 7)\}$

or $\quad\quad\quad\quad\quad ^+5 - ^-2 = ^+5 + ^+2 = ^+7.$

(iii) $\{(5, 0)\} - \{(0, 2)\} = \{(5, 0)\} + \{(2, 0)\} = \{(7, 0)\}$

or $\quad\quad\quad\quad\quad ^-5 - ^+2 = ^-5 + ^-2 = ^-7.$

(iv) $\{(5, 0)\} - \{(2, 0)\} = \{(5, 0)\} + \{(0, 2)\} = \{(5, 2)\} = \{(3, 0)\}$

or $\quad\quad\quad\quad\quad ^-5 - ^-2 = ^-5 + ^+2 = ^-3.$

etc.

From the information given by statements of withdrawals and deposits into the bank accounts of shop-keepers, we have so far discovered an operation and its inverse which we can use to combine any two integers to form a third integer which is equivalent to the resultant change.

On looking back at the second row of Table 4, we see that the change in the balance of Mr Brown's account, due to the transactions of 3rd May, was a gain of £3 and that the change in his balance, due to the transactions of 4th May, was also a gain of £3. If, on looking back at his statements of withdrawals and deposits for the week ending on Sunday, 7th May, Mr Brown finds that the change in his balance for each day was a gain of £3, he can conclude that, if this state of affairs remains unchanged for the coming week, in four days time he will be £12 better off, and that by the end of the week, he will be £21 better off. He will also realise that on Thursday, 4th May, he was £9 worse off than he is today, Sunday,

7th May, and that he can show how much better off he was or will be, if the change in his balance continues to be a gain of £3 per day, than he is today as follows:

### Mr Brown's Table

| £18 | £15 | £12 | £9 | £6 | £3 |
|---|---|---|---|---|---|
| worse off | worse off | worse off | worse off | worse off | worse off |
| Mon. | Tues. | Wed. | Thurs. | Fri. | Sat. |
| 1st May | 2nd May | 3rd May | 4th May | 5th May | 6th May |

| | £3 | £6 | £9 | £12 | £15 |
|---|---|---|---|---|---|
| | better off | better off | better off | better off | better off |
| Sun. | Mon. | Tues. | Wed. | Thurs. | Fri. |
| 7th May | 8th May | 9th May | 10th May | 11th May | 12th May |

We can improve the entries in Mr Brown's Table by using integers to indicate whether Mr Brown is better or worse off and to distinguish between days past and days to come, as follows:

| $-18$ | $-15$ | $-12$ | $-9$ | $-6$ | $-3$ | | $+3$ | $+6$ | $+9$ | $+12$ | $+15$ | $+18$ |
|---|---|---|---|---|---|---|---|---|---|---|---|---|
| $-6$ | $-5$ | $-4$ | $-3$ | $-2$ | $-1$ | Sun. 7th May | $+1$ | $+2$ | $+3$ | $+4$ | $+5$ | $+6$ |

If, on the other hand, Mr Brown had found that the change in his balance for each day, was a loss of £3, he would have concluded that, if this state of affairs remains unchanged for the coming week, in five days time he will be £15 worse off and that by the end of the week, he will be £21 worse off than he is today. He would also have realised that on Wednesday, 3rd May, he was £12 better off than he is today, and so on. These results we can tabulate as follows:

| $+18$ | $+15$ | $+12$ | $+9$ | $+6$ | $+3$ | | $-1$ | $-6$ | $-9$ | $-12$ | $-15$ | $-18$ |
|---|---|---|---|---|---|---|---|---|---|---|---|---|
| $-6$ | $-5$ | $-4$ | $-3$ | $-2$ | $-1$ | Sun. 7th May | $+1$ | $+2$ | $+3$ | $+4$ | $+5$ | $+6$ |

From these results we see that this type of situation implies an operation of 'multiplication' between integers. In the particular instance when Mr Brown realised that on Wednesday, 3rd May, he would have been £12 better off than he is today, if the daily change in his balance was a loss of £3, we seem to have

$$-3 \times -4 = +12.$$

As we have seen however, an integer is an equivalence class of ordered pairs of natural numbers and so the question now arises, how can we 'multiply' an equivalence class by a second equivalence class? But first we must devise a way of multiplying ordered pairs.

Let us now go back and investigate what happens when Mr Brown's daily change in his balance is a loss of £3.

Suppose Mr Brown's run of bad luck started seven days ago, that is, on Monday, 1st May, and that, in fact, his daily withdrawal from his bank account was £8 and that his daily deposit was £5. His loss per day can thus be represented by (8, 5).

Today is 7th May. Over the seven days that Mr Brown has sustained this loss, he has withdrawn £56 from his bank account and paid in £35. This change in his balance can be denoted by (56, 35).

Let us look on four days, that is, to 11th May. This interval of time can be represented by (7, 11). By 11th May, Mr Brown will have withdrawn £88 from his bank account and paid in £55. This change in his balance can be denoted by (88, 55).

The state of his affairs on the 11th is expected to differ from that on the 7th, by (88, 55) − (56, 35) but

$$(88, 55) - (56, 35) = (88, 55) + (35, 56) = (123, 111)$$

so we must have $\quad$ $(8, 5) \times (7, 11) = (123, 111)$.

Looking the other way, Mr Brown may also say 'Today is 7th May, how did the state of my affairs on the 3rd, compare with the state of my affairs now?' By 3rd May the change in his balance was (24, 15). By 7th May, it is (56, 35). Thus the state of his affairs on the 3rd, differed from that on the 7th, by (24, 15) − (56, 35) but

$$(24, 15) - (56, 35) = (34, 15) + (35, 56) = (59, 71)$$

that is $\quad$ $(8, 5) \times (7, 3) = (59, 71)$

Now we must generalise this argument to cover all similar situations.

Suppose our shop-keeper makes a daily profit (or loss) represented by $(a, b)$ where $a$ represents his daily withdrawal of £$a$ from his bank account and $b$ represents his daily deposit of £$b$ and that this has happened for $c$ days to date. If we let $d$ represent the number of days from the start of this period of constant change in our shop-keeper's balance, to the day under consideration, then $(c, d)$ represents the interval of time, from the present, with which we are concerned.

During the $c$ days our shop-keeper has had this constant change in his daily balance, he has withdrawn £$ac$ from his bank account and paid in £$bc$. This change in his balance can be represented by $(ac, bc)$.

During the $d$ days our shop-keeper has had this constant change in his daily balance, he has withdrawn £$ad$ from his bank account and paid in £$bd$. This change in his balance can be represented by $(ad, bd)$ and so in the interval of time represented by $(c, d)$, the change in his balance is

$$(ad, bd) - (ac, bc) = (ad, bd) + (bc, ac) = (ad+bc, ac+bd).$$

We can thus take as our definition of multiplication of ordered pairs of natural numbers, the relation

$$(a, b) \times (c, d) = (ad+bc, ac+bd). \tag{3}$$

Now we must consider what happens when the terms on the left-hand side of equation (3), are replaced by other members of the equivalence classes to which they belong.

Suppose $(a, b)$ and $(a', b')$ are members of the same equivalence class, then

$$a+b' = a'+b \tag{4}$$

and that $(c, d)$ and $(c', d')$ are members of another equivalence class, then

$$c+d' = c'+d. \tag{5}$$

On multiplying equation (4) by $c$, we get

$$ac+b'c = a'c+bc.$$

On multiplying equation (4) by $d$, we get

$$ad+b'd = a'd+bd.$$

Thus $\qquad ad+b'd+a'c+bc = ac+b'c+a'd+bd. \tag{6}$

On multiplying equation (5) by $a'$, we get

$$a'c+a'd' = a'c'+a'd.$$

On multiplying equation (5) by $b'$, we get

$$b'c+b'd' = b'c'+b'd.$$

Thus $\qquad a'c+a'd'+b'c'+b'd = a'c'+a'd+b'c+b'd'. \tag{7}$

From equations (6) and (7) we get

$$ad+b'd+a'c+bc+a'c'+a'd+b'c+b'd'$$
$$= ac+b'c+a'd+bd+a'c+a'd'+b'c'+b'd,$$

that is, $\qquad ad+bc+a'c'+b'd' = a'd'+b'c'+ac+bd.$

120

But this is the condition for $(ad+bc, ac+bd)$ and $(a'd'+b'c', a'c'+b'd')$ to be equivalent, and so if the terms on the left-hand side of equation (3), are replaced by other terms in the same equivalence classes, the resulting terms on the right-hand side of equation (3), all belong to the same equivalence class. For example,

$$(1, 4) \times (6, 2) = (2+24, 6+8) = (26, 14),$$
$$(1, 4) \times (4, 0) = (0+16, 4+0) = (16, 4),$$
$$(0, 3) \times (6, 2) = (0+18, 0+6) = (18, 6),$$
$$(0, 3) \times (4, 0) = (0+12, 0+0) = (12, 0).$$

(1, 4) and (0, 3) belong to the equivalence class $\{(0, 3)\}$; (6, 2) and (4, 0) belong to the equivalence class $\{(4, 0)\}$, and (26, 14), (16, 4), (18, 6) and (12, 0) belong to the equivalence class $\{(12, 0)\}$. Thus we can define the operation of multiplication of equivalence classes and hence the operation of multiplication of integers, by the relation,

$$\{(a, b)\} \times \{(c, d)\} = \{(ad+bc, ac+bd)\}. \qquad (8)$$

Hence

(i) $\quad \{(0, 2)\} \times \{(0, 5)\} = \{(0+0, 0+10)\} = \{(0, 10)\}$

or $\qquad\qquad ^+2 \times {}^+5 = {}^+10.$

(ii) $\quad \{(0, 2)\} \times \{(5, 0)\} = \{(0+10, 0+0)\} = \{(10, 0)\}$

or $\qquad\qquad ^+2 \times {}^-5 = {}^-10.$

(iii) $\quad \{(2, 0)\} \times \{(0, 5)\} = \{(10+0, 0+0)\} = \{(10, 0)\}$

or $\qquad\qquad ^-2 \times {}^+5 = {}^+10.$

(iv) $\quad \{(2, 0)\} \times \{(5, 0)\} = \{(0+0, 10+0)\} = \{(0, 10)\}$

or $\qquad\qquad ^-2 \times {}^-5 = {}^+10.$

The operation of multiplication of integers, as defined by equation (8), also has the following properties:
(i) it is commutative,

$$\{(a, b)\} \times \{(c, d)\} = \{(c, d)\} \times \{(a, b)\},$$

for $\qquad \{(a, b)\} \times \{(c, d)\} = \{(ad+bc, ac+bd)\},$
$$= \{(da+cb, ca+db)\},$$
$$= \{(cb+da, db+ca)\},$$
$$= \{(c, d)\} \times \{(a, b)\},$$

121

since $a$, $b$, $c$ and $d$ are natural numbers which are commutative with respect to addition and multiplication;

(ii) it is associative,

$$\{(a, b)\} \times [\{(c, d)\} \times \{(e, f)\}] = [\{(a, b)\} \times \{(c, d)\}] \times \{(e, f)\}$$

for $\quad \{(a, b)\} \times [\{(c, d)\} \times \{(e, f)\}] = \{(a, b)\} \times \{(cf + de, ce + df)\},$

$$= \{(a(ce + df) + b(cf + de), a(cf + de) + b(ce + df))\}$$
$$= \{(ace + adf + bcf + bde, acf + ade + bce + bdf)\},$$
$$= \{((ad + bc)f + (ac + bd)e, (ad + bc)e + (ac + bd)f)\}$$
$$= \{(ad + bc, ac + bd)\} \times \{(e, f)\},$$
$$= [\{(a, b)\} \times \{(c, d)\}] \times \{(e, f)\},$$

since $a$, $b$, $c$, $d$, $e$ and $f$ are natural numbers which are commutative and associative with respect to addition and multiplication and multiplication is distributive over addition;

(iii) there is a unique identity element, for in the set of integers there exists $\{(0, 1)\}$ which has the following property

$$\{(a, b)\} \times \{(0, 1)\} = \{(a + 0, 0 + b)\} = \{(a, b)\},$$

that is, there exists an element of the set of integers which when multiplied by an element of the set of integers, leaves that element unaltered. Thus the set of integers has an identity element $\{(0, 1)\}$ and this identity element is unique because if there exists $\{(c, d)\}$ such that

$$\{(a, b)\} \times \{(c, d)\} = \{(a, b)\},$$

then $\quad\quad\quad\quad \{(ad + bc, ac + bd)\} = \{(a, b)\}.$

For these integers to represent the same set of ordered pairs of natural numbers, we require $\quad (ad + bc, ac + bd) \equiv (a, b)$

for all $a$ and $b$, that is $\quad ad + bc + b = ac + bd + a,$

that is, $\quad\quad\quad\quad ad + b(c + 1) = a(c + 1) + bd$

for all $a$ and $b$, thus $\quad\quad\quad c + 1 = d$

for all $a$ and $b$, that is, $\quad\quad c + 1 = d + 0$

for all $a$ and $b$, but this is the condition for the ordered pairs $(c, d)$ and $(0, 1)$ to be equivalent and so

$$\{(c, d)\} = \{(0, 1)\}.$$

Thus the identity element of the set of integers is unique;

(iv) it is distributive over the operation of addition of integers,

$$\{(a, b)\} \times [\{(c, d)\} + \{(e, f)\}] = [\{(a, b)\} \times \{(c, d)\}] + [\{(a, b)\} \times \{(e, f)\}],$$

for

$$\{(a, b)\} \times [\{(c, d)\} + \{(e, f)\}] = \{(a, b)\} \times \{(c+e, d+f)\},$$
$$= \{(a(d+f) + b(c+e), a(c+e) + b(d+f))\},$$
$$= \{(ad + af + bc + be, ac + ae + bd + bf)\},$$
$$= \{(ad + bc, ac + bd)\} + \{(af + be, ae + bf)\},$$
$$= [\{(a, b)\} \times \{(c, d)\}] + [\{(a, b)\} \times \{(e, f)\}],$$

since $a$, $b$, $c$, $d$, $e$ and $f$ are natural numbers which are commutative and associative with respect to addition and multiplication, and multiplication is distributive over addition.

Thus from the information given by statements of withdrawals and deposits into the bank accounts of shop-keepers, we have formed a set of objects called the integers, on which two binary operations, addition and multiplication, are defined such that

(i)   addition is commutative and associative,

(ii)  multiplication is commutative and associative,

(iii) multiplication is distributive over addition.

The set of integers, therefore, mimic the natural numbers in the operations of addition and multiplication when the integers are used to represent changes between quantities which have taken place in one of two possible ways. In other words they form a number system.

# BOUND VECTORS AND FREE VECTORS

*by* T. J. FLETCHER

'There should be a more vigorous treatment of rectors'
Typist's error

The question 'What is a vector?' is a perennial one wherever the teaching of mathematics is discussed; and the question is understandable when the word is used in a number of contexts with apparently differing shades of meaning. Most new schemes of work are agreed in developing geometry with a rather greater stress on vector ideas, and in including some of the elementary ideas of algebraic vectors also.

At some time, as the course develops, it will be necessary to reconcile these two kinds of vector and to show the relations between them. In a way this is only the old distinction between 'bound' and 'free' vectors all over again; but there is a difference, in that if we seek to elucidate the relation between bound and free vectors in a contemporary setting we find that the relation is precisely the same as that between certain parts of the number system. This being so, time spent studying this relation is a better investment than it was, for now we clarify other situations at the same time.

We consider the problem that arises when students know the affine properties of the Euclidean plane—that is, the properties of parallelograms—expressed in vector language, and when they are familiar with algebraic vectors and their laws of addition, this knowledge having been gained by studying 'shopping lists' and other intuitively acceptable instances of the structure. The problem is to relate the two fields of study. The discussion will proceed, using ideas such as 'group' and 'equivalence class', not because we imagine that every child receiving a modern programme of instruction will master these ideas early on, but because they are working tools whose value will become understood over the years by using them as opportunity arises. This is one suitable opportunity.

The approach here is not an axiomatic one, for we are not assuming that we have reached the stage of mathematical sophistication when we have become aware of what our axioms are. We are merely building logical bridges between structures with which we have become familiar through exploration. Throughout the discussion our geometry will be informal,

125

i.e. not axiomatically based; but we will seek to formalize the algebra as much as we can.

We know that if we have any three points in space $o$, $a$, $b$, then there is a unique fourth point $x$, such that $oaxb$ is a parallelogram. We have said 'in space' and not 'in a plane' because the number of dimensions in which we are working is immaterial. This enables us to put forward a definition. We choose an arbitrary point in space as origin and call it $o$.

### DEFINITION I

Given points $a$ and $b$, $x = a \oplus b$ is the fourth vertex of the parallelogram $oaxb$.

This is the definition of the operation which we denote by $\oplus$. Note that we have defined a rule whereby we propose to add a *point* to a *point*, getting a *point*. It may be objected that we do not add points in this way! The objection is over-ruled. In mathematics we may define any operations we please, so long as they are meaningful and we do not contradict ourselves, and this is an operation which we have chosen to define. Our experience of Euclidean space enables us to assert:

## Property 1

Addition is commutative and associative.

## Property 2

With the operation $\oplus$ Euclidean space is a commutative group. The second property is established if in addition to property 1 we note that adding $o$ to any point $a$ gives $a$, so that $o$ is the identity element of the group, and given any point $a$ we may find another point $a'$, such that $a \oplus a' = 0$, $a'$ is the inverse of $a$.

We are not calling these results theorems for two reasons. We do not propose to give a formal proof, and in any case, if it came to constructing one, these properties might turn out to be so fundamental that they corresponded to properties of Euclidean space which we would be inclined to take as axioms. Observe in passing that the commutative law $a \oplus b = b \oplus a$ can be interpreted as saying that a unique parallelogram is specified if we are given a vertex and two sides through it. The associative law, $(a \oplus b) \oplus c = a \oplus (b \oplus c)$, can be interpreted as saying that a unique parallelepiped is specified if we are given one vertex with three edges through it. This being so, three-space seems to realise the fundamental properties of vectors more typically than two-space.

Let us denote the commutative group which we have just described by **G1**. It is called the group of *bound vectors* at $o$.

We now take ordered pairs of elements of **G1** and define an equivalence relation between them. Intuitively speaking, we wish to be able to say that line segments are equivalent when they are equal and parallel, but we need a way of saying this with the algebraic resources at our disposal. If $ab$ and $cd$ are equal and parallel then $abdc$ is a parallelogram. The midpoints of $ad$ and $bc$ coincide. This means that $\frac{1}{2}(a \oplus d) = \frac{1}{2}(b \oplus c)$, and this motivates a convenient algebraic definition.

### DEFINITION 2

$$(a, b) \equiv (c, d) \quad \text{if and only if} \quad a \oplus d = b \oplus c.$$

In our geometrical knowledge this is familiar as an equivalence relation; what is the corresponding formal algebra?

*Theorem 1*   Definition 2 defines an equivalence relation.

*Proof.*
$$(a, b) \equiv (c, d) \Leftrightarrow a \oplus d = b \oplus c,$$
$$(c, d) \equiv (e, f) \Leftrightarrow c \oplus f = d \oplus e.$$

*Adding*
$$a \oplus d \oplus c \oplus f = b \oplus c \oplus d \oplus e,$$
$$\Rightarrow a \oplus f = b \oplus e,$$
$$\Rightarrow (a, b) \equiv (e, f).$$

This shows that the relation $\equiv$ is transitive. The reflexive and symmetric properties are very easily shown; thus we have an equivalence relation.

The algebraic equivalence relation employs a particular point $o$ as origin. Can we be sure that we get the *same* equivalence relation if we start with a different origin? This question has no significance in the formal algebraic structure which we are seeking to develop. It is a geometrical question to which we can if we wish give a geometrical answer, but let us see how the algebra builds up.

Having defined an equivalence relation let us denote the class of ordered pairs equivalent to $(a, b)$ by $\{(a, b)\}$. From our geometrical background we recognise these equivalence classes as free vectors. What is the appropriate way to add classes? If addition of classes is denoted by $+$ it is natural to define it by:

### DEFINITION 3

$$\{(a, b)\} + \{(x, y)\} = \{(a \oplus x, b \oplus y)\}.$$

For this definition to be satisfactory it is necessary to show that the operation $\oplus$ and the equivalence relation are compatible; this ensures that whatever representatives we pick from two equivalence classes we get the *same* class as the sum. This class will, in general, be represented by different elements, but they will be equivalent (defn. 2) and so this will not matter.

*Theorem 2*    $\oplus$ and the equivalence relation are compatible.

*Proof.*
$$(a, b) \equiv (a', b') \Leftrightarrow a \oplus b' = b \oplus a', \Big\}$$
$$(x, y) \equiv (x', y') \Leftrightarrow x \oplus y' = y \oplus x', \Big\}$$
$$\Rightarrow a \oplus b' \oplus x \oplus y' = b \oplus a' \oplus y \oplus x',$$
$$\Rightarrow (a \oplus x) \oplus (b' \oplus y') = (b \oplus y) \oplus (a' + x'),$$
$$\Rightarrow (a \oplus x, b \oplus y) \equiv (a' \oplus x', b' \oplus y'),$$
$$\Rightarrow \{(a, b)\} + \{(x, y)\} = \{(a', b')\} + \{(x', y')\}.$$

*Theorem 3*    Equivalence classes form a group under $+$.

*Proof.* The details of the proof are largely matters of routine which we may omit. It is easy to prove closure and associativity. The identity element of the group is the class $\{(a, a)\}$, and the inverse of the class $\{(a, b)\}$ is the class $\{(b, a)\}$.

This group we will denote by **G2**. It is called the group of free vectors.

It may well seem that some of the above points have been spelt out in rather pedantic detail. But pedantic detail of this kind can bring a dividend, for if we look closely at the argument we see that it will apply equally well in other circumstances.

The method of constructing **G2** from **G1** does not depend at all on any of the physical properties of space. It will apply to any commutative group. From any commutative group we may construct a second commutative group using equivalence classes or ordered pairs of the first one. This might seem a fairly striking theorem. Unfortunately it turns out to be almost trivial, for the two groups are always 'the same' in the sense that they are isomorphic—there is a one-one correspondence between them.

The groups are isomorphic because the equivalence classes of **G2** may be represented by the particular members of the form $(o, b)$. Then $\{(o, b)\} + \{(o, d)\} = \{(o, b \oplus d)\}$ in **G2** corresponds to adding $b$ and $d$ to get $b \oplus d$ in **G1**.

Bound and free vectors are easily confused because their groups are isomorphic—that is to say from an abstract, algebraic point of view they have the same group. On the other hand the two geometric systems which are the realisations of the groups are quite distinct. A number of writers comment that free vectors are equivalence classes of bound vectors, but adopt an asymmetric definition of addition (the triangle law) in which although an arbitrary choice may be made of the representative from the first equivalence class, a special representative has to be chosen from the second—the member whose 'tail' coincides with the 'head' of the member of the first class. The approach here gives the complete freedom that is needed. Any member may be chosen from either equivalence class, and the sum is always a member of the resultant class.

This kind of detailed analysis sometimes causes a certain impatience. Is it worth going into such detail merely to prove that two easily confused things, the groups of bound and free vectors, are isomorphic? If this were all perhaps not, but there is more to come. If we examine theorems 1, 2, 3 we see that by no means all the properties of the group **G1** are actually used in the proofs. The group properties, as usually stated are (i) closure, (ii) associativity, (iii) the existence of an identity element, (iv) the existence of an inverse for each element.

Our proofs certainly use (i) and (ii), but (iii) is not assumed, for even if **G1** did not have an identity element we could still construct the equivalence class which is the identity element of **G2**. (iv) may appear to be used in the proof of theorem 1 at the transition from line 3 to line 4. The inverse of $c+d$ is, it would seem, added to both sides of the equation. But this can be seen another way. The deduction remains valid if we appeal only to a cancellation law

$$(\text{iv}a) \quad a \oplus x = b \oplus x \Rightarrow a = b.$$

This is a weaker assumption than the assumption that every element has an inverse, and it is not merely a theoretical point because some mathematical systems which are not groups possess properties (i), (ii) and (iv$a$). The natural numbers form such a system.

The elements we start with, and denote by $a$, $b$, $c$, ...could be natural numbers. The argument may be picked up at definition 2 and then followed step by step. The algebra is identical letter by letter, but it receives a new interpretation. Starting with the natural numbers in this way we construct the integers. An integer is an equivalence class of ordered pairs of natural numbers. They are an additive group, and a subset of them is isomorphic to the integers. Incidentally, since property (iii) is not used we have confirmation that it does not matter greatly whether or not zero is defined as a natural number.

Is this all?

No, we may take yet another point of view. If the letters $a$, $b$, $c$,... denote integers (excluding zero), and the sign $\oplus$ denotes *multiplication* of integers, then proceeding in exactly the same way we may construct the rationals (excluding zero) as equivalence classes of ordered pairs of integers, and show that they form a group with respect to multiplication. (Why do we have to be so careful to exclude zero?) Again, there is a subset which is isomorphic to the integers.

These three situations are major steps in a mathematical education—the introduction of 'fractions', the introduction of 'directed numbers' and the introduction of free vectors. The discussion shows that these are not three problems but one. The three superficially different procedures are identical, step by step and symbol by symbol, provided that they are seen from a suitably abstract algebraic point of view.

# THE HUMAN ELEMENT IN MATHEMATICS

## by C. GATTEGNO

It may be a fitting tribute to a person who devoted a great deal of his energy and thinking to reduce suffering, and tried to understand the reasons behind the existence of confusing issues, to attempt to write a section for this book that will bring out a mood rather than facts.

The human element has, over the years, become more and more a source of inspiration and insight. Today I can say that I am able to trace, through the last forty years, the emergence, the blossoming and the present state of my awareness of the relevance of this human element, to the point that its story reflects the unfolding of my inner life as related to the intellectual part. Since Geoff Sillitto has been associated with me at some points on this road, I feel his presence as I write the following thoughts, which I offer to our colleagues as part of a book that is intended to make the reader feel in contact with him.

My permanent feeling as a student was one of awe whenever I turned my mind to the field of mathematics. Anyone whose name was connected with the subject received at once my deepest respect. The Greeks who developed the science of geometry, the founders of modern analysis in the seventeenth century, the pioneers like Lagrange, Cauchy and Riemann overpowered me, and I read their works in the way others approach the sacred books of their religion.

I could not escape the feeling that the company I was keeping, stretching far away in time and space, was in its quality similar to sitting at the feet of great masters, and generated in me not only humility because of the distance that separated my mind from theirs, but also pride at being allowed this spiritual contact.

Mathematics had an existence of its own; I saw it as a collection of sculptured chapels forming one large and beautiful temple. The demands it made were not merely on my intellectual powers, but on the whole of myself. I, the pygmy, could roam freely in that holy space, reverencing much and learning a number of its laws as literally as I could, even if at at times I did not altogether know what they were stating.

My library grew; I read extensively and often wondered at the meaning of some of the titles of the *Notes à l'Académie des Sciences,* written by the geniuses of the time. What I had actually mastered was so insignificant that it barely served me in my attempt at passing examinations. Never did I for a moment believe that the gifts of writers of memoirs or books could belong to people like myself. Once, when one of my former mathematics teachers, whom I respected for his erudition, said to a group of young men, including me, that perhaps one day there would be some Calebian integral (reminiscent in sound of Abelian) I felt a rush of blood to my head as well as a surge to my pride. The shame came from being identified with what I revered, and the pleasure from the fact that no greater flattery could be heard.

The seriousness with which histories of mathematics were written also helped to sustain my feeling of reverence.

Nevertheless, some writers on non-Euclidean geometry and set theory, some anecdotes from the pens of eminent writers such as Henri Poincaré and Felix Klein, were opening a breach in the high wall that I had put around mathematics.

For a long time mathematician after mathematician had failed to understand the nature of a postulate and found it very hard to comprehend that Euclid's postulate did not need either to be proved or accepted. The history of this long episode showed me that my religious attitude was not due to my own intellectual servility or idiosyncracy but was a very common one. And as a result of this new awareness I was able to see that creation in mathematics came from within, from a deliberate movement of the mind translated into new definitions and axioms.

Soon afterwards, I discovered a flaw in a proof by a well-known and productive mathematician and managed to find a new proof which rescued his theorem. The study of what happened to me helped me to separate those parts of the temple where men still showed their imperfections, from those others where gods seemed to be the architects. In the former I could now see more clearly—but not yet very well—the impact of prejudice, belief and fashion. The latter I set beyond my sight so that I need not even dream of taking a critical look.

Forty years ago Cantor's work was new even among working mathematicians. Since I was self-taught, and under the random influence of whatever I could lay my hands on, Cantor's ideas (as they appear in the numerous monographs published by Emile Borel) were the fabric of my thought from 1930 onwards. I learned of the opposition of Kronecker and Felix Klein to the theory of sets; I read of the enthusiasm of the French and of the new theories they produced; of the efforts of Peano, Bertrand

Russell, Hilbert and others to clarify their foundations, which were still considered shaky because of the numerous antimonies which they revealed.

The trend that dominated discussions between the two World Wars could be summarised by what Paul Dienes said to me in 1946 in reference to Brouwer and his intuitionistic logic: that mathematicians work as they have always done on weekdays—and worry about foundations on Sundays. Indeed, a schizophrenic situation existed in mathematics: looking at the edifice nobody would believe that anything could be wrong with the foundations, but a look at the foundations seemed to make an illusion of the vision of the edifice.

In France, the team known as the Bourbakis initiated a complete rethinking of mathematics and in 1936 started publishing their *Elements*. Their work held far-reaching consequences. The mere fact that a 'small' collection of chapters could replace the whole of the mathematics evolved up to our day was in itself unsettling; the edifice which had seemed to have a majesty that covered all of mankind's evolution was now to be presented as a deductive system. A few sets of axioms, well 'chosen', could provide *all* the mental equipment which, with the machinery of 'mathematical reasoning' or 'method', would produce *all the content* of mathematics. Mathematics would henceforth be independent of all other experience; it would be an intellectual game played by those who excelled in it and enjoyed it.

This conception of a mathematic (singular) as a tapestry, woven by the able hands of the people who had learned the axiomatic method, was adopted almost universally soon after the war as world communications were restored.

The crises at the turn of the century, and the plea for help from psychologists, led to an auto-psychoanalysis on the part of mathematicians who looked at their deepest levels of mental structuration and found there 'structures' and 'relations'. Venerable chapters of mathematics were abandoned and replaced by the study of underlying structures. As if fully grown trees had suddenly lost their appeal and only the water, the air, the nitrates, etc., that were needed for their growth had beauty, mathematicians were busy producing the machine tools that, it was presumed, would permit a close examination of these various components. The aesthetic experience was no longer acquired by gazing at the edifice, but by accumulating the bricks and mortar from which it had been made.

When those vast entities called 'categories' had been spotted, it seemed that the 'abstractors' had reached their goal; that from how on we could only go down into the 'concrete' of entities constructed by choice and taste, much as artists use canvas and paint to produce pictures which only depend on the mood, know-how and opportunities of the particular painter.

A new tension was being created. The analysis of *most* mathematical

133

notions led to some or other of the singled-out structures, and their behaviour could be forecast from the nature of these structures. A universal and compelling quality of mathematics was still to be found in the nature of the structures, which now appeared to be mental structures, revealing themselves through a process of purification called abstraction.

However, besides this universal quality in the minds of mathematicians (of which they take advantage when they tell laymen that it makes them competent in all fields of rational study), the individual slant, the unpredictable twist was also let in; so that, whereas Hilbert in 1900 could voice on behalf of the body of working mathematicians the few most important challenges that lay in the future and would need the most determined efforts, in 1968 anyone's guess about the future of mathematics is equally valid. It could even become a trivial occupation for idle minds.

Mathematics thus reflects, like any other human activity, the personal, the individual human qualities which make its future as completely open as it must have been for the various phases of its past just before these occurred—even though this can only be apparent when we look back.

Mathematics is secreted by the minds of mathematicians. Its eternal quality coincides with the belief that men will always exist, rather than with the picture of a realm of permanent ideas into which men can enter to pick some up.

To rewrite the history of mathematics from the point of view that whatever has been produced reflects the preoccupations of men in their respective societies, will make a fascinating task which I see as both easily done and extremely useful.

For instance, there was no great need for mathematics during the early Middle Ages because people were concerned with the salvation of their souls, an undertaking which seemed to them full of pitfalls. Later, when men looked at Creation with their reason—starting from the premise that the mind of a fallen creature and the content of the world were of the same level and essence—mathematics took its inspiration from the Natural World and was looked at by the same minds. Galileo, Descartes, Fermat, Newton, ... were at the same time mathematicians, physicists, astronomers, etc. The study of man's habitat over the last 300 years has required mental tools (mathematics) as well as material instruments. Their co-existence made Poincaré and others look to mathematics as having to justify the 'reality' of imaginary numbers. They saw the 'reality' of non-Euclidean spaces as a challenge to their consciousnesses.

I hope that some readers will see that it is possible to produce many interesting studies of the content of the consciousness of mathematicians—

beginning with the Egyptians, Babylonians and Greeks, and on to the more numerous instances of the last three centuries—and thus shed light on the history of mathematics from within.

In 1954, for the Amsterdam Congress of Mathematicians, I toyed with the idea that there may be a psychosomatic basis for people electing to become algebraists, topologists, analysts, probabilists, etc. I had for three years prior to that used an instrument I called a Gayograph (after A. Gay, its inventor) for some studies of the structures of the mind[1] and it seemed an adequate tool for the production of tracings reflecting what mathematicians on a couch were doing when thinking about a problem.

The ground for my belief that we could analyse the tracings produced by mathematicians at work, and reach a quality that might throw some light on whether or not there is a temperamental basis for the choice of one's field of study, is to be found in a session we had at Melun (France) in 1952, when we asked a few mathematicians (among whom were Gustave Choquet, Jean Dieudonné and André Lichnerowicz) to think of the same classical theorem—Bolzano's. We saw variations in the tracings which suggested there and then that one of them argued using a line as a support (and he agreed he did), while another used a two-dimensional support to his thinking (which he also agreed he did). A third was caught being muddled at first and was then questioned about what he was doing whilst the tracing was being observed (and he said that he had lost the thread of his argument at first and was then trying to consider the converse of the theorem using an analytic non-geometric model).

This experiment proved that the problem I posed was not altogether idle and that the Gayograph is an instrument for such studies. The project was abandoned before the Congress took place because of lack of funds but I still believe it will teach us something important, perhaps vital. I am personally interested in co-operating with anyone who

(*a*) believes in personality and its role in our behaviours, of which mathematical thinking is one,

(*b*) can administer such a research project.

For the general reader it tells of one more aspect of the human element in mathematics.

When one has lived through as many shocks as I have while studying the attitudes of mathematicians over the centuries—finding that the Greeks

[1] Gattegno, C. and Gay, A., *Un Nouveau Phénomène Psychosomatique*,' Delachaux et Niestlé, Neauchâtel and Paris, 1952, as well as Volume II, of Gattegno, C., *For the Teaching of Mathematics*, Educational Explorers Ltd, Reading, 1963.

could not make themselves look at some numbers (which they called irrational) in the way that they looked at others; that, as Vieta said, only infidels could treat unknown quantities as if they were known; that it took much courage to write, publish and teach non-Euclidean geometry when orthodoxy only supported Euclid; that Euler never really thought about continuity; that Riemann did not see that a particular point in his work was uncertain, the proof of which required Hilbert and Hadamard to propose new ideas; that Cantor had to fight to be heard by his colleagues on what has since become the *ABC* of mathematics; that even today the foundations of mathematics are uncertain because people disagree with each other—one can see that an extremely interesting moment in history has been reached, and ask: 'Where will mathematicians find new sources for the continuing renewal of the challenges and problems which occupy their minds?'

Rather than extrapolate from the past, I take leave to continue with a study in self-awareness that has served me well, enabling me to renew myself repeatedly in every one of the fields in which I have worked during this life.

Since mathematics is the outcome of mental activity it is obvious to me that only awareness of the mind at work generates the problems the mind apprehends.

Hence when I look at the innumerable problems that the mind puts to itself for the greater clarification of its own functioning, I have no worry about the future of mathematics. Indeed, mathematics can be seen as that special activity of the mind which can be made to accompany any other, and which produces special kinds of models, so that the mind can contemplate these other activities with the tools it already owns. To isolate the mental activity called mathematics is as easy as to merge it with any other, for *it is a property of the mind to isolate and merge, to stress and ignore*, particularly when it does it to itself.

In this context, one of the most promising directions for the development of mathematics will be the awareness of what is entailed by the various mental functionings called speech.

This paper is not the place to undertake a detailed study of this question. Indeed, after years of contemplation I am not yet really able to be coherent enough for enemies and indifferent people to find the patience to listen. Only friends, intimate friends, are my audiences today (another human aspect not to be forgotten), and so far they have said only that it seems very interesting but mightily complex.

What I can say to the general public is that the literature on linguistics suggests that the problem of learning to talk is extremely complex, since speech presents so many variables and structures that legions of linguists are not sufficient to fathom, classify and fully understand it. Each of us did, however, learn to talk before or around the age of two. The mental equipment for mastering this skill must actually exist and it proves its existence by functioning. Mathematics could attempt to produce a working model to display those features which a study of what speech is to its users will bring to the fore.

When linguists use mathematics to describe their awareness, they borrow models from the existing literature, models which were originally produced for an entirely different purpose and which, more often than not, fail to provide a deeper understanding of the situation. This use of existing mathematics seems to linguists as legitimate as it does to engineers, physicists or biologists. What I am proposing here is the reverse process: the creation of a new mathematics and its problematics for the purpose of formalising the awareness of the dynamics of speech.

One of the difficulties resides in the fact that the grasp of meanings precedes verbalisation and that words *per se* are not the message, but only one of the possible vehicles for the message. Hence the mathematics of speech cannot in fact result from the analysis of sentences, but can only arise through an understanding of the mysterious ways in which these carry meanings. To have a working model—a mathematics—it is necessary to shake speech free of all its unnecessary adornments and reach the way in which meanings select their own expressions and place them adequately and correctly on the flow of speech in order to provide, through a set of *transformations*, the required equivalences. It is my hunch today that *equivalence*, which carries within itself the dynamic component of transformation, is the cardinal concept of mathematics.

Perhaps one day I shall be able to tell the story of 'equivalence through transformation' and its place in the study of speech.

However disjointed this paper may appear, its unity exists and is in myself. We can only reach the human element in mathematics when we remember that behind each scientific paper there is a *person* who has written it after days, weeks or even years of fumblings, doubts, certainties, minute examinations of special cases (never before mentioned), often with a feeling that the task as it stands is not yet completed and needs re-examination. First come mathematicians and only then mathematics. The ambiguity in the situation is created by the co-existence of a number of mathematicians. Some represent the past (they embody the edifice, the institution) and some the future.

The future to me is more fascinating than the past and I strive to be in it as truly as I have been in the past when I was mesmerised by it to the point of paralysis. The unknown future does not seem to operate in the same manner. It is more welcoming; in fact more real.

# ANALYTICAL METHODS IN TRANSFORMATION GEOMETRY

*by* G. GILES

## A MAPPING GAME

The class of ten-year-olds waits expectantly, chattering quietly as I pin up the large sheets of inch-squared paper.

'Have you ever been in a town where all the streets run either north and south or east and west?'

Some have, but they've all got imagination.

'This could be a map of a town like that, couldn't it?' I run my finger along the lines of the first sheet.

'Suppose you went for a walk, starting here...' I mark an intersection with a black cross. 'How might you go?'

Once they get the idea they are soon giving me a route, section by section. 'Two north!' 'Three west!' 'Two more west!' 'Five south!'...I follow it with my finger.

'Now suppose I go for a walk too, starting here...' I mark a green cross on the paper. 'But suppose that I have no choice where I go. Suppose I have to obey this secret Rule...' I slip a card in my breast pocket.

'Let's see what happens if we start from the crosses and take alternate moves. You move first.' (fig. 1).

I draw in the moves as they are made, black for them, green for me. In only a few moves they have guessed what my Rule is: '*Move the same distance in the opposite direction*'.

We now turn the situation into a challenge: can they move so that I am forced to move to the same corner as they move to? Their thought now becomes purposeful and the insight they have already gained is enough to let them 'catch' me quite efficiently.

When the jubilation dies down we start again from the same initial points so that others can participate in guiding the chase. They quickly catch me again—and at the same point!

'Did you expect to catch me at the same place?'

Some, by their surprise, obviously did not expect this, others had not reached the stage of expecting anything, but a few say that of *course* it was the same place—and it would be the same place if we did it again...(see fig. 6.)

We now start again with a fresh sheet, and I have a new Rule: '*Move twice the distance in the same direction*'. Again they soon know my Rule but it takes them longer to catch me. With most of them a lot of guesswork is involved and they are confused also because they associate the word 'catch' so strongly with the word 'chase'.

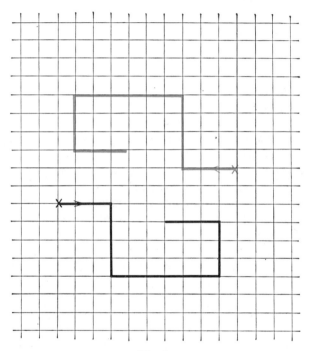

Fig. 1

We start again from the same crosses using this second Rule. After a few moves I ask them 'Do you think we're going to meet at the same corner?' (fig. 2).

An interesting discussion develops.

Later I use a third Rule: '*Face the direction in which they moved, turn left and then move forward the same distance*'. Once again the Rule is quite easy to deduce, although it is more difficult to put into words. But to work out the consequences and plan an efficient route is another matter. However they eventually manage to catch me, and once again they find that if we start at the same places they always meet me at the same corner.

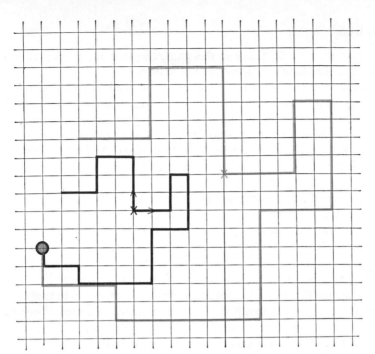

Fig. 2

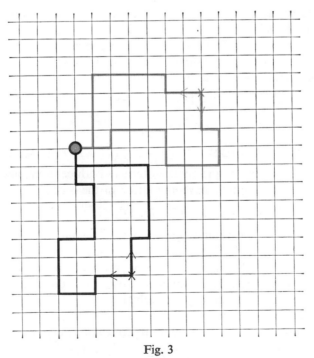

Fig. 3

Through their participation in this game they are building up an understanding of simple mappings of the plane on to itself. When they want to talk about what they are doing they meet the need to create new words. They may want to make up their own or they may be happy to use mine— mapping, corresponding point, image, fixed point, rotation, dilatation, transformation. But new words are brought in only when they are needed; they are just labels to tie on to important ideas. And all the time their geometrical intuition is growing, sometimes because of and sometimes in spite of the square grid.

This approach to the geometry of the plane links the basic concepts behind transformation geometry with the square-lattice structure of the plane that lies behind analytical geometry. It is natural to wish to develop this approach at a later stage by formalising it through the language and notation of conventional co-ordinate geometry, but this is not possible. This language is not suitable both on the practical grounds that it is inappropriate for the description of mappings of the plane on to itself and on the theoretical grounds that it implies the existence of a special point, the origin, whereas the plane is essentially a homogeneous set of points. (The further difficulty that the existence of a square lattice conflicts with the isotropic nature of the plane will have to be faced later.)

But analytical geometry is still a main topic in secondary school mathematics and seems likely to remain so in the foreseeable future. So those who continue their mathematical education at school are faced with the prospect of graduating from transformation geometry to analytical geometry and finding they have virtually nothing in common.

If school mathematics is to be a well-integrated whole, this gulf must be filled in. The purpose of this paper is to suggest a way in which this can be done.

## A GENERALIZATION OF ANALYTICAL GEOMETRY

Children using a square grid think in terms of 'three along and one up'. It follows that they should have a notation of the form

$$\text{`}AB \text{ is } (3, 1)\text{'}$$

as this matches their natural way of thinking. The difficulty lies in making a notation of this sort respectable. The question whether the numbers involved are natural numbers, integers, rationals or real numbers is relatively unimportant. The vital matter is to decide precisely what is meant by $AB$, by (3, 1), and by the verb 'is'.

I make no apology for attempting to provide a firm axiomatic basis for the 'vector notation', as a satisfactory treatment is a necessity not a luxury.

But I am aware that most readers will wish to skip quickly over the next page or two.

We assume the properties of the real number system and proceed thus:

(1) We define **V** to be the set of ordered pairs of real numbers with addition and multiplication by a real number defined in the usual way so that, for example,

$$\binom{2}{7}+\binom{4}{1} = \binom{6}{8} \quad \text{and} \quad 2\binom{1}{4} = \binom{2}{8}.$$

It follows at once that **V** is a vector space of dimension two over the real numbers.

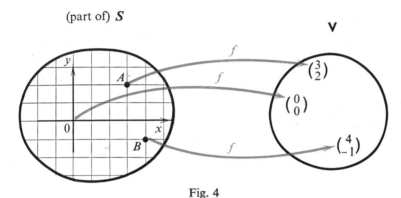

Fig. 4

(2) We define the plane to be set *S* of elements, which we call points, such that there exists a bijection (i.e. a one-to-one mapping) *f* of *S* on to **V**. It is this foundation mapping *f* that is the fundamental link between the geometric and analytic aspects of the theory, and it serves also to keep them apart. In effect we have now the co-ordinate or arithmetic plane with its special point the origin, *O*, which maps on to the zero vector of **V**, but we deliberately refrain from saying that a point *is* its ordered pair of co-ordinates.

We now regain the homogeneity of the plane by sidestepping the difficulty of the unique origin.

(3) We say that each ordered pair of points, (*P*, *Q*), has a *step*, $s(P, Q) \in$ **V**, defined by

$$s(P, Q) = f(Q) - f(P).$$

This is a mapping of the Cartesian product, *S*×*S*, on to **V**.

This definition of *step* has three important consequences:

(*a*) It is intuitively obvious that *s*(*P*, *Q*) is independent of 'the position of the origin' although it does depend on the square grid with its *x* and *y*-

directions. Thus, in so far as we do not refer back to the foundation mapping but only play around with these steps, the plane is homogeneous.

(*b*) It is easily proved (by going back to the definition) that, whatever foundation mapping is used,

$$s(A, B) + s(B, C) = s(A, C)$$

for all points *A*, *B* and *C*.

This fundamental property is of special interest as, in addition to ignoring the origin, it does not depend on the particular *x* and *y* directions chosen. We are reminded that our ultimate goal must be an analytical treatment of a homogeneous and isotropic plane.

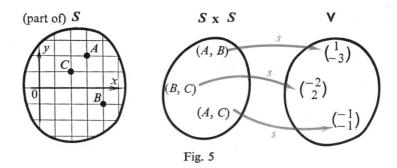

Fig. 5

(*c*) As steps are elements of the vector space **V** it follows at once that for every real number *k*,

$$k(s(A, B) + s(B, C)) = ks(A, B) + ks(B, C).$$

At a later stage in the development of the axiomatic theory this leads to basic geometrical properties of similarity, but we need not follow this up just now.

Alternative notations for $s(A, B)$ are $\overrightarrow{AB}$, which is convenient for blackboard work, and **AB**, which is far easier to set in type and which will be used from now on. It should be noted that there is no hint of movement in the statement

$$s(A, B) = \overrightarrow{AB} = \mathbf{AB} = \begin{pmatrix} 1 \\ -3 \end{pmatrix}.$$

Nor is there any suggestion of a 'path' connecting *A* to *B*, although the conventional way of thinking of 'vector *AB*' is as a directed line segment starting at *A* and finishing at *B*.

But we can of course use these notations in describing changes of position such as the moves in the mapping game. Indeed we can do this at two different levels: we can talk of the move $\binom{3}{0}$ and the corresponding move, under the first Rule, $\binom{-3}{0}$; and we can specify the Rule itself in the form

$$\mathbf{Q_1 Q_2} = -\mathbf{P_1 P_2},$$

where $\mathbf{Q_1 Q_2}$ is the move that corresponds to their move $\mathbf{P_1 P_2}$.

It may be noted that this work is in no way inconsistent with the basic language of analytical geometry but is an extension and generalization of it. The conventional techniques are still available but as they are almost all concerned with the equations of straight lines and other loci they are of little help in this present investigation. New techniques are required for transformation geometry, techniques which will enable us to describe, manipulate and systematize mappings of the plane on to itself.

To define a mapping of the plane the image of every point of the plane must be specified. That the first Rule (with the two initial points) does indeed define a mapping can be shown by proving that the line segment joining each point $P$ to its image $Q$ is always bisected by the point $A$ at which green and black coincide.

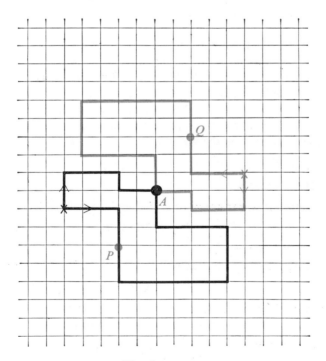

Fig. 6

This unique point $A$ maps on to itself. We now see that the mapping can be defined in the following way:

$$P \leadsto Q: \mathbf{AQ} = -\mathbf{AP}.$$

Similarly the second Rule gives a transformation which is defined by

$$P \leadsto Q: \mathbf{AQ} = 2\mathbf{AP},$$

where once again $A$ is the fixed point of the mapping.

This notation provides a framework against which our geometrical intuitions may be reconsidered. We confirm, for example, that the first two Rules do define one-to-one mappings, that in each case only one point maps on to itself, and that each mapping is a dilatation about $A$. And we notice that the enlargement factor ($-1$ and $2$) appears as the coefficient of $\mathbf{AP}$ in the equation. We can guess that a tenfold enlargement is a mapping of the form

$$P \leadsto Q: \mathbf{AQ} = 10\mathbf{AP}$$

but can we be sure that there is always a fixed point $A$?

*If a transparent inch to the mile map is laid over a corresponding $\frac{1}{4}$ inch to the mile map is there always a point which maps on to itself? Do you wish to assume that the maps are similarly orientated?*

Invitations like this to investigate further abound. What about the Rule '*Move the same distance in the same direction*'? Are successive dilatations always equivalent to a single dilatation? Even if the fixed points are not the same? And there is still that third Rule...

Let us now look at the kind of formal structure that arises naturally out of investigations like these; we use the above notation and develop any techniques we need on the way.

## TRANSLATIONS

A translation is a transformation of the plane defined by

$$P \leadsto Q: \mathbf{PQ} = \mathbf{k},$$

where $\mathbf{k} \in \mathbf{V}$ is a constant.

This mapping could just as well have been defined by writing

$$Q \leadsto R: \mathbf{QR} = \mathbf{k},$$

as the symbols given to the representative points are irrelevant. We make use of this when considering the composition of two translations.

Suppose the mapping

$$P \leadsto Q: \mathbf{PQ} = \begin{pmatrix} 5 \\ 2 \end{pmatrix}$$

is followed by the mapping

$$Q\frown R\colon \mathbf{QR} = \begin{pmatrix} 4 \\ -6 \end{pmatrix}$$

the result is the mapping

$$P\frown R\colon \mathbf{PR} = \mathbf{PQ} + \mathbf{QR}$$

$$= \begin{pmatrix} 5 \\ 2 \end{pmatrix} + \begin{pmatrix} 4 \\ -6 \end{pmatrix} = \begin{pmatrix} 9 \\ -4 \end{pmatrix}$$

which is a translation.

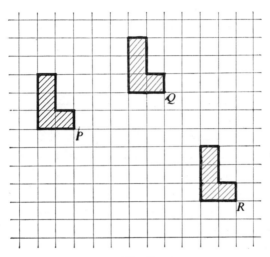

Fig. 7

By taking these translations in the other order,

$$P\frown Q\colon \mathbf{PQ} = \begin{pmatrix} 4 \\ -6 \end{pmatrix} \quad \text{and then} \quad Q\frown R\colon \mathbf{QR} = \begin{pmatrix} 5 \\ 2 \end{pmatrix},$$

we can verify that the composition of these translations is commutative.

As every element of **V** defines a translation and composition of translations is isomorphic to addition in **V**, we see that the set of translations is not only a commutative group but a vector space as well.

## DILATATIONS

To specify a dilatation one needs a point about which the dilatation takes place and a nonzero real number or factor which gives the proportional enlargement. For example we can talk of the dilatation $(A, 3)$ by which we mean the transformation

$$P\frown Q\colon \mathbf{AQ} = 3\mathbf{AP}.$$

147

We note that if the factor is positive but less than one there is a contraction rather than an enlargement, and if it is negative the image appears upside down on the opposite side of the fixed point.

The composition of dilatations having the same fixed point is always simple. For example

$$P \curvearrowright Q: \mathbf{AQ} = 3\mathbf{AP}$$

followed by

$$Q \curvearrowright R: \mathbf{AR} = -\tfrac{1}{4}\mathbf{AQ}$$

gives the resultant mapping

$$P \curvearrowright R: \mathbf{AR} = -\tfrac{1}{4}\mathbf{AQ} = -\tfrac{1}{4}(3\mathbf{AP}) = -\tfrac{3}{4}\mathbf{AP}$$

(by eliminating $\mathbf{Q}$ between the two equations) which is the dilatation centre $\mathbf{A}$ and factor $-\tfrac{3}{4}$.

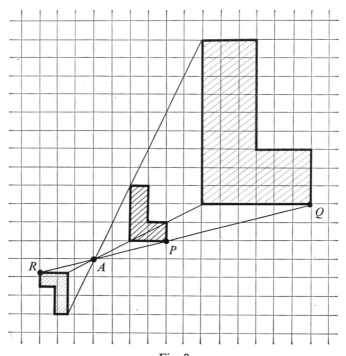

Fig. 8

As every nonzero real number defines a dilatation about a fixed point $A$, and composition of dilatations is isomorphic to multiplication in these real numbers, the set of dilatations about $A$ form not only a commutative group but also a vector space of dimension one.

When different centres are involved the situation is more interesting.

148

Consider the composition of the dilatations $(A, a)$ and $(B, b)$. These are defined by

$$P \curvearrowright Q: \mathbf{AQ} = a\mathbf{AP}$$

and

$$Q \curvearrowright R: \mathbf{BR} = b\mathbf{BQ},$$

and by eliminating $Q$ blindly we find that the resultant mapping is

$$P \curvearrowright R: \mathbf{BR} = b(\mathbf{AQ} - \mathbf{AB})$$
$$= b(a\mathbf{AP} - \mathbf{AB}), \tag{1}$$

but while this enables us to calculate the position of a final image it does not help us to see what is happening.

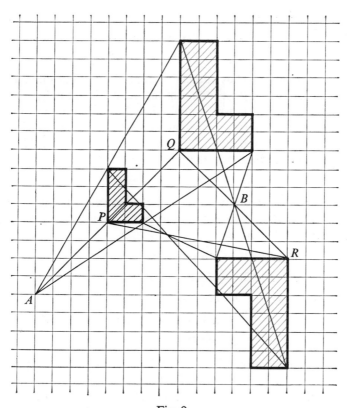

Fig. 9

When we study the diagram of a particular case our intuitive conclusions may strengthen into conviction, but the important point is that with insight we can take our theory a stage further. All we need to see is that if the resultant mapping is itself a dilatation then it must have a fixed point, say

149

$C$. This means that under the two consecutive mappings $C$ must map on to itself. But we already know that a point $P$ will map on to a point $R$ where $\mathbf{BR} = b(a\mathbf{AP}-\mathbf{AB})$ so, substituting $C$ for both $P$ and $R$, we have

$$\mathbf{BC} = b(a\mathbf{AC}-\mathbf{AB})$$

and we are able to find the position of $C$ relative to $A$ thus:

$$\mathbf{AC}-\mathbf{AB} = ab\mathbf{AC}-b\mathbf{AB}$$

so
$$(1-ab)\,\mathbf{AC} = (1-b)\,\mathbf{AB}$$

and
$$\mathbf{AC} = \frac{1-b}{1-ab}\,\mathbf{AB} \quad \text{if } ab \neq 1. \tag{2}$$

This forces us to consider the special case of $ab = 1$. The mapping (1) becomes

$$P \leadsto R: \mathbf{BR} = \mathbf{AP}-b\mathbf{AB}$$

i.e.
$$P \leadsto R: \mathbf{PR} = (1-b)\,\mathbf{AB}$$

which is a translation. Thus successive dilatations about different points give a dilatation only if the product of the factors is not unity.

But we have not yet shown formally that the composition of the dilatations $(A, a)$ and $(B, b)$ do give a dilatation, $(C, c)$ say, when $ab \neq 1$. We have shown that a fixed point $C$ exists, and we can hardly doubt that $c = ab$ and that the resultant mapping is

$$P \leadsto R: \mathbf{CR} = ab\mathbf{CP} \tag{3}$$

but it is a good opportunity to try out the notation. Using the point $C$ defined by (2) it should be possible to put mapping (1) in the form (3) assuming $ab \neq 1$. We have

$$P \leadsto R: \mathbf{BR} = b(a\mathbf{AP}-\mathbf{AB})$$

i.e.
$$
\begin{aligned}
P \leadsto R: \mathbf{CR} &= ab\mathbf{AP}-b\mathbf{AB}-\mathbf{BC} \\
&= ab\mathbf{CP}-b\mathbf{AB}+\mathbf{AB}-\mathbf{AC}+ab\mathbf{AC} \\
&= ab\mathbf{CP}+(1-b)\,\mathbf{AB}-(1-ab)\,\mathbf{AC} \\
&= ab\mathbf{CP}.
\end{aligned}
$$

At first this manipulation seems heavy, but not when one gets used to it.

Is it obvious that $C$ lies on $AB$? Thinking geometrically, the image of $A$ under the dilatations $(A, a)$ and then $(B, b)$ must lie on line $AB$ so $C$, the centre of the composite dilatation must lie on $AB$ as well. Thinking analytically, we see that (2) states that $C$ lies on the line $AB$. Indeed we can go further and say that *the fact that it is possible* to find the centre of the resultant dilatation by the above method implies that this centre lies on $AB$—no other position could be specified as $A$ and $B$ are the only fixed points.

Thinking geometrically again, we see that we have in effect proved Menelaus' Theorem, for $A$, $B$ and $C$ divide the sides of the triangle $PQR$ in the ratios $-1/a$, $-1/b$, and $-c$ and the product of these is $-1$. This aspect of successive dilatations is investigated in David Morris's contribution to this book.

The set of dilatations of the plane does not form a group by itself, but it is easily shown that if we include the set of translations we then have a group. That this group is not commutative can be seen either geometrically or analytically.

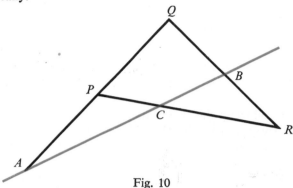

Fig. 10

## THE QUARTER TURN

Consider the quarter turn about $A$ shown in the diagram. This is the kind of transformation we get when we use the third Rule in the mapping game,

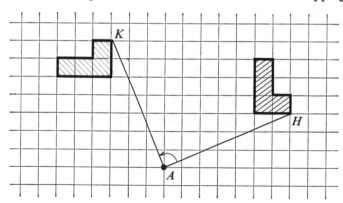

Fig. 11

and we soon see that the techniques that we have developed so far do not help at all. A new method must be evolved and this requires a heuristic approach to the whole problem. We shall use reasoning that is plausible

6                                        151

rather than precise in our investigation; the logical implications and possible inconsistencies will be left in the air until later.

The anticlockwise rotation of 90° about $A$ maps $H$ on to $K$, and we note that

$$\mathbf{AH} = \begin{pmatrix} 7 \\ 3 \end{pmatrix} \quad \text{and} \quad \mathbf{AK} = \begin{pmatrix} -3 \\ 7 \end{pmatrix}.$$

This is a particular example of a general relationship that can be used to define the quarter turn. The difficulty in stating this relationship makes the definition clumsy:

$P{\curvearrowright}Q$: 'AQ is obtained by taking the components of **AP**, reversing them and then changing the sign of the first one.'

(Incidentally, this is equivalent to a reflection in the line $x = y$, taking $A$ as the origin, followed by a reflection in the line $x = 0$, these two lines being at 45° which is half the 90° turn required. See *Some Lessons in Mathematics*, p. 279.)

If we are to follow up this line of thought it is clear that we must find a more concise way of expressing these ideas. Let us define a symbol which will stand for this operation on an element of **V**. Let us call the operator $\mathscr{J}$, where

$$\mathscr{J}\begin{pmatrix} x \\ y \end{pmatrix} = \begin{pmatrix} -y \\ x \end{pmatrix}.$$

Now we can define the quarter turn about $A$ as the transformation

$$P{\curvearrowright}Q: \mathbf{AQ} = \mathscr{J}\mathbf{AP}.$$

At this stage we could look further into the algebra involved. When $\mathscr{J}$ operates on a vector the result is a vector which in turn may be added to a vector, multiplied by a number or operated on by $\mathscr{J}$ again. How does $\mathscr{J}$ behave in such manipulation? Or we could look at the geometrical aspect. A quarter turn about $A$ followed by a quarter turn about $A$ gives a half turn about $A$—which is a dilatation with factor $-1$. Putting this into the notation we have

$$P{\curvearrowright}Q: \mathbf{AQ} = \mathscr{J}\mathbf{AP}$$

$$Q{\curvearrowright}R: \mathbf{AR} = \mathscr{J}\mathbf{AQ}$$

which gives the composite transformation

$$P{\curvearrowright}R: \mathbf{AR} = \mathscr{J}(\mathscr{J}\mathbf{AP}).$$

We can confirm analytically that this is a dilatation with factor $-1$ for if

$$\mathbf{AP} = \begin{pmatrix} x \\ y \end{pmatrix} \quad \text{then} \quad \mathscr{J}\mathbf{AP} = \begin{pmatrix} -y \\ x \end{pmatrix}$$

and

$$\mathscr{J}(\mathscr{J}\mathbf{AP}) = \begin{pmatrix} -x \\ -y \end{pmatrix} = -\mathbf{AP}.$$

The algebra seems to fit the geometry, and we push on with more confidence.

This operation of a quarter turn about a particular point $A$ generates a group of transformations with four elements:

$P\curvearrowright Q: \mathbf{AQ} = \mathcal{J}\mathbf{AP}$    (quarter turn)

$P\curvearrowright Q: \mathbf{AQ} = -\mathbf{AP}$    (half turn, or dilatation with factor $-1$)

$P\curvearrowright Q: \mathbf{AQ} = -\mathcal{J}\mathbf{AP}$    (threequarter turn, or quarter turn backwards)

$P\curvearrowright Q: \mathbf{AQ} = \mathbf{AP}$    (identity transformation)

(or $P\curvearrowright P$)

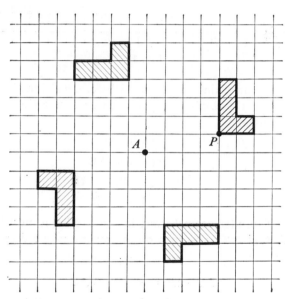

Fig. 12

This group of rotations is isomorphic to the multiplicative group

$$\{i, -1, -i, 1\},$$

both being examples of the cyclic group of order four.

If we now consider successive quarter turns about different points,

$$P\rightleftharpoons Q: \mathbf{AQ} = \mathcal{J}\mathbf{AP}$$

$$Q\curvearrowright R: \mathbf{BR} = \mathcal{J}\mathbf{BQ}$$

153

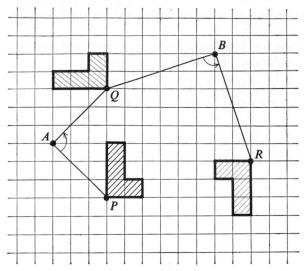

Fig. 13

we have a more interesting situation. As before, we should arrive at the composite mapping by combining these and eliminating $Q$. We have, using plausible reasoning,

$$P \curvearrowright R: \mathbf{BR} = \mathscr{J}(\mathbf{AQ}-\mathbf{AB})$$
$$= \mathscr{J}(\mathscr{J}\mathbf{AP}-\mathbf{AB})$$
$$= \mathscr{J}(\mathscr{J}\mathbf{AP})-\mathscr{J}\mathbf{AB} \quad (?)$$
$$= -\mathbf{AP}-\mathscr{J}\mathbf{AB}.$$

If this is a half turn (as geometrically it seems to be) it must have a fixed point, say $C$. And as $C$ must map on to itself we take a deep breath and write

$$\mathbf{BC} = -\mathbf{AC}-\mathscr{J}\mathbf{AB}$$

i.e. $$\mathbf{AC}-\mathbf{AB} = -\mathbf{AC}-\mathscr{J}\mathbf{AB}$$

i.e. $$2\mathbf{AC} = (1-\mathscr{J})\mathbf{AB} \quad (?)$$

i.e. $$\mathbf{AC} = (\tfrac{1}{2}-\tfrac{1}{2}\mathscr{J})\mathbf{AB} \quad (?)$$
$$= \tfrac{1}{2}\mathbf{AB}-\tfrac{1}{2}\mathscr{J}\mathbf{AB}. \quad (?)$$

This gives the position of $C$ relative to $A$ and, consulting the diagram, we find that the resultant half turn does indeed have this point as centre. This encouraging sign suggests that it will certainly be worthwhile to sort out the theory properly.

Just as with the set of dilatations, the set generated by the quarter turn becomes a group only when the set of translations is included as well.

## THE FIELD OF OPERATORS

We called $\mathcal{J}$ an operator because it changed the vector that followed it. If we are to be consistent we should call 3 an operator when it appears in a similar way, for example

$$3\binom{2}{5} = \binom{6}{15}.$$

These 'numerical operators' are elements of the field over which the vector space **V** is defined. If the operator $\mathcal{J}$ is to have the same status it must not only obey the same laws but also be an element of the field. Thus the field over which **V** is defined should be the extension generated by the real numbers (or operators) **R** and the new element $\mathcal{J}$.

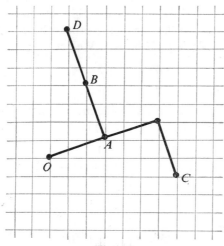

Fig. 14

Whether we call the real numbers 'operators' or $\mathcal{J}$ a 'number' is immaterial but relevant. We could say that we now have the field of complex numbers, but it is preferable to talk of the field of operators which is isomorphic to the field of complex numbers. By doing this we maintain the strong link with geometry and give our geometrical intuition more opportunity to guide our progress.

The validity of this last point can be judged by considering the nature of the 'field of operators' in terms of a diagram. As $\mathbf{AB} = \mathcal{J}\mathbf{OA}$ we have

$$\mathbf{OB} = \mathbf{OA} + \mathcal{J}\mathbf{OA}$$

which we can write $\qquad \mathbf{OB} = (1 + \mathcal{J})\,\mathbf{OA}.$

155

Here is the geometrical significance of addition in the field of operators, and we can check that it is both commutative and associative. Similarly

$$\mathbf{OC} = (2-\mathscr{J})\,\mathbf{OA}$$

and
$$\mathbf{OB}+\mathbf{OC} = (1+\mathscr{J})\,\mathbf{OA}+(2-\mathscr{J})\,\mathbf{OA}$$
$$= 3\,\mathbf{OA}.$$

Further, a quarter turn about $O$ maps $C$ on to $D$ and we have

$$\mathbf{OD} = \mathscr{J}\mathbf{OC}$$
$$= \mathscr{J}[(2-\mathscr{J})\,\mathbf{OA}]$$
$$= [\mathscr{J}(2-\mathscr{J})]\,\mathbf{OA}.$$

This enables us to consider the product of operators geometrically. That multiplication is indeed distributive over addition can be proved from first principles, but we get the flavour of the process here by 'multiplying out the brackets' and replacing $\mathscr{J}^2$ by $-1$. We get

$$\mathbf{OD} = (1+2\mathscr{J})\,\mathbf{OA}$$

which we can see is correct.

The algebraic study of operators is identical to that of complex numbers, so the multiplicative inverse of $(1+2\mathscr{J})$ is

$$\frac{1}{1+2\mathscr{J}} = \frac{1-2\mathscr{J}}{(1+2\mathscr{J})\,(1-2\mathscr{J})}$$
$$= \frac{1-2\mathscr{J}}{5},$$

and thus
$$\mathbf{OA} = \frac{1}{1+2\mathscr{J}}\,\mathbf{OD}$$
$$= (\tfrac{1}{5}-\tfrac{2}{5}\,\mathscr{J})\,\mathbf{OD}.$$

It is by playing with statements like

$$\mathbf{CD} = (3+\mathscr{J})\,\mathbf{AB}, \quad \mathbf{AC} = -\,\mathscr{J}\mathbf{OB} \quad \text{and} \quad \mathbf{BC} = (1\tfrac{1}{2}-\tfrac{1}{2}\mathscr{J})\,\mathbf{AC}$$

that we realise the implications of the field extension. Our vector space **V** is now of dimension one—every pair of vectors is linearly dependent. For every set of three (distinct) points, $A$, $P$ and $Q$, there is an operator $z$ such that
$$\mathbf{AQ} = z\mathbf{AP},$$

where $z$ is of the form $a+b\mathscr{J}$ where $a$ and $b$ are real numbers.

But a further and more important point is that this operator $z$ is not affected by a change of square grid. In the diagram, for example, we see that the positions of $P$ and $Q$ relative to $A$ can be stated in many ways:

$$\mathbf{AP} = (4+2\mathscr{J})\,\mathbf{u}, \qquad \mathbf{AQ} = (6+8\mathscr{J})\,\mathbf{u};$$
$$\mathbf{AP} = 2\mathbf{v}, \qquad \mathbf{AQ} = (4+2\mathscr{J})\,\mathbf{v};$$
$$\mathbf{AP} = (1+\mathscr{J})\,\mathbf{w}, \qquad \mathbf{AQ} = (1+3\mathscr{J})\,\mathbf{w};$$

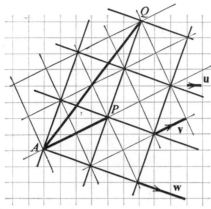

Fig. 15

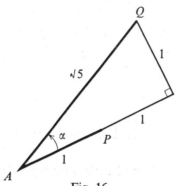

Fig. 16

but in each case it is true that

$$\mathbf{AQ} = (2+\mathscr{J})\,\mathbf{AP}.$$

It follows that the mapping defined by

$$P \curvearrowright Q: \mathbf{AQ} = (2+\mathscr{J})\,\mathbf{AP}$$

is in no way affected by the choice of grid—indeed the presence of a grid is often a distraction. When we remove all the grids in the above diagram it becomes easier to see that this transformation is made up of a rotation of angle $\alpha$ where $\tan\alpha = \frac{1}{2}$, and a dilatation of factor $\sqrt{5}$. We see also that this transformation can be expressed

$$P \curvearrowright Q: \mathbf{AQ} = \sqrt{5}(\cos\alpha + \sin\alpha \mathscr{J})\, \mathbf{AP},$$

and so we are able to describe, and presumably to manipulate, rotational dilatations.

Before going on to consider these fully, consider the simple rotation of angle $\theta$ about $A$:

$$P \curvearrowright Q: \mathbf{AQ} = (\cos\theta + \sin\theta\,\mathscr{J})\, \mathbf{AP}$$
$$= \cos\theta\mathbf{AP} + \sin\theta\,\mathscr{J}\mathbf{AP}$$
$$= \mathbf{AN} + \mathbf{NQ}.$$

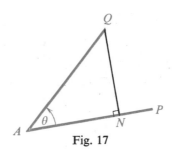

Fig. 17

A further rotation of angle $\theta$ about $A$, which we can write

$$Q \curvearrowright R: \mathbf{AR} = (\cos\theta + \sin\theta\,\mathscr{J})\, \mathbf{AQ},$$

gives the composite transformation

$$P \curvearrowright R: \mathbf{AR} = (\cos\theta + \sin\theta\,\mathscr{J})^2\, \mathbf{AP},$$

which is clearly a rotation of $2\theta$ about $A$.

It is interesting to note that Demoivre's theorem, when thought of in terms of operators, reduces to

    '$n$ successive rotations of angle $\theta$ are equivalent to a single rotation of angle $n\theta$.'

## THE ROTATIONAL DILATATIONS

A rotational dilatation may be described briefly and defined formally in two different ways. Algebraically we have the transformation $(A, z)$ defined by
$$P \curvearrowright Q: \mathbf{AQ} = z\mathbf{AP}$$
while geometrically it is more appropriate to use the form $(A; \theta, k)$ defined by
$$P \curvearrowright Q: \mathbf{AQ} = k(\cos\theta + \sin\theta\,\mathscr{J})\, \mathbf{AP}.$$

158

The former is very suitable for algebraic manipulation, but the latter promotes valuable geometrical insight as we have already seen.

Consecutive rotational dilatations about the same point give no difficulty at all and little interest. It is enough to state the results:

$(A, z_1)$ followed by $(A, z_2)$ is equivalent to $(A, z_1 z_2)$;

$(A; \theta, k_1)$ followed by $(A; \phi, k_2)$ is equivalent to $(A; \theta+\phi, k_1 k_2)$.

In the case of different fixed points one might expect trouble, but we find that the treatment is exactly similar to that for consecutive dilatations. The transformations

$$P \curvearrowright Q: \mathbf{AQ} = z_1 \mathbf{AP}$$

and

$$Q \curvearrowright R: \mathbf{BR} = z_2 \mathbf{BQ}$$

give the resultant mapping

$$P \curvearrowright R: \mathbf{BR} = z_2(z_1 \mathbf{AP} - \mathbf{AB}).$$

If this is a rotational dilatation it has a fixed point, say $C$, which maps on to itself and is thus defined by:

$$\mathbf{BC} = z_2(z_1 \mathbf{AC} - \mathbf{AB}).$$

Solving for $\mathbf{AC}$ we have

$$\mathbf{AC} - \mathbf{AB} = z_2(z_1 \mathbf{AC} - \mathbf{AB}),$$

so

$$(1 - z_1 z_2)\mathbf{AC} = (1 - z_2)\mathbf{AB}$$

and

$$\mathbf{AC} = \frac{1 - z_2}{1 - z_1 z_2} \mathbf{AB} \quad \text{if } z_1 z_2 \neq 1.$$

If $z_1 z_2 = 1$ we see intuitively that there is no rotation and no enlargement and hence the composite transformation is a translation. In every other case a fixed point $C$ exists as defined above and it can be shown, just as with the dilatations, that the resultant mapping is

$$P \curvearrowright R: \mathbf{CR} = z_1 z_2 \mathbf{CP}.$$

A group is formed by the union of the rotational dilatations and the translations. This is the group of direct similarities or, more fundamentally, of angle-preserving transformations of the plane.

## THE GROUP OF ANGLE-PRESERVING TRANSFORMATIONS

In every transformation that we have considered, shape has been conserved without any need for 'turning over'. We can state this precisely thus:

> 'for all points $P_1$, $P_2$ and $P_3$, with images $Q_1$, $Q_2$ and $Q_3$, angle $P_1 P_2 P_3$ = angle $Q_1 Q_2 Q_3$, where these are signed angles.'

159

It is a useful exercise to prove that the converse is also true, that we have in fact covered all possible cases of direct similarity.

Within this major group of transformations there are many subgroups, the main ones being the group of size-preserving transformations (the direct isometries), the group of direction-preserving transformations and their intersection, the group of translations.

**Group of angle-preserving transformations**

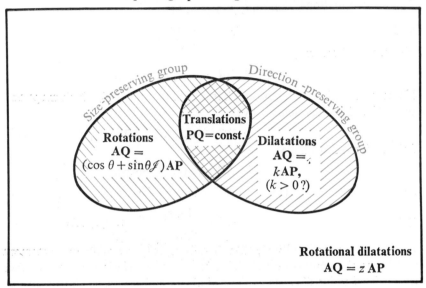

Fig. 18

To see these transformations in better perspective we should relate them also to more general groups. For example, our major group of direct similarities is a subgroup of the group of transformations in which parallel lines map on to parallel lines (e.g. shears), and this itself is a subgroup of the group of projective transformations in which collinearity is preserved. We see that although our new techniques are powerful their range of application is distinctly limited.

Another technique for studying transformations of the plane involves matrices. It is instructive to compare these methods, and we can do this easily in the many cases where they can be used to describe the same transformation:

(a) $\begin{pmatrix} X \\ Y \end{pmatrix} = \begin{pmatrix} 2 & 0 \\ 0 & 2 \end{pmatrix} \begin{pmatrix} x \\ y \end{pmatrix}$      $\mathbf{OQ} = 2\mathbf{OP},$

(b) $\begin{pmatrix} X \\ Y \end{pmatrix} = \begin{pmatrix} 0 & -1 \\ 1 & 0 \end{pmatrix} \begin{pmatrix} x \\ y \end{pmatrix}$      $\mathbf{OQ} = \mathscr{J}\mathbf{OP},$

(c) $\begin{pmatrix} X \\ Y \end{pmatrix} = \begin{pmatrix} 2 & -1 \\ 1 & 2 \end{pmatrix} \begin{pmatrix} x \\ y \end{pmatrix}$      $\mathbf{OQ} = (2 + \mathscr{J})\,\mathbf{OP},$

(d) $\begin{pmatrix} X \\ Y \end{pmatrix} = \begin{pmatrix} \cos\theta & -\sin\theta \\ \sin\theta & \cos\theta \end{pmatrix} \begin{pmatrix} x \\ y \end{pmatrix}$      $\mathbf{OQ} = (\cos\theta + \sin\theta\,\mathscr{J})\,\mathbf{OP}.$

(a)

(b)

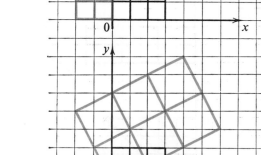

(c)

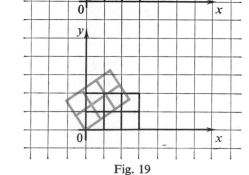

(d)

Fig. 19

We see that every operator $a+b\mathscr{J}$ has an equivalent matrix $\begin{pmatrix} a & -b \\ b & a \end{pmatrix}$, and so, as one would expect, these matrices also form a field isomorphic to that of the complex numbers. We could use them throughout our investigation in place of the operators if we wished.

But there are other two-by-two matrices which can be used to describe transformations such as reflection, stretch and shear,

$$\begin{pmatrix} X \\ Y \end{pmatrix} = \begin{pmatrix} -1 & 0 \\ 0 & 1 \end{pmatrix} \begin{pmatrix} x \\ y \end{pmatrix}, \quad \begin{pmatrix} X \\ Y \end{pmatrix} = \begin{pmatrix} 2 & 0 \\ 0 & 1 \end{pmatrix} \begin{pmatrix} x \\ y \end{pmatrix}, \quad \begin{pmatrix} X \\ Y \end{pmatrix} = \begin{pmatrix} 1 & 1 \\ 0 & 1 \end{pmatrix} \begin{pmatrix} x \\ y \end{pmatrix}$$

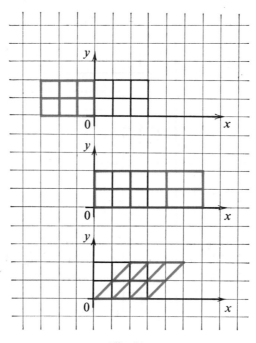

Fig. 20

so it is natural to wish to replace the operators not just by the isomorphic field of matrices but by the *whole* set of two-by-two matrices. But while this extends the range of description it limits immediately the power of the associated algebra because these matrices do not form a field (for example multiplication is not commutative) and thus **V** is no longer a vector space. How drastic the effect of this is, and what can be done about it, I do not know.

What about translations? Whichever field the vector space **V** is defined over we would still normally define a translation by

$$P\!\curvearrowright\!Q: \mathbf{PQ} = \mathbf{k}.$$

But without this type of approach we are in trouble. What has unfortunately become the conventional treatment of transformations using matrices makes no distinction between a point and its co-ordinates. Instead of an operator acting on a set of 'relative positions' of points the matrix acts in effect on the point itself. This necessitates and emphasises not only the existence of the origin but also special directions in the plane. And we find that it is necessary to increase the matrix size to cope with translations:

$$\begin{pmatrix} X \\ Y \\ 1 \end{pmatrix} = \begin{pmatrix} 1 & 0 & 4 \\ 0 & 1 & 3 \\ 0 & 0 & 1 \end{pmatrix} \begin{pmatrix} x \\ y \\ 1 \end{pmatrix} \qquad \mathbf{PQ} = \begin{pmatrix} 4 \\ 3 \end{pmatrix} \quad \text{or} \quad \mathbf{OQ} = \mathbf{OP} + \mathbf{OA}.$$

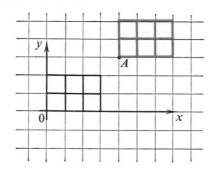

Fig. 21

Another way of comparing the operator and matrix approaches to transformations I find particularly interesting. Think of playing the Mapping Game with two quite separate sheets of squared paper, mapping from one sheet on to the other. The aim of the game at once disappears as 'catching' is no longer possible. But, once we have agreed on corresponding directions, we can just as easily make our moves and the mathematics seems almost the same. It was with a bit of a jolt that I realised that there was now no such thing as a translation, that there could not be because **PQ** does not exist if $P$ and $Q$ are not on the same plane.

We can handle such mappings from one plane to another equally correctly with either operators or matrices, using statements like

$$\mathbf{Q_1 Q_2} = 2\mathbf{P_1 P_2}$$

which still defines explicitly the Rule of the game. It is only when we map from a plane on to itself that we can get translations. And this is when, and possibly why, the normal matrix method runs into difficulties.

The same objection can be raised in the case of the Argand diagram. We say 'the point $(4+3i)\ldots$' but we do not take this to its logical conclusion and talk of 'the points $A$, $B$ and $(A+B)\ldots$' and write equations like $A+B = C$ and $AB+C = D$. But perhaps when we say 'the point $(4+3i)$' we really mean 'the point which represents the complex number $(4+3i)$', in which case all we have is a diagrammatic representation of the complex numbers. The fact that interesting geometrical relationships arise does not imply that here is an appropriate way to tackle geometry, it merely suggests that there is an interesting connection between geometry and the field of complex numbers that should become clearer when geometry is studied in a suitable way.

The two new notations that we have developed from the basic concept of the 'step', as an element of the vector space **V**, bridge the gap between the traditional notations of analytical geometry and the Argand diagram.

$$P(x,y)$$

$$\text{OP} = \begin{pmatrix} x \\ y \end{pmatrix}$$

$$\text{OP} = (x+y\mathscr{G})\,\mathbf{u},$$

$$P(x+iy)$$

They provide a language that is both flexible and powerful, a language which makes possible an algebraic study of geometry rather than a geometrical representation of algebra.

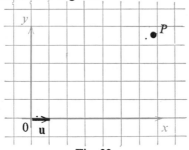

Fig. 22

But not only does this generalisation of analytical geometry make possible a fuller study of parts of Euclidean geometry, it also makes available ways of thinking and explicit techniques in algebra which existed only at the intuitive level in working with the Argand diagram.

*Example:* Solve $z^3 + 8 = 0$.

The complex numbers are isomorphic to the field of operators so we can handle this equation geometrically. We have $z^3 \mathbf{u} = -8\mathbf{u}$, where $z$ is an operator, or, in words, 'what operation when performed three times gives the operation $-8$?'

We can think of the operator $-8$ as a combination of a dilatation factor 8 and a rotation of 180°, so the required operator will give a dilatation of factor 2 and a rotation of a third of 180° (mod 360). This gives the three solutions

$$z_1 = 2(\cos 60° + \sin 60° \; \mathscr{J}),$$
$$z_2 = 2(\cos 180° + \sin 180° \; \mathscr{J}),$$
$$z_3 = 2(\cos 300° + \sin 300° \; \mathscr{J}),$$

which are illustrated by the vectors $\mathbf{OP_1} = z_1 \mathbf{u}$, etc.

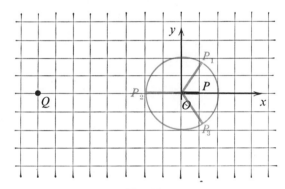

Fig. 23

## CONCLUSION

To be acceptable, a proposed change in school mathematics must be thoroughly respectable mathematically. To be *desirable* it should satisfy two broad criteria:

(*a*) Is it appropriate to the children concerned? Does it stimulate their interest, insight and understanding?

(*b*) Does it simplify and clarify at the formal level, either in the particular branch of mathematics concerned or in the relation between the branches?

It is on the first of these counts that motion geometry shows up so well, as those who use it in the classroom know. But now that it is becoming a recognised part of school mathematics the second criterion is important and must be satisfied if possible.

One formal continuation of motion geometry is to denote the transformations by symbols and to embark on an algebraic study. This is discussed in the chapter on geometry in *Some Lessons in Mathematics* and continued in Geoff Howson's contribution to this book.

The continuation that I am concerned with here involves the wider task of the modernisation and generalisation of analytical geometry with the specific aim of promoting the integration of school mathematics. Only that part of the work directly relevant to the composition of geometric transformations has been treated in this article.

I am well aware that there will be defects and inconsistences in this work; I hope that they will be drawn to my attention. Many questions are unanswered, and many more have not yet been asked. But this must be expected of a theory that is still being worked out. The great need now is for criticism, creative where possible but destructive where necessary, and for further investigation.

# A GROUP CALCULUS FOR GEOMETRY

## by A. G. HOWSON

Even before World War I attempts were made to base school geometry upon the study of such plane transformations as reflections, rotations, translations and enlargements (see, for example, Dobbs[1]). Why these attempts failed is not clear but one can only surmise that the rigidity of the examination system was to blame in part. Possibly a more cogent reason was that no allied attempt was made to reform school algebra. If transformation geometry is only to be used to establish the standard results of Euclidean geometry, then its claim on a place in the school syllabus is seriously weakened. Its great advantage over the traditional Euclidean approach is its relevance to other branches of mathematics. It is, therefore, only when functions, matrix algebra, groups, etc. are included in the syllabus that the case for the study of transformation geometry begins to build up.

It is this alliance between algebra and transformation geometry that has led to the recent widespread interest in the subject. As far as England is concerned this awakening of interest dates from the beginnings of *Some Lessons in Mathematics*[2], and A. G. Sillitto, through this book and those of the S.M.G. and S.M.P.—he was the author of the section on transformation geometry in the *Teacher's Guide to Book T*[3]—played a major part in it. In 1962 one could not assume any knowledge of the subject on the part of teachers, and this is reflected in the choice of material in the relevant

---

[1] Dobbs, W. J. in *A School Course in Geometry*, Longmans Green, 1913, and in *Math. Gazette*, VII, 1913.

Interest was not confined to this side of the Atlantic, for even earlier D. E. Smith had written in *The Teaching of Geometry*, Boston and London, 1911, '...The efforts usually made to improve the spirit of Euclid are trivial...But there is a possibility, remote though it may be at present, that a geometry will be developed that will be as serious as Euclid's, and as effective in the education of the thinking individual. If so, it seems probable that it will not be based upon the congruence of triangles, but upon certain postulates of motion...It will be through some effort as this, rather than through the weakening of the Euclid-Legendre style of geometry, that any improvement is likely to come...'

[2] Fletcher, T. J. (Ed.), *Some Lessons in Mathematics*. Cambridge University Press, 1964.

[3] School Mathematics Project, *Teacher's Guide to Book T*, Cambridge University Press, 1965.

chapter of *Some Lessons in Mathematics*. Since that time teachers have become increasingly familiar with this topic and, in particular, with the underlying algebraic ideas. The object of these notes is to look in more detail at some of the notions briefly mentioned in that chapter and to indicate how certain ideas can be developed.

In chapter 10 of *Some Lessons in Mathematics* we met the four types of plane isometries—reflections, rotations, translations and glide-reflections—and we saw that these isometries form a group under the operation of combination.

Two features of this group are of especial interest, namely, (i) the group is *generated* by the set of reflections in a line, that is, any isometry can be written as the product of reflections (more than this, we learned that rotations and translations can always be expressed as the product of two reflections, while a glide-reflection can be expressed as the product of three), (ii) the only non-identity elements of the group that are *self-inverse* are reflections in lines and half-turns (or point-reflections). It is interesting to note that line- and point-reflections are also distinguished by being the only plane isometries defined by one element of the plane: they are fixed once the mirror-line and point of rotation respectively are known. Two pieces of information must be given when we define the other isometries.

In these notes we shall be concerned almost entirely with line- and point-reflections and we shall refer to them using the letters denoting the lines or points defining them—reflections in the lines $l$, $m$, $n$,...will be denoted by **l**, **m**, **n**,...and reflections in the points $A$, $B$, $C$,...by **A**, **B**, **C**,... We shall follow the convention that **mA** denotes first **A** and then **m** (this differs from the usage in *Some Lessons in Mathematics*).

Early experimentation with reflections leads to the discovery that the relation **lm** = **ml** (**l** $\neq$ **m**) is satisfied if and only if the lines $l$ and $m$ are perpendicular. **lm** then represents a point-reflection **P**, say, where $P$ is the point of intersection of $l$ and $m$.

We note that the relation
$$\mathbf{lm} = \mathbf{ml}$$

can be expressed in other ways. In particular, it is equivalent to

$$\mathbf{lmlm} = (\mathbf{lm})^2 = \mathbf{I} \quad \text{(where } \mathbf{I} \text{ is the identity transformation)}$$

and to
$$\mathbf{lml} = \mathbf{m}.$$

The former is equivalent to saying that **lm** is self-inverse and, in fact, we can say that the two lines $l$ and $m$ are perpendicular if and only if **lm** is self-inverse. The significance of the second mode of presentation will become apparent later.

Other geometric facts of a less obvious nature can also be described by means of such relations and some examples are as follows:

(a)  $\mathbf{lPlP} = \mathbf{I}$          $P$ lies on $l$;

(b)  $\mathbf{PQRS} = \mathbf{I}$       $PQRS$ is a parallelogram (possibly degenerate);

(c)  $\mathbf{PRQR} = \mathbf{I}$,  $\mathbf{P} \neq \mathbf{Q}$    $R$ is the mid-point of $PQ$;

(d)  $\mathbf{PlQl} = \mathbf{I}$        $l$ is the mediator (perpendicular bisector) of $PQ$;

(e)  $\mathbf{a(bac)^2\,a(cab)^2 = I}$,    The triangle bounded by $a$, $b$ and $c$ is
      $\mathbf{(bac)^2 \neq I}$        isosceles with equal sides along $b$ and $c$;

(f)  $\mathbf{(abc)^2 = I}$        $a$, $b$ and $c$ are concurrent or parallel—in either case we have $\mathbf{abc} = \mathbf{d}$ for some $\mathbf{d}$.

To prove these assertions we make use of certain stock results such as:

(i) A point-reflection can be expressed as the product of two line-reflections. We are free to choose the direction of the axis of one reflection, the axis of the other reflection is then fixed (the two axes are at right-angles).

(ii) The product of two point-reflections is a translation.

(iii) The product of two reflections in parallel lines is a translation (through twice the distance between the lines).

(iv) Non-zero translations are never self-inverse.

The ability to express geometrical facts in terms of relations between the elements of a group presents us with a novel method for proving geometrical theorems. The procedure is simply to translate the given geometrical facts into algebraic terms and then to carry out purely algebraic operations until we arrive at the algebraic equivalent to our geometrical result. This method is, of course, the one used in Cartesian geometry—the novelty here lies in the fact that we are concerned solely with the elements of a group and with a *single* group operation. The algebraic structure is simpler than that of the vector space underlying Cartesian geometry. Moreover, there is no question of having to select any particular co-ordinate system.

As an example we prove that the mediators of a triangle are concurrent.

Let $l$ and $m$ be the mediators of the sides $AB$ and $BC$ respectively and let them intersect at $D$ (see fig. 1).

Denote the line $BD$ by $p$.

Translated into group relations we have:

$$\mathbf{AlBl} = \mathbf{I} \qquad \text{(from (d) above)} \qquad\qquad \text{(i)}$$

$$\mathbf{BmCm} = \mathbf{I} \qquad \text{(from (d) above)} \qquad\qquad \text{(ii)}$$

$$\mathbf{pB} = \mathbf{Bp} \qquad \text{(from (a) above)} \qquad\qquad \text{(iii)}$$

169

Let $\quad\quad\quad\quad\quad$ **lpm = n** $\quad\quad$ (from ($f$) above) (iv).

Then, $\quad\quad$ **AnCn = AlpmCn** from (iv),

$\quad\quad\quad\quad\quad\quad\quad$ = **lBpmCn** from (i),

$\quad\quad\quad\quad\quad\quad\quad$ = **lpBmCn** from (iii),

$\quad\quad\quad\quad\quad\quad\quad$ = **lpmCCn** from (ii),

$\quad\quad\quad\quad\quad\quad\quad$ = **lpmn** $\quad$ since **CC = I**,

$\quad\quad\quad\quad\quad\quad\quad$ = **I** $\quad\quad\quad$ from (iv).

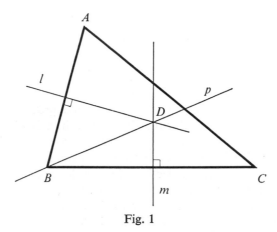

Fig. 1

Hence, from ($d$), $n$ is the mediator of $AC$. Moreover, **n = lpm** implies that $l$, $m$, $n$ and $p$ are parallel (which is not the case) or are concurrent, i.e. $n$ passes through $D$. Hence, the three mediators meet at $D$.

This method of proof is by no means easy—at first sight one can see little reason for the introduction of $p$ and the definition of **n**. These steps become clearer when one realises that the transformation in which we are interested is a reflection mapping $C$ onto $A$. **lm** will map $C$ onto $A$ (via $B$), but it is a rotation. We need, therefore, to introduce a further reflection but one that will not affect the final image of $C$—**p** inserted after **m** will, of course, do the trick since it leaves $B$ unchanged.

Nevertheless, there are certain aspects of this method of proof that are quite appealing. To obtain a result we need only show that the group element obtained by combining a certain finite set of elements in a particular fashion is the identity element. As the logical steps involved in moving from one line of the proof to the next are stereotyped one might ask whether a computer would be capable of producing such proofs. Alternatively, can we generate countless theorems using a computer? Is there a geometrical theorem corresponding to every group relation?

As an example of this type of reasoning we return to the result of Thomsen's[1] quoted in *Some Lessons in Mathematics*. If $a$, $b$ and $c$ are any three lines in the plane (neither concurrent nor parallel), then **abc** is a glide-reflection and $(\mathbf{abc})^2$ is a translation. Similarly, $(\mathbf{bca})^2$ is a translation. Since translations commute, we have

$$(\mathbf{abc})^2 (\mathbf{bca})^2 = (\mathbf{bca})^2 (\mathbf{abc})^2$$

or $\qquad$ **abcabcbcabcacbacbcbacb** $= \mathbf{I}$

for all **a, b, c**. (If $a$, $b$ and $c$ are concurrent or parallel, this relation is more easily seen to be true, for then $(\mathbf{abc})^2 = \mathbf{I}$.)

This is a non-trivial group relation and presumably represents some geometrical theorem. But what theorem?

It is possible then to generate theorems whose geometrical content is by no means obvious. More to the point is whether or not we can obtain all the obvious results by this means.

That we cannot is shown by the following example: given that $a$, $b$ and $c$ are concurrent and that $a$, $b$ and $d$ are concurrent, we imply that $a$, $b$, $c$ and $d$ meet at a point. However, it is not true in a general group that if **a, b, c** and **d** are group elements then

$$\mathbf{a}^2 = \mathbf{b}^2 = \mathbf{c}^2 = \mathbf{d}^2 = (\mathbf{abc})^2 = (\mathbf{abd})^2 = \mathbf{I} \quad \text{implies} \quad (\mathbf{acd})^2 = \mathbf{I}.$$

The reason for this is that so far we have only spoken about line- and point-reflections and the fact that they are self-inverse. Yet one can define these transformations in geometries other than Euclid's, for example, using Klein's spherical model for elliptic geometry[2] we can define reflections in great circles and reflections in points on the surface of the sphere. We should not expect then to be able to prove results belonging to Euclidean geometry unless we build into our system, in the form of group relations, certain conditions that will characterise this particular geometry.

In order to see how this can be done, we shall approach the problem from a totally different point of view and show how a geometry can be associated with a given group. Only certain groups are eligible; in fact, we shall only be interested in groups that are generated by a set of *self-inverse* elements **a, b, c, d,** .... To these elements will correspond our 'lines' $a$, $b$, $c$, $d$, .... A 'point' will be associated with a self-inverse element of the group that can be written as the product of two of the generators: if, for example, $\mathbf{P}^2 = \mathbf{I}$ and $\mathbf{P} = \mathbf{ab}$, then we associate with **P** the 'point' $P$.

We note that from these relations we obtain

$$\mathbf{abab} = \mathbf{I},$$

---

[1] Thomsen, G. The Treatment of Elementary Geometry by a Group Calculus. *Math. Gazette*, xvii, 1933.

[2] See for example, Adler, C. F. *Modern Geometry*, McGraw-Hill, 1958.

which is equivalent to

**ab = ba**   (since **a** and **b** are self-inverse).

This suggests the definition: the distinct lines $a$ and $b$ are perpendicular if and only if **ab = ba.**

Other geometrical relations can be defined in a similar manner, for example, looking back at the relations listed on p. 169, we see that a suitable definition of incidence is: the point $P$ lies on the line $l$ if and only if

**Pl = lP,**

that is, if and only if **Pl** is self-inverse.

Groups giving rise to interesting geometries will of necessity be complicated and contain many elements. However, it is interesting to consider some elementary groups.

The smallest group of interest is Klein's four-group. This group contains four elements **I, a, b, ab** and, presented in terms of generators and relations, it is the group

$$\{a, b\colon a^2 = b^2 = I, ab = ba\}.$$

The associated geometry, therefore, consists of the two lines $a$ and $b$ together with their point of intersection $C$ (**C = ab**); the two lines are, of course, perpendicular. Little more can be said of this geometry!

The group table of the non-abelian group of order 6 is

|   | I | a | b | c | φ | ψ |
|---|---|---|---|---|---|---|
| **I** | I | a | b | c | φ | ψ |
| **a** | a | I | φ | ψ | c | b |
| **b** | b | ψ | I | φ | a | c |
| **c** | c | φ | ψ | I | b | a |
| **φ** | φ | c | a | b | ψ | I |
| **ψ** | ψ | b | c | a | I | φ |

The group can be presented in terms of generators and relations by

$$\{a, b, c\colon a^2 = b^2 = c^2 = I, ab = bc = ca, ac = ba = cb\}.$$

The corresponding geometry consists of the three lines $a$, $b$ and $c$. Although simple, this geometry is not without interest for it suggests a possible definition of angle bisector. (Compare relation $(c)$ on p. 169 and note the examples of duality which arises in this table of relations. What is the dual of relation $(d)$?)

The two groups we have just discussed are, of course, the symmetry groups of the rectangle and the equilateral triangle, and it is interesting to note the connection between these figures and the geometries defined by the groups.

Another group with three generators is the group of order 8 given by

$$\{a, b, c: a^2 = b^2 = c^2 = I, ab = ba, bc = cb, ac = ca\}.$$

In the associated geometry we have three lines $a$, $b$ and $c$, and three points $X$ ($X = ab$), $Y$($Y = bc$) and $Z$($Z = ac$). The lines $a$ and $b$ meet at $X$, $b$ and $c$ at $Y$, and $a$ and $c$ at $Z$. It is a little disconcerting to note that the lines $a$, $b$ and $c$ are mutually perpendicular (yet $X$, $Y$ and $Z$ are known to be distinct), but we know that such a state of affairs can exist in spherical geometry. A more perplexing problem is raised by the element $\mathbf{abc}$, for this too is self-inverse. Is it, then, to be associated with a point, a line, or neither?

Clearly, if we are to obtain geometries with which we are familiar, and in particular plane Euclidean geometry, then we must impose further conditions upon the groups underlying the geometries. This is done by constructing a set of axioms based on the properties we wish our points and lines to have. The following set of axioms is taken from Bachmann.[1]

Suppose we are given a group $\mathbf{G}$ generated by the set of self-inverse elements $\mathbf{a, b, c, d,}$ ... and that $\mathbf{P, Q, R, S,}$ ... are the self-inverse elements of $\mathbf{G}$ that can be expressed as products of two members of the set of generators.

We demand:

*Axiom 1:* Given $\mathbf{P}$ and $\mathbf{Q}$, there exists a $\mathbf{g}$ such that $\mathbf{Pg}$ and $\mathbf{Qg}$ are self-inverse (i.e. there exists a line $\mathbf{PQ}$ ($= \mathbf{g}$)).

*Axiom 2:* If $\mathbf{Pg}$, $\mathbf{Qg}$, $\mathbf{Ph}$ and $\mathbf{Qh}$ are all self-inverse, then either $\mathbf{P} = \mathbf{Q}$ or $\mathbf{g} = \mathbf{h}$ (i.e. $PQ$ is unique if $P \ne Q$).

*Axiom 3:* If $\mathbf{Pa}$, $\mathbf{Pb}$ and $\mathbf{Pc}$ are all self-inverse, then there exists a $\mathbf{d}$ such that $\mathbf{abc} = \mathbf{d}$.

*Axiom 4:* If $\mathbf{ag}$, $\mathbf{bg}$ and $\mathbf{cg}$ are all self-inverse, then there exists a $\mathbf{d}$ such that $\mathbf{abc} = \mathbf{d}$.

(These two somewhat puzzling axioms are referred to in Example (12) on p. 291 of *Some Lessons in Mathematics*.)

*Axiom 5:* There exist $\mathbf{g}$, $\mathbf{h}$ and $\mathbf{j}$ such that $\mathbf{gh}$ is self-inverse but $\mathbf{gj}$, $\mathbf{hj}$ and $(\mathbf{gh})\mathbf{j}$ are not (i.e. there is at least one right-angled triangle in our geometry).

An important property of a group satisfying these axioms is that if $\mathbf{l}$ and $\mathbf{P}$ are elements corresponding to a line and a point respectively, then:

   (i) if $\mathbf{m}$ corresponds to a line, then so do $\mathbf{lml}$ and $\mathbf{PmP}$;

   (ii) if $\mathbf{Q}$ corresponds to a point, then so do $\mathbf{lQl}$ and $\mathbf{PQP}$.[2]

---

[1] Bachmann, F., *Aufbau der Geometrie aus dem Spielungsbegriff*, Springer, 1959.
[2] See example (7) on p. 290 of *Some Lessons in Mathematics*.

A. G. HOWSON

If we now define such terms as mid-point, angle bisector and mediator using relations such as are given on p. 169, then we can begin to explore the theorems of our geometry.

For example:

*Theorem:* Given that $P$ lies on $a$ and $b$ and that both $a$ and $b$ are perpendicular to $g$, it follows that $a = b$.

*Proof* (1) Suppose $P$ lies on $g$.

Then $P$ lies on $a$ and on $g$, and $a$ is perpendicular to $g$.

This implies that $\mathbf{P} = \mathbf{ag}$ (some details of proof are omitted here).

Similarly, $\mathbf{P} = \mathbf{bg}$.

Hence, $\mathbf{ag} = \mathbf{bg}$ which, since $\mathbf{a}$, $\mathbf{b}$ and $\mathbf{g}$ are group elements, implies $\mathbf{a} = \mathbf{b}$.

 (2) Suppose $P$ does not lie on $g$ $(\mathbf{P} \neq \mathbf{gPg})$.

 $P$ lies on $a$ and $b$ and so, by the definition of incidence and the property of the group quoted above, the point $gPg$ lies on the lines $gag$ and $gbg$. However, since $g$ is perpendicular to $a$ and $b$,

$$\mathbf{gag} = \mathbf{a} \quad \text{and} \quad \mathbf{gbg} = \mathbf{b}.$$

Hence, $gPg$ lies on $a$ and $b$.

Since the points $P$ and $gPg$ are not coincident, it then follows from Axiom 2 that $a = b$.

(In this proof we have assumed that $\mathbf{P} \neq \mathbf{g}$; the significance of this assumption will become clear later (see p. 176).)

But given this geometry, can we define a corresponding 'transformation geometry'? That is, if we associate lines and points with group elements, how can we describe reflections in lines and reflections in points? If one considers the properties of these transformations, then a suitable definition suggests itself. Both these transformations map points onto points and lines onto lines in a way that preserves such relations as incidence, 'bisects' and 'is perpendicular to'. We wish then to define mappings of the elements of our base group that will map generators onto generators and self-inverse elements onto self-inverse elements, and which will preserve certain group relations. Moreover, there must be a mapping corresponding to every point and line. Since the group structure is to be preserved, we are interested in isomorphisms which map the group onto itself, that is, in *automorphisms* of the group. One particular class of automorphisms is suggested by the special form of many of the relations on p. 169—the *inner automorphisms*. The inner automorphism associated with the element $\mathbf{x}$ of the group $\mathbf{G}$ is the mapping that maps the element $\mathbf{g} \in \mathbf{G}$ onto the element $\mathbf{x}^{-1}\mathbf{gx}$. We note that if $\mathbf{g}$ and $\mathbf{h}$ are any two elements of $\mathbf{G}$, then

(i) $$\mathbf{gh} \to \mathbf{x}^{-1}(\mathbf{gh})\,\mathbf{x}$$
$$= (\mathbf{x}^{-1}\mathbf{gx})\,(\mathbf{x}^{-1}\mathbf{hx}),$$

174

that is, multiplication is preserved,

(ii) $$\mathbf{x^{-1}gx = x^{-1}hx \Rightarrow g = h,}$$

that is, the mapping is one-one, and

(iii) given $\mathbf{k} \in \mathbf{G}$, then $(\mathbf{xkx^{-1}}) \to \mathbf{k}$, that is, the mapping is onto.

This shows that the mapping is an isomorphism.

In particular we note that $\mathbf{x} \in \mathbf{G}$ is mapped onto itself by the inner automorphism associated with $\mathbf{x}$.

We are, therefore, led to the following definitions of line- and point-reflections:

If $l$ is a line, then we define reflection in the line $l$ to be the inner automorphism associated with $\mathbf{l}$.

If $P$ is a point, then we define reflection in the point $P$ to be the inner automorphism associated with $\mathbf{P}$.

The combination of transformations is straightforward—a reflection in the line $l$ followed by a reflection in the point $P$ would be the inner automorphism defined by

$$\mathbf{g \to P^{-1}(l^{-1}gl)P \quad (= PlglP).}$$

It is a consequence of the property quoted on p. 173 that, for groups satisfying our axiom system, such a combination of transformations will always map a point onto a point and a line onto a line.

It is easily shown that, for any group $\mathbf{G}$, the inner automorphisms of $\mathbf{G}$ form a group. It can be proved that, given our axiom system, the group of inner automorphisms of $\mathbf{G}$ is isomorphic to $\mathbf{G}$ itself (this would not be true of the group of inner automorphisms associated with the Klein four-group). When proving this result one establishes the fact that, in a group satisfying our axioms, all self-inverse elements are points or lines (that is, we are not embarrassed by the existence of elements like $\mathbf{abc}$ in the group of order 8 discussed on p. 173). This follows from the result that every element of such a group can be expressed as the product of at most three generators.

What we cannot prove is that the product of three generators is never the identity element or, what is equivalent, that the set of all elements which can be expressed as the product of two generators form a *proper* subgroup (the group of *direct* isometries). It is possible to find groups that satisfy our axiom system and have generators $\mathbf{a}$, $\mathbf{b}$, $\mathbf{c}$ for which $\mathbf{abc = I}$. Geometrically we have a polar triangle (see fig. 2).

$$\mathbf{abc = I \Rightarrow ab = c}$$

$$\Rightarrow \mathbf{ab} \text{ is self-inverse}$$

$$\Rightarrow \mathbf{ab} \text{ defines a point.}$$

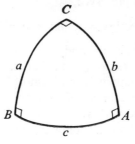

Fig. 2

That is, we can associate a line $c$ with a point $C$ (the intersection of the lines $a$ and $b$).

If we wish to restrict ourselves to Euclidean geometry, we must add a further axiom:

*Axiom 6:* There are no elements **a, b** and **c** for which **abc** = **I**.

This axiom was assumed when we proved the theorem on p. 174: it is, of course, obvious that this theorem does not hold in spherical geometry.

The object of this note is, as stated earlier, merely to outline a group approach to geometry and any reader wishing to study this approach in more detail is recommended to consult Bachmann (see p. 173).

# ANGLES, CIRCLES AND MORLEY'S THEOREM

### *by* R. C. LYNESS

1  There have been changes in school geometry and arithmetic recently which suggest that more accurate notation might be used in measuring angles. Rotations and reflections and modular arithmetic are investigated in a way that was not common twenty years ago.

In this article I am not concerned with geometry as an axiomatic system in the sense that the *whole* of it can be deduced from a set of primitive symbols and statements with rules by which new statements can be correctly made. I expect the acceptance of statements and rules which appear intuitively obvious, and the acceptance of a notation which can be used to prove more than conventional notation can prove without the consideration of special cases. To establish the generality of the 'new' notation it is of course necessary to consider different cases, but once established the new notation is a powerful economiser of thought.

An axiomatic feature of the new notation is that it can be used without looking at the geometrical configuration to which it applies. This is not entirely true of course, but school geometry is applied mathematics and having set up some words and symbols 'abstracted' from a physical situation we can follow a mathematical process without thinking of the physics and arrive at later statements which are physically interesting. This process is often in a derogatory way called 'mere' manipulation, but it is part of the essential nature of mathematics, and it is what most distinguishes mathematics from other disciplines.

I shall start by describing some ways of measuring angles and then show the use of the accompanying notation (for which no originality is claimed) in a proof of Morley's theorem about the trisectors of the angles of a triangle.[1]

2  All points in this and later sections are assumed to be in the same plane, on which a positive sense of rotation is specified.

[1] Morley, F. and Morley, F. V., *Inversive Geometry*. London, 1933.

177

## 2.1 *Signed angles*

The size of the signed angle *PQR*, written $\angle PQR$, is the amount of rotation (positive or negative) required to rotate the ray *QP* on to the ray *QR*. Equality of signed angles is equality modulo 360°. The principal value of $\angle PQR$, written pr.$\angle PQR$, is its value in the interval $(-180°, +180°]$. $\angle PQR = -\angle RQP$.

In fig. 1, $\angle BCA = 40°$, $400°$, $-320°$, ... and $\angle ACL = -20°$, $340°$, ....
If *M* is a point such that

$$2 \angle BCM = \angle BCA$$

then $\angle BCM = 20°$ (mod 180°) and *M* is on the line passing through *C* and *L*, possibly on *LC* produced.

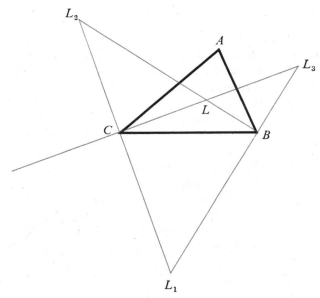

Fig. 1

## 2.2 *Crosses*

The size of the cross *PQR*, written $\measuredangle PQR$, is the amount of rotation (positive or negative) required to rotate the whole line through *Q* and *P* on to the whole line through *Q* and *R*. Equality of crosses is equality modulo 180°. The principal value of $\measuredangle PQR$, written pr.$\measuredangle PQR$, is its value in the interval $[0°, 180°)$. $\measuredangle PQR = -\measuredangle RQP$.

In fig. 1, $\measuredangle BCL = 20°$, $200°$, $-160°$, ... and

$$\measuredangle BLC = \measuredangle BLL_3 = \measuredangle BL_1C.$$

178

If $M$ is a point such that $2 \, \measuredangle BCM = \measuredangle BCA$

then $M$ is on either the internal or the external bisector of angle $ACB$.

Crosses are unnecessary if one uses signed angles and equality (mod 180°) but it is easier to write $\angle$ and $\measuredangle$ than to write (mod 360°) and (mod 180°) after every equality or to write

$$\angle PQR + 360n° \quad \text{or} \quad \measuredangle PQR + 180n°,$$

though it may sometimes be profitable to think in these terms.

## 2.3  Unsigned angles

The size of an unsigned angle $PQR$, written $P\hat{Q}R$, is that one of the principal values of $\angle PQR$ and $\angle RQP$ which is positive or zero.

2.4  The notation of signed angles and crosses is used also with rays and lines thus: $\angle(OP, OQ) = \angle POQ$ and $\measuredangle(l_1, l_2)$ is the rotation required to make $l_1$ parallel to $l_2$.

2.5  Several well-known facts have an unusual appearance in the notation of signed angles and crosses:

*Angles at a point:* If $A$, $B$, $C$, $D$ and $O$ are distinct points on a plane, then $\angle AOB + \angle BOC + \angle COD = \angle AOD$. The same is true with crosses.

*Angles of a triangle:* If $A$, $B$ and $C$ are non-collinear points, then pr. $\angle ABC$, pr. $\angle BCA$ and pr. $\angle CAB$ have the same sign and their sum is $+180°$ or $-180°$.

*Angles of a polygon:* If $A$, $B$, $C$, ..., $M$, $N$ are $p$ distinct points on a plane, then

$$\angle ABC + \angle BCD + \angle CDE + ... + \angle MNA + \angle NAB = 0° \quad \text{if } p \text{ is even,}$$

and $\qquad\qquad\qquad\qquad\qquad\qquad\qquad\qquad\quad = 180° \quad \text{if } p \text{ is odd.}$

With crosses $0° = 180°$.

*Cyclic quadrilateral:* The use of crosses enables us to say that if $A$, $B$, $C$ and $D$ are distinct points on a circle, then $\measuredangle ABC = \measuredangle ADC$. This brings together the properties of angles in the same segment and of opposite angles of a cyclic quadrilateral, and the order of the points round the circumference does not matter.

Crosses are useful when the order of points on a line is unknown.

3.1  Let us apply some of this notation to the well-known configuration of a triangle and its internal and external angle-bisectors (fig. 1). We shall investigate the sizes of angle $CMB$ where $M$ is one of the four points of intersection of the bisectors of angle $ABC$ and the bisectors of angle $BCA$. First we note that $\angle MBC = \frac{1}{2}\angle ABC \Leftrightarrow M$ is on the internal bisector of angle $ABC$, and $\angle MBC = \frac{1}{2}\angle ABC + 90° \Leftrightarrow M$ is on the external bisector of angle $ABC$.

Now
$$\angle CLB + \angle LBC + \angle BCL = 0°$$

and
$$\angle LBC = \tfrac{1}{2}\angle ABC, \quad \angle BCL = \angle\tfrac{1}{2}BCA;$$

hence
$$\angle CLB = -\tfrac{1}{2}(\angle ABC + \angle BCA)$$
$$= -\tfrac{1}{2}(180° - \angle CAB)$$
$$= \tfrac{1}{2}\angle CAB + 90°.$$

If we substitute $L_1$ for $L$, then
$$\angle L_1 BC = \tfrac{1}{2}\angle ABC + 90° \quad \text{and} \quad \angle BCL_1 = \tfrac{1}{2}\angle BCA + 90°$$

and we have
$$\angle CL_1 B = \tfrac{1}{2}\angle CAB + 90°.$$

Both $L$ and $L_1$ are on the circle $\{X: \angle CXB = \tfrac{1}{2}\angle CAB + 90°\}$. By substituting $L_2$ and $L_3$ for $L$ it follows similarly that $L_2$ and $L_3$ are on the circle $\{Y: \angle CYB = \tfrac{1}{2}\angle CAB\}$.

**3.2**  If we assume that $L$ and $L_1$ lie on the internal bisector of angle $CAB$ and that $L_2$ and $L_3$ lie on its external bisector (these facts cannot be proved by angle properties alone), and if we assume that a circle can cut a straight line in at most two points, we have the following

*Lemma:* If $\angle CMB = \tfrac{1}{2}\angle CAB$ and $M$ lies on the external bisector of angle $CAB$, or if $\angle CMB = \tfrac{1}{2}\angle CAB + 90°$ and $M$ lies on the internal bisector of angle $CAB$, then $M$ is an in-centre or ex-centre of triangle $ABC$.

## 4   TRISECTORS

If $3\angle PQM = \angle PQR$, three times the rotation from $QP$ to $QM$ will rotate $QP$ to $QR$, and if we know that
$$\angle PQR = 42°, 402°, -318°, \ldots$$

then
$$\angle PQM = 14°, 134°, -106°, \ldots$$

and $M$ is on one of three rays inclined to each other at $120°$. A signed angle, then, has three trisectors. But we have been accustomed to saying that the unsigned angle $P\hat{Q}R$ has *two* trisectors. When $P\hat{Q}R = 42°$ we have called these trisectors $QM$ and $QN$ where $P\hat{Q}M = M\hat{Q}N = N\hat{Q}R = 14°$. We recognise $QN$ as a trisector of $\angle RQP$ but *we will no longer admit $QN$ as a trisector of $\angle PQR$*.

We must however distinguish between the three trisectors of $\angle PQR$ and we do not want them as half-lines, but as whole lines.

180

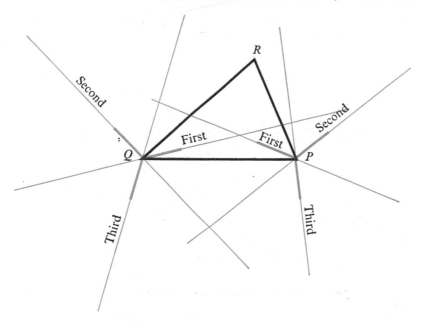

Fig. 2. The trisectors of $\angle PQR$ and $\angle QPR$

## Definitions

The first trisector of the signed angle $\angle PQR$ is the line $\{M_1\}$ such that $\measuredangle PQM_1 = \frac{1}{3}\text{pr.}\angle PQR$. The second trisector is the line $\{M_2\}$ such that $\measuredangle PQM_2 = \frac{1}{3}\text{pr.}\angle PQR \pm 120°$ and the third trisector is the line $\{M_3\}$ such that $\measuredangle PQM_3 = \frac{1}{3}\text{pr.}\angle PQR \pm 240°$ where the plus or minus sign is taken according as $\text{pr.}\angle PQR$ is positive or negative. (To obtain the ray-trisectors substitute $\angle$ for $\measuredangle$ in these definitions.)

Visually, we get the second trisector of $\angle PQR$ by rotating $QP$ about $Q$ through $\frac{1}{3}\text{pr.}\angle PQR$ and continuing the rotation in the same sense through a further 120°; a further continuation of 120° gives the third trisector.

We are now in a position to state Morley's theorem.

## 5  MORLEY'S THEOREM[1]

If in any triangle $ABC$ the first trisector of $\angle BCA$ meets the first trisector of $\angle CBA$ at $L'$, the first trisector of $\angle CAB$ meets the first trisector of $\angle ACB$ at $M'$, and the first trisector of $\angle ABC$ meets the first trisector of $\angle BAC$ at $N'$, then triangle $L'M'N'$ is equilateral.

And this is true if either the word 'second' or the word 'third' is substituted throughout for the word 'first'.

[1] Dobbs, W. J., Morley's Triangle: *Math. Gazette*, February 1938.

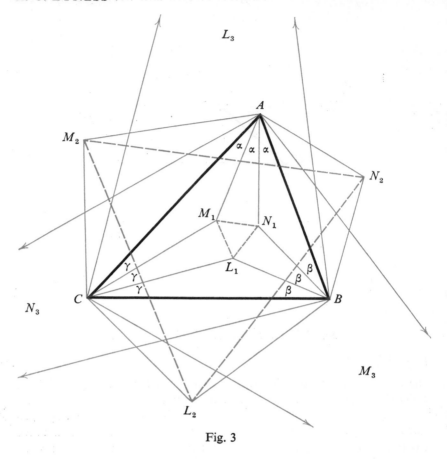

Fig. 3

## 6   PROOF OF MORLEY'S THEOREM

The method of the proof is to start with an equilateral triangle $LMN$ and construct a triangle which proves

   (i)  to be equiangular to the given triangle $ABC$, and

   (ii) to have $L$, $M$, $N$ as the intersections of appropriate pairs of its angle trisectors.

   The theorem with first trisectors is relatively easy to prove with unsigned angles. Starting with triangle $LMN$ in fig. 4 the positions of $P, Q$ and $R$ are fixed by the angles of the given triangle $ABC$ and thus points $A_1$, $B_1$ and $C_1$ are determined. We now show that $C_1 \hat{L} B_1 = 90° + \frac{1}{2} C_1 \hat{P} B_1$ with $L$ on the internal bisector of $C_1 \hat{P} B_1$ and we deduce that $L$, $M$, $N$ are the in-centres of triangles $PB_1 C_1$, $QC_1 A_1$, $RA_1 B_1$ respectively and thus that Morley's theorem holds for triangle $A_1 B_1 C_1$.

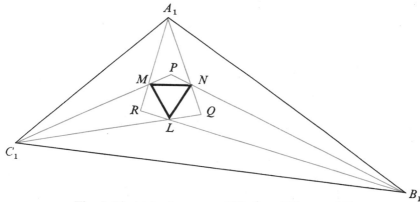

Fig. 4. First trisectors: $\alpha_1 = 35°$; $\beta_1 = 10°$; $\gamma_1 = 15°$

In this proof one assumes from the figure that $L$ is inside triangle $PB_1C_1$. Such assumptions are unnecessary when one uses signed angles and crosses and this notation also makes the generalisation of the theorem to second and third trisectors (where some in-centres may become ex-centres) a relatively simple matter. Indeed it is not even easy to *state* Morley's general theorem without using signed angles. And so it is a good theorem to show off the notation.

**6.1**   Define the positive sense of rotation so that $\text{pr}.\angle ABC$ is positive and define $\alpha_1$, $\beta_1$, $\gamma_1$ by

$$\alpha_1 = \tfrac{1}{3}\text{pr}.\angle CAB, \quad \beta_1 = \tfrac{1}{3}\text{pr}.\angle ABC, \quad \gamma_1 = \tfrac{1}{3}\text{pr}.\angle BCA.$$

Then
$$\alpha_1 + \beta_1 + \gamma_1 = 60°.$$

**6.2**   Take an equilateral triangle $LMN$ where $\angle LMN = +60°$ and on $MN$, $NL$, $LM$ as bases construct isosceles triangles with vertical angles $\angle MPN = 60° + 2\alpha_1$, $\angle NQL = 60° + 2\beta_1$, and $\angle LRM = 60° + 2\gamma_1$. Let the whole lines $RM$ and $QN$ meet at $A_1$, $PN$ and $RL$ at $B_1$, $QL$ and $PM$ at $C_1$.

$$\angle PNM + \angle NMP + \angle MPN = 180°$$
$$\Rightarrow \angle PNM + \angle NMP = 180° - (60° + 2\alpha_1) = 120° - 2\alpha_1.$$

Since triangle $MPN$ is isosceles
$$\measuredangle PNM = \measuredangle NMP = 60° - \alpha_1,$$

and since $B_1$, $P$, $N$ are collinear and $C_1$, $P$, $M$ are collinear
$$\measuredangle B_1NM = \measuredangle NMC_1 = 60° - \alpha_1.$$
$$\measuredangle B_1NL = \measuredangle B_1NM + \measuredangle MNL$$
$$= 120° - \alpha_1$$

7                                                     183

and $$\measuredangle LMC_1 = \measuredangle LMN + \measuredangle NMC_1$$
$$= 120° - \alpha_1.$$

Similarly, by applying the permutation $T = (ABC)(PQR)(LMN)(\alpha_1\beta_1\gamma_1)$ to the preceding argument, $\measuredangle C_1LM = 120° - \beta_1$, and, by applying the permutation $T^2 = T^{-1}$, $\measuredangle NLB_1 = 120° - \gamma_1$.

$$\measuredangle C_1LB_1 = \measuredangle C_1LM + \measuredangle MLN + \measuredangle NLB_1$$
$$= 120° - \beta_1 - 60° + 120° - \gamma_1$$
$$= -(\beta_1 + \gamma_1)$$
$$= \alpha_1 - 60°.$$

Since triangles $MPN$ amd $MLN$ are isosceles, $L$ lies on the internal bisector of angle $MPN$. Hence $L$ lies either (i) on the internal or (ii) on the external bisector of angle $C_1PB_1$.

If (i) $$\angle C_1PB_1 = \angle MPN = 60° + 2\alpha_1$$
and $$\measuredangle C_1LB_1 = 90° + \tfrac{1}{2}\angle C_1PB_1.$$

If (ii) $$\angle C_1PB_1 = 180° + \angle MPN = -120° + 2\alpha_1$$
and $$\measuredangle C_1LB_1 = \tfrac{1}{2}\angle C_1PB_1$$

so that, by the lemma, $L$ is an in-centre or ex-centre of triangle $C_1PB_1$, and

$$\measuredangle B_1C_1L = \measuredangle LC_1P; \quad \measuredangle C_1B_1L = \measuredangle LB_1P.$$

Similarly $M$ is an in-centre or ex-centre of triangle $A_1QC_1$ and

$$\measuredangle QC_1M = \measuredangle MC_1A_1.$$

Hence $$\measuredangle B_1C_1L = \measuredangle LC_1M = \measuredangle MC_1A_1.$$

Now $$\measuredangle MC_1L + \measuredangle C_1LM + \measuredangle LMC_1 = 0°$$
$$\Rightarrow \measuredangle LC_1M = 240° - (\alpha_1 + \beta_1)$$
$$= \gamma_1;$$

therefore $$\measuredangle B_1C_1A_1 = \measuredangle B_1C_1L + \measuredangle LC_1M + \measuredangle MC_1A_1$$
$$= 3\gamma_1.$$

Similarly $$\measuredangle C_1A_1B_1 = 3\alpha_1 \quad \text{and} \quad \measuredangle A_1B_1C_1 = 3\beta_1.$$

It follows that $\angle B_1C_1A_1 = 3\gamma_1 + 180n°$, $\angle C_1A_1B_1 = 3\alpha_1 + 180l°$ and $\angle A_1B_1C_1 = 3\beta_1 + 180m°$ where $l$, $m$, $n$ are integers.

Since, modulo $360°$, $\angle B_1C_1A_1 + \angle C_1A_1B_1 + \angle A_1B_1C_1 = 180°$ and $3\alpha_1 + 3\beta_1 + 3\gamma_1 = 180°$, either all the integers $l$, $m$, $n$ are even or only one, say $n$, is even. In the latter case we have a contradiction for pr.$\angle C_1A_1B_1$ and pr.$\angle A_1B_1C_1$ are negative and pr.$\angle B_1C_1A_1$ is positive. Hence $\angle C_1A_1B_1 = \angle CAB$, $\angle A_1B_1C_1 = \angle ABC$, and the triangles $A_1B_1C_1$ and $ABC$ are directly equiangular.

**6.3**   Now $\not\prec B_1 C_1 L = \gamma_1 = \frac{1}{3}\text{pr}.\angle BCA = \frac{1}{3}\text{pr}.\angle B_1 C_1 A'$ and so $C_1 L$ is a first trisector of $\angle B_1 C_1 A_1$. Applying $T^{-1}$ to $\not\prec MC_1 A_1 = \gamma_1$ we have $\not\prec LB_1 C_1 = \beta_1$ and so $\not\prec C_1 B_1 L = -\beta_1 = \frac{1}{3}\text{pr}.\angle CBA = \frac{1}{3}\text{pr}.\angle C_1 B_1 A_1$ and $B_1 L$ is a first trisector of $\angle C_1 B_1 A_1$. Similarly the other trisectors are first trisectors, and thus Morley's theorem with first trisectors is true for triangle $A_1 B_1 C_1$.

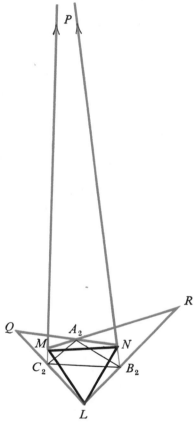

Fig. 5. Second trisectors: $\alpha_2 = 35° + 120°$; $\beta_2 = 10° + 120°$; $\gamma_2 = 15° + 120°$.

**6.4**   The proof for second trisectors comes by writing

$$\alpha_2 = \alpha_1 + 120°, \quad \beta_2 = \beta_1 + 120° \quad \text{and} \quad \gamma_2 = \gamma_1 + 120°,$$

and substituting suffix 2 for suffix 1 throughout section 6.2. In section 6.3 we have

$$\not\prec B_2 C_2 L = \gamma_2 = \frac{1}{3}\text{pr}.\angle BCA + 120°$$
$$= \frac{1}{3}\text{pr}.\angle B_2 C_2' A_2 + 120°$$

and so $C_2 L$ is a second trisector of angle $B_2 C_2 A_2$.

185

R. C. LYNESS

As in 6.3  $\measuredangle C_2 B_2 L = -\beta_2.$

So  $\measuredangle C_2 B_2 L = -\beta_1 - 120° = \frac{1}{3} \mathrm{pr}. C_2 B_2 A_2 - 120°$

and $B_2 L$ is a second trisector of $\angle C_2 B_2 A_2$. Similarly the other trisectors are second trisectors and Morley's theorem with second trisectors is true for triangle $A_2 B_2 C_2$.

6.5  Similarly, writing $\alpha_3 = \alpha_1 + 240°$, etc., Morley's theorem with third trisectors is true for triangle $A_3 B_3 C_3$.

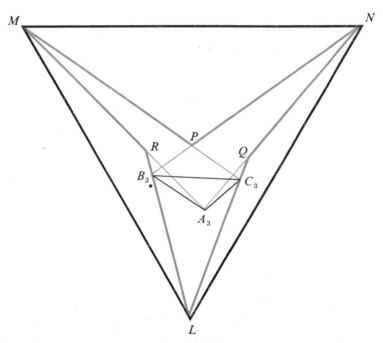

Fig. 6. Third trisectors: $\alpha_3 = 35° + 240°$; $\beta_3 = 10° + 240°$; $\gamma_3 = 15° + 240°$

6.6  What we have shown is that Morley's theorem for first, second and third trisectors is true for triangles $A_1 B_1 C_1$, $A_2 B_2 C_2$ and $A_3 B_3 C_3$ respectively, and that these triangles are all equiangular to the arbitrary given triangle $ABC$. Now if the theorem is true for a particular triangle it must be true for every triangle equiangular to it. Hence Morley's theorem is true for any arbitrary triangle $ABC$.

7  The reader will have seen that assumptions (e.g. about concurrencies of the angle bisectors of a triangle and about the symmetry of isosceles

triangles) have been made. But my object was not to avoid making assumptions but to show the value of the $\angle$, $\measuredangle$ notation. It is no use introducing notation if it does not help one to think more automatically; after a little practice I hope the reader will find that the notation advocated here is valuable. The whole of 6.2 can be written out without reference to the three figures which show the three types of trisector.

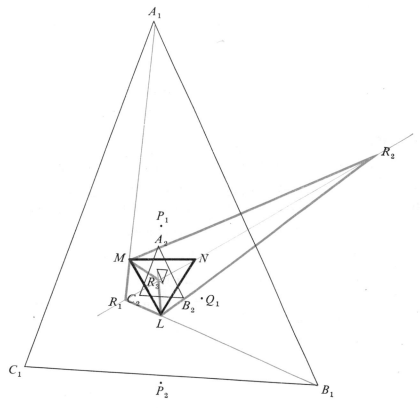

Fig. 7. Combined figure: $\alpha_1 = 15°$; $\beta_1 = 20°$; $\gamma_1 = 25°$

**8**   My object of persuading others of the value of the $\angle$, $\measuredangle$ notation may perhaps be defeated by choosing Morley's theorem to exemplify it for this is not one of the simpler theorems to prove.

**8.1**   Signed angles are of course necessary in trigonometry and algebraic geometry, where the 'general angle' and gradients are considered. If $OX$ is the positive $x$-axis the gradient of the line $OP$ is tan $\measuredangle XOP$.

**8.2**  If $\tan \sphericalangle BPA = k$, then

$$k = \tan \sphericalangle (BP, AP)$$
$$= \tan[\sphericalangle(BP, OX) + \sphericalangle(OX, AP)]$$
$$= \tan[\sphericalangle(OX, AP) - \sphericalangle(OX, BP)].$$

If $A$ and $B$ are the fixed points $(c, O)$ and $(-c, O)$, $c \neq O$, and $P$ the variable point $(x, y)$, where $x^2 \neq c^2$,

$$\tan \sphericalangle BPA = k$$

$$\Leftrightarrow \frac{y}{x-c} - \frac{y}{x+c} = k\left(1 + \frac{y^2}{x^2 - c^2}\right)$$

$$\Leftrightarrow k(x^2 + y^2 - c^2) - 2cy = 0$$

$$\Leftrightarrow P \text{ lies on a circle through } A \text{ and } B.$$

**8.3**  If $\cos \angle BPA = h$, $h \neq 1$, then

$$(x-c)^2 + y^2 + (x+c)^2 + y^2 - 4c^2 = 2h\sqrt{\{(x-c)^2 + y^2\}} \cdot \sqrt{\{(x+c)^2 + y^2\}},$$

where $\sqrt{\phantom{x}}$ means the positive square root. Hence $P$ lies on an arc of one of two circles. We can rationalise this equation of two circular arcs by squaring,

$$4(x^2 + y^2 - c^2)^2 = 4h^2[(x^2 + y^2 + c^2)^2 - 4c^2x^2]$$

$$\Rightarrow \qquad (x^2 + y^2 - c^2)^2 = h^2[(x^2 + y^2 - c^2)^2 + 4c^2y^2]$$

$$\Rightarrow \sqrt{(1 - h^2)}\,(x^2 + y^2 - c^2) = \pm 2hcy$$

which is the whole of two circles, coincident when $h = 0$. But the squaring has introduced $\cos \angle BPA = -h$.

# A MATHEMATICAL ACTIVITY

## INTRODUCTION

If students of mathematics are not to be mere spectators of someone else's game then the writing that is allowable must include the unfinished, the non-formal, the exploratory, the mistaken, the debatable and the idiosyncratic as well as the so-called formally enunciated, rigorously defended piece.

'There seems to be no settled language in the literature by which to describe $T_n$, and it is difficult, if not impossible, to invent one which serves as a calculus. We have therefore not hesitated, in the present state of the art, to use pictorial methods of description rather than to obscure meaning for the sake of complete rigour.'[1]

There is no sense in which Griffiths is not attempting to discuss a rigorous piece of mathematics but a decision on 'common language' had to be made. An investigation may start at quite a different level. David Morris and Sillitto corresponded on transformations and Menelaus. Some notes were written and Morris said 'after struggling for some weeks, I couldn't get the development I'd hoped for'.

The editor discussed the problem and someone agreed to look at the work, largely because it was felt that the statement of the unfinished and the atmosphere of development were important.

It is impossible yet to reproduce the discussions and arguments that surround attempts to sort out, clear up and draw conclusions, and the product is duller and less rich than the sum of all the acts that have led to its production. But is this not the case with every 'piece of mathematics'?

As an example, in the piece that follows you will note that there are four assumptions listed on the first page. In Morris's notes there were only three but on the second page was a parenthetic '(Note that if $L(B) = C$, then $L \in BC$)'. This is a demonstration of flexible axiomatics. When a discovery is made that another assumption is required then make it...we can perhaps change it later.

'Now to make any progress at all, we *need* to associate the 7 with the $7_1$—we *need* the associativity of addition in $Z$. Let's have it then!'[2]

[1] Griffiths, H. B., 'Automorphisms of a 3-dimensional handlebody'. *Abh. Math. Sem. Univ. Hamburg* (26) 1964, pp. 191–210.
[2] Sillitto, A. G., 'A teaching approach to the definition of a group'. *Mathematics Teaching*, **33** (1965).

# ENLARGEMENTS—AN INVESTIGATION, CONTINUATION AND INVITATION

MORRIS, Brookes...

There are different levels at which an investigation can be started. One may be affected by special problems of simple enlargement or contraction on a plane surface; one may attempt to consider abstractly transformation of the plane where properties correspond to what we would expect enlargements to have; one may combine these two in an attempt to look at an interesting situation from different points of view. The importance of a group structure for a set of transformations may affect the investigation. This implies that *closure*, being an important limiting feature of a mathematical investigation, is arranged. The issue of unique inverses and identities in the solution of more complex problems will be very much in mind.

So we start, with hope, but not necessarily with a clear idea as to where we shall finish.

## A NOTATION

$\mathbf{L} = (L, \lambda)$ denotes an enlargement, centre on point $L$ and with a scale factor $\lambda$, where $\lambda$ is rational.

$\mathbf{M.L}$ is the composition of the two enlargements $(L, \lambda)$ followed by $(M, \mu)$.

$AB$ is a line segment.

$\overline{AB}$ is the length of line segment $AB$.

$\langle AB \rangle$ is the line through $A$, $B$.

$\mathbf{L}(A) = B$ means that point $A$ is transformed by $\mathbf{L}$ to point $B$.

Similarly we can have
$$\mathbf{L}(\langle AB \rangle) = \langle CD \rangle,$$
$$\mathbf{L}(AB) = CD.$$

## Some assumptions

(i) If $\mathbf{L}(A) = A$, either $A = L$ or $\lambda = 1$.

(ii) If $\mathbf{L}(AB) = AB$, where $A \neq B$, then $\lambda = 1$.

(iii) $\mathbf{L}(A) = B$, iff $L \in \langle AB \rangle$.

(iv) $\mathbf{M.L}$ is an enlargement $(N, \nu)$ where $N \in \langle ML \rangle$ and $\nu = \lambda\mu$, provided $\lambda\mu \neq 1$.

## *An example*

Consider a line segment $AB$ transformed by **L** and then by **M**.

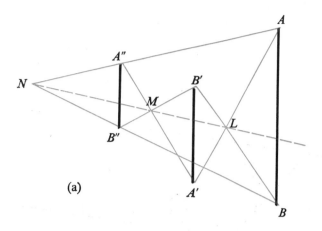

(a)

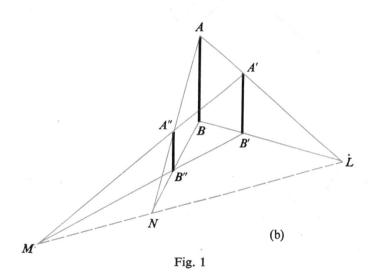

(b)

Fig. 1

$$A''B''||A'B', \quad A'B'||AB, \quad \overline{A''B''} = \lambda\mu\overline{AB}.$$

From assumption (iv) $\qquad$ **M.L = X,**

where $\qquad\qquad\qquad$ $\mathbf{X} = (X, \lambda\mu)$

and $\qquad\qquad\qquad$ $X \in \langle ML \rangle.$

Hence $\qquad\qquad\qquad \mathbf{X}(A) = A''$

and $\qquad\qquad\qquad\quad \mathbf{X}(B) = B'',$

and by assumption (iii) $\qquad X \in \langle AA'' \rangle$

$$X \in \langle BB'' \rangle$$

If $N$ is the intersection of $\langle AA'' \rangle$ and $\langle BB'' \rangle$ then $X = N$ and $L, M, N$ are collinear.

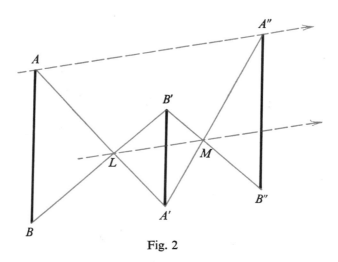

Fig. 2

If $\lambda\mu = 1$, with $A''B''$ and $AB$ distinct, then

$$\overline{A''B''} = \overline{AB} \quad \text{and} \quad \langle AA'' \rangle // \langle LM \rangle.$$

If we are to keep the group idea of the set of enlargements we must regard this translation as an enlargement, $\nu = 1$, with centre at infinity in the direction of the translation. In this group treatment $\lambda = 0$ is barred as having no inverse.

If $\lambda\mu = 1$ and $A''B''$ are *not* distinct, then $L = M$ and $\mathbf{M.L} = \mathbf{I}$, the identity enlargement.

There are already many things to investigate in this set of transformations. For example, with different $\lambda$, $\mu$: $-ve$, $+ve$, $>1$, $<1$, and different $L, M$ what range of things can be said about the composition enlargement $\mathbf{N} = (N, \lambda\mu)$? What happens if the $\mathbf{M}, \mathbf{L}$ are followed by a third enlargement $\mathbf{N.(M.L)}$?

Are the enlargements associative?

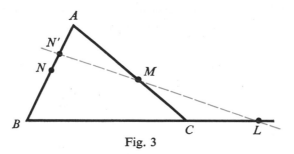

**Fig. 3**

*The Menelaus configuration* may be considered as a special case of the following general situation.

With a given triangle $ABC$ choose points $L, M, N$ such that $\mathbf{L}(B) = C$, $\mathbf{M}(C) = A$, $\mathbf{N}(A) = B$. By assumption (iii) this means that the points $L, M, N$ are contained in $\langle BC \rangle$, $\langle CA \rangle$, $\langle AB \rangle$, respectively. If the associated scale factors are $\lambda$, $\mu$, $\nu$ respectively interest lies in what can be said when $\lambda\mu\nu = 1$. (Note that $\lambda, \mu, \nu$ are the negative inverses of the ratios as they normally appear in a non-vector treatment of Menelaus theorem in school texts.)

We can consider different cases:

## CASE I

$L, M, N$ *not* collinear and $\lambda\mu\nu \neq 1$. From $\mathbf{L}(B) = C$; $\mathbf{M}(C) = A$; $\mathbf{N}(A) = B$, we have $\mathbf{N}.\mathbf{M}.\mathbf{L}(B) = B$ (associativity assumed).

By assumption (i) $B$ is the centre of enlargement $\mathbf{N}.\mathbf{M}.\mathbf{L}$ or $\lambda\mu\nu = 1$. But as $\lambda\mu\nu \neq 1$ then $B$ is the centre of enlargement.

As will be seen in Cases II, III a more detailed analysis into pairs of enlargements helps to show the difficulties that arise when $\lambda\mu\nu = 1$.

For case I: $\qquad \mathbf{M}.\mathbf{L}(B) = A \quad$ and as $\quad \mathbf{M}.\mathbf{L} = \mathbf{N}'$

by assumptions (iii) and (iv)

$$N' = \langle LM \rangle \cap \langle AB \rangle.$$

As $N \neq N'$, $\mathbf{N}.\mathbf{N}'$ has a centre of enlargement on $\langle NN' \rangle$, that is, on $\langle AB \rangle$. But $\mathbf{N}.\mathbf{N}'(B) = \mathbf{N}.\mathbf{M}.\mathbf{L}(B) = B$ and as before this implies $B$ to be the centre of enlargement.

## Illustrations

(a) $\lambda = \mu = \nu = -1$, $\lambda\mu\nu = -1$ (fig. 4).

(b) $\lambda = \frac{1}{3}$, $\mu = -3$, $\nu = -\frac{9}{11}$, $\lambda\mu\nu = \frac{9}{11} \simeq 1$ (fig. 5).

(c) $\lambda = -\frac{2}{3}$, $\mu = -\frac{2}{3}$, $\nu = 2$, $\lambda\mu\nu = \frac{8}{9}$ (fig. 6).

193

In fig. 4, $\lambda\mu = 1$ and **M.L** is a translation; $\lambda\mu\nu = -1$ and **N.M.L** is a half-turn about $B$, that is, the enlargement $(B, -1)$.

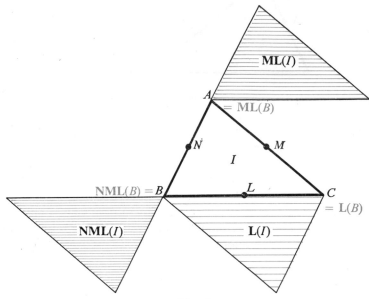

Fig. 4

In fig. 5, $\lambda\mu = -1$ and **M.L** is a half-turn about $N'$, the mid-point of $AB$; $N' = \langle LM \rangle \cap \langle AB \rangle$.

$\lambda\mu\nu = +\frac{9}{11}$ and **N.M.L** is the enlargement $(B, \frac{9}{11})$.

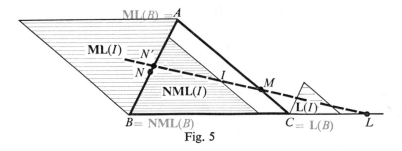

Fig. 5

In fig. 6, **N.M.L** is the enlargement $(B, \frac{8}{9})$.

In Case I where $\lambda\mu\nu \neq 1$ and $L(B) = C$, $M(C) = A$, $N(A) = B$, the centre of enlargement for **N.M.L** is $B$. Similarly the centre of enlargement for **M.L.N** is $A$ and for **L.N.M** is $C$. What are the centres for the other three orders of operation?

194

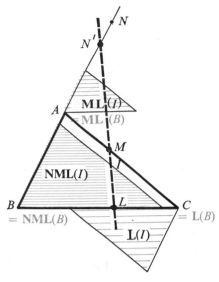

Fig. 6

## CASE II

$L, M, N$ defined in the same way with $\lambda\mu\nu = 1$.

$\mathbf{N.M.L} = \mathbf{I}$ and hence $\mathbf{N.M.L}(A, B, C) = A, B, C$.

$\mathbf{M.L} = \mathbf{N'}$, hence $\mathbf{N.N'} = \mathbf{I}$ and $N = N'$, that is, $L, M, N$ are collinear.

Though in this case $\mathbf{N.M.L}(B) = B$ as in case I, and $\lambda\mu\nu = 1$, $B$ is not necessarily the centre of enlargement. In fact the centre of enlargement of $\mathbf{M.L}$ is at $N'$ but $N = N'$ and so the centre of enlargement of $\mathbf{N.N'}(= \mathbf{N.M.L})$ is at $N'$. Similarly $\mathbf{M.L.N}$ is at $M$, $\mathbf{L.N.M}$ is at $L$.

$$\mathbf{L} = (L, -\tfrac{1}{2}), \quad \mathbf{M} = (M, \tfrac{3}{2}), \quad \mathbf{N} = (N, -\tfrac{4}{3}), \quad \lambda\mu\nu = 1.$$

We see that for $\lambda\mu\nu \neq 1$ the centre is defined but for $\lambda\mu\nu = 1$ the centre of the identity enlargement is not strictly defined. What is the 'direction' of the null (identity) translation?

## CASE III

Given $L, M, N$ as before but $L, M, N$ collinear.

In this case $N' = N$ and $\mathbf{N.M.L}(B) = B$.

But $\mathbf{N.M.L}(N) = \mathbf{N.N'}(N) = N$.

Again when this condition holds $B$ is the centre or $\lambda\mu\nu = 1$, but this applies to the second conclusion. Hence either we have a trivial reduction to a single point or $\lambda\mu\nu = 1$.

195

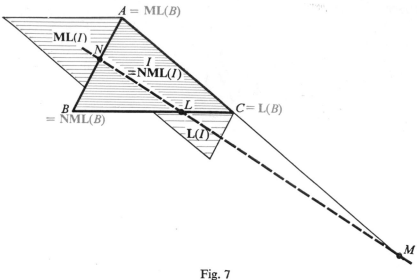

Fig. 7

## SOME APPLICATIONS

There is a relation between 'transformation geometry' and 'descriptive geometry'. Problems in the latter are often concerned at one level with the problem of drawing diagrams. This develops into the more abstract problems of the existence of solutions of drawing with given information and eventually to the development of theoretical structures. Classical projective geometry is an example of this.

The development of algebras of transformations allows a more immediate control of construction theory. In the following work the construction of centres of enlargement in a number of situations is investigated. Again we start with some situations and hope.

## THREE UNEQUAL CIRCLES

Given three circles $\Gamma_1, \Gamma_2, \Gamma_3$, with centres $C_1, C_2, C_3$ and radii $a_1, a_2, a_3$. $S_{12}$ is the external centre of enlargement for $\Gamma_1$ and $\Gamma_2$, and $\mathbf{S}_{12} = (S_{12}, a_2/a_1)$. Note that $\mathbf{S}_{21} = (S_{21}, a_1/a_2)$.

The points $S_{12}$ and $S_{21}$ are identical to the point which is one of the centres of similitude of $\Gamma_1$ and $\Gamma_2$.

As $\mathbf{S}_{23} . \mathbf{S}_{12} = \mathbf{S}_{13}$ then $S_{13} \in \langle S_{12} S_{23} \rangle$. These three centres of enlargement are collinear. Similarly we may show that $S_{13}$ is collinear with $S'_{12}$ and $S'_{23}$, where the primes indicate internal centres of enlargement, that is $\mathbf{S}'_{12} = (S'_{12}, -a_1/a_2)$. The ratios are negative.

196

Hence the six centres of similitude lie by threes on four straight lines. Note that each centre has two names. The diagonal point triangle of the complete quadrilateral so formed is the triangle $C_1 C_2 C_3$. Note that multiplicity of names need not worry us. For example, this triangle has six names based on the letters $C_1, C_2, C_3$.

If $a_1 = a_2$, $S_{23} S_{13}$ and $S'_{23} S'_{13}$ are parallel to $C_1 C_2$.

If $a_1 = a_2 = a_3$ a mid-point theorem can be enunciated...

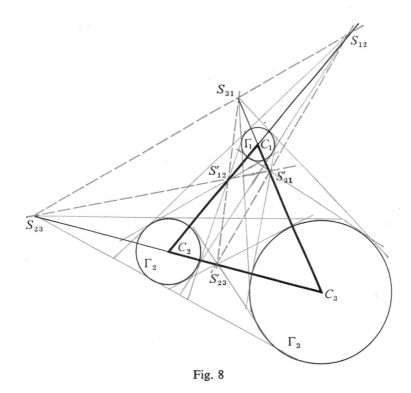

Fig. 8

## THREE UNEQUAL SQUARES WITH THE SAME ORIENTATION

The construction of rectilinear figures raises questions of symmetry.

As for the three circles the six centres of enlargement lie by threes on four straight lines. They can be seen as the centres of similitude of associated circles, for instance, the three inscribed or the three circumscribed circles.

The three squares have twelve sides between them and one may ask whether in the construction of the six centres, each of the twelve may be

197

used. A single pair of corresponding parallel sides determines the corresponding centre of enlargement. Is it possible then to choose the six necessary pairs so that each of the twelve sides is used once and once only? As two opposite enlargements make a direct one it is not possible. Why?

Another question may well ask for the minimum number of the twelve sides that need be used to construct the centres.

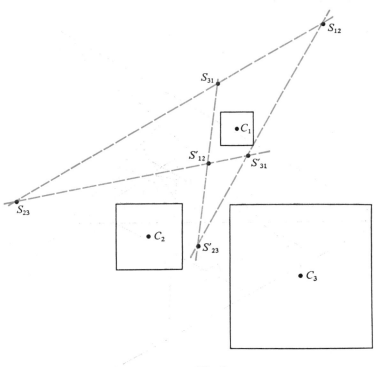

Fig. 9

Other sets of regular figures will have this same relationship, provided corresponding sides are parallel, that is, similarly oriented regular figures. For example, three regular octagons, similarly situated, will have six centres of enlargement lying, by threes, on four straight lines. Will this hold even when the octagons overlap or when one lies entirely within another? Sketch these two cases.

Do the figures have to be regular? What are the minimum conditions which they must satisfy for this relationship to hold?

Investigation of these two questions can lead to the observation that as a side $AB$ of one figure must be related by external enlargement to one side of a second figure and by internal enlargement to the opposite side of that figure, our figures need only have *half-turn* symmetry. Hence the basic standard geometrical figures having this property are similar parallelograms, similarly situated.

As shown in fig. 10, we only need one side of one of the parallelograms and the parallel sides of the other two.

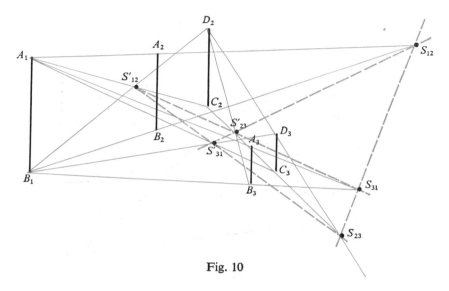

Fig. 10

From fig. 10 we can obtain a simple solution to the problem: Given two lines, $p_1, p_2$, meeting at an inaccessible point $Q$, to draw, through a given point $R$, the line $\langle RQ \rangle$.

Fig. 11

199

Through $R$ draw a pair of lines $r_1$, $r_2$, to cut $p_1$, $p_2$ at $A_2$, $B_2$ as shown.

Take $\qquad\qquad A_1 \in r_1,\ B_1 \in r_2,\ A_3 \in p_1,\ B_3 \in p_2$

such that $\qquad\qquad A_1 B_1 // A_2 B_2 // A_3 B_3$.

Then $P = \langle A_1 A_3 \rangle \cap \langle B_1 B_3 \rangle$ gives another point on the required line. In the notation of the previous diagrams $Q = S_{23}$, $P = S_{31}$, and $R = S_{12}$.

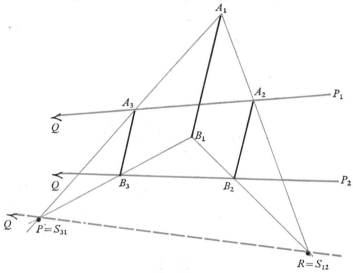

Fig. 12

A further question linked with the original Menelaus investigation concerns the identity enlargements associated with the sets of three centres of similitude on each of the four lines. In other words, what can be said about the centres of enlargement for the composite enlargements:

$$S_{31}.S_{23}.S_{12},\quad S'_{31}.S_{23}.S'_{12},\quad S_{31}.S'_{23}.S'_{12},\quad S'_{31}.S'_{23}.S_{12}?$$

Consider the first of these and a quadrilateral $A_1 B_1 C_1 D_1$. With centre $S_{12}$ and appropriate scale factor $\nu$

$$S_{12}(A_1 B_1 C_1 D_1) = A_2 B_2 C_2 D_2$$

and with centre $S_{23}$ and scale factor $\mu$

$$S_{23}(A_2 B_2 C_2 D_2) = A_3 B_3 C_3 D_3.$$

Hence $\qquad S_{23}.S_{12}(A_1 B_1 C_1 D_1) = A_3 B_3 C_3 D_3 = S_{13}(A_1 B_1 C_1 D_1)$

with scale factor $\qquad\qquad \mu\nu = 1/\lambda,$

where $\lambda$ is scale factor associated with $S_{31}$.

If we take a point $N' \neq S_{31}$ on $B_1 B_3$ and scale factor $\lambda'$ such that $\mathbf{N}'(B_3) = B_1$, then as we saw before $\mathbf{N}'.\mathbf{S}_{23}.\mathbf{S}_{12}$ will be an enlargement with centre $B_1$ provided $\lambda' \neq 1/\mu\nu$. That is as $N'$ approaches $S_{31}$, $\lambda.\mu\nu$ will tend to 1 but as long as actual equality is not reached the centre of enlargement remains at $B_1$.

No definite conclusion is reached about centres of such identity enlargements. On the other hand the behaviour of different sequences of triads $(\lambda, \mu, \nu)$ associated with the composition of three enlargements is largely unexplored. Further investigation could throw light on the behaviour in the limit.

It is noted also that the original approach to this problem may well have resulted in an inadequate symbol for an enlargement. Would it not be more appropriate to use $\mathbf{L}_\lambda$ where the two characteristics are properly identified rather than $\mathbf{L}$ with no specific statement about $\lambda$? This has special cases such as $\mathbf{L}_{-1}$, which will be a half turn about $L$, and $\mathbf{L}_1$ which will be the identity.

Reference can be made to M. Jeger, *Transformation Geometry*, George Allen and Unwin, 1966, for some discussion of this particular transformation. For the moment it rests here but others may want to pursue it or describe solutions already achieved.

# THE SIGNIFICANCE OF CONCRETE MATERIALS IN THE TEACHING OF MATHEMATICS

*by* W. SERVAIS

Mathematics is an abstract science; we could say, it is the science of abstraction. Learning mathematics is learning to abstract, to handle abstraction and to use it.

Doubtless this is why some teachers believe it proper to present abstractions ready-made. It would be better if they put their pupils in a situation expressed abstractly, and then helped them to work out their procedures, representations and concepts, and move from one level of abstraction to a higher one. More determinedly and consciously abstract than traditional mathematics, with more precise concepts and a more concise formalism, 'modern' mathematics may tempt a teacher who is anxious to get on quickly and efficiently to offer his pupils without delay the finished product of adult thinking. On the other hand, there are those who take intuitive mathematics to the limit and who would replace conceptualisations by visual percepts and proofs by physical actions.

The formalists have great fun underlining the misconceptions and mistakes of the intuitionists and denouncing their mathematical juggling as a fraudulent conversion of the currency.

Those who nevertheless value the support of intuition sometimes come to suffer from the lack of mathematical respectability in their position.

I remember particularly vividly the frankness with which Geoffrey Sillitto, when showing a model made of paper or cardboard, would stress the modesty of the means. As if these needed any excuse!

What matters is that the material perform its task effectively. Far from being a sign of poverty, simplicity is often a token of productivity. The aim of material is not to produce an attachment to the concrete but, on the contrary, to free the mind. We are not concerned to study for themselves the models or pieces of apparatus as a technician or a physicist would. When we are aiming at mathematical activity, it is the release of mathematical thinking which we must develop and not manual dexterity, however interesting this may be. The simplicity of a material, first of all, allows all children to take advantage of it, whatever their skill may be. So a child, even the very worst at drawing, can make accurate figures of polygons on the geoboard introduced by C. Gattegno, merely by stretching rubber bands between the nails on the board. But since the aim is to discover an abstract structure from the concrete model, it is desirable that the structure show itself as clearly as possible. This condition of transparency is best met in structured materials like the Cuisenaire rods or the Dienes Multibase Arithmetic Blocks. It accounts for their value as teaching aids.

To be effective, concrete material must allow action, since this is a better means to learning than contemplation. Materials which can be handled at leisure by the pupils so that they become completely familiar are much more valuable than any corresponding teaching aids used by the teacher for authoritarian demonstrations. The concrete actions of the pupils, however, are not the only ones which stimulate and give significance to the material in their hands. There is no real action which does not duplicate itself in a mental representation which becomes more and more conscious and increasingly distinct from that action. This representation in the mind is already a spontaneous abstraction since it contains only a simplified and rapidly stereotyped view of the concrete procedure. The development of an imagery of figures in this way is the first step towards geometry and topology. The mental representation of a succession of virtual actions, the realisation of how they arrange themselves in a certain order and how they allow of being inverted, is the approach to order structures and algebraic structures.

The traditional geometrical figures have a large perceptive content but this will remain unassimilated unless the study of them has been truly active. One needs to compare the parts of a figure, to imagine rebuilding the figure from its elements, and to see what happens when such and such a deformation is applied. The ability to do this is not immediate and the figures printed in the classical texts do not encourage it.

New means enable us to improve this state of things considerably. Plane or three-dimensional articulated models can, by their movements, help us grasp what is invariant in a structure. Polygons and working models of geometrical transformations made from Meccano have become familiar. I would like to stress all the things that can be shown by binding several knitting needles together with elastic so that they can pivot as well as slide. Four needles are enough to suggest all possible quadrilaterals, skew as well as plane, and to pass by deformation from a simple square to the complete quadrilateral of projective geometry.

Light is a natural form of projection. Much can be derived from it. The rays from a pocket torch can replace all the costly and complicated devices for demonstrating conic sections. It is enough to change the inclination of the cone of light shone on to the surface of a wall to obtain all the sections and to pass continuously from one to another.

Another method requiring a darkened room, is to cut across a model made of string or thread with a plane of light from an illuminated slit.

All the devices mentioned so far give the pupils themselves the power to change at will the elements of a geometrical figure.

Films are a powerful means for displaying geometry dynamically and the films by Nicolet and Fletcher—to mention a farsighted pioneer and an accomplished producer—succeed in a remarkable fashion. By their means the teacher can put before his pupils' eyes those situations involving movement which he wants them to absorb into their mental imagery.

It is appropriate to point out here that good mathematical films dispense with commentaries and do not try to reproduce the proofs in the textbooks. Their purpose is quite different: before the silent attention of the watchers they represent an orderly game played with variable structures. They are food for the imagination.

The materials we have mentioned so far have been linked, in a direct and obvious way, with visual perception. In a sense they present a phenomenology of mathematics. It is therefore essential that, in going beyond the experimental data, the percept becomes the concept, as with all abstract geometrical figures. In this connection, concrete experience can be misleading. For example, if one cuts a ruler into two parts it falls into two separate pieces whereas an interior point of a segment does not determine a partition of it into two disjoint segments.

One of the particular features of theoretical mathematics is the way in which it can be organised deductively, starting from systems of axioms and developing by means of theorems and definitions.

Most of the advocates of intuitive mathematics hold that it is a way of leading up to deductive mathematics. In fact, by using Venn's refinement of the method that Euler used to represent relations and operations on sets, we see that we can use a diagram of three intersecting circles to deal with all the questions of classical logic. It is enough to shade the regions which are empty and mark with a cross those which have at least one element.

Dienes has developed a logical game from Venn diagrams using hoops and geometrical blocks of different shapes and colours. The same diagrams, eventually drawn in colours, are used to begin the study of sets.

We still have a concrete material, but it is used to illustrate a variety of different situations. The appeal of the diagrams is entirely to the intuition—

which makes them suspect to those who believe in rigour—but the multiplicity of the interpretations which can be given to them makes them a truly abstract material. To show this it is only necessary to represent two straight lines by a Venn diagram, for example, and mark it to illustrate the possible positions of the lines. We have then produced a concrete example of the abstract significance of the incidence and parallel axioms. Venn diagrams make the Boolean algebra of the subsets of a set completely tangible.

Another well known representation is by means of switching circuits. We thus have a way of handling the operations of propositional logic concretely. Punched cards offer a fresh illustration. Finally, a game like WFF'N PROOF gives an approach, which is in fact completely formal, to the same logic. So with the help of isomorphic concrete models we can comprehend how mathematics has the power to unify through abstraction.

Within mathematics itself, digital and analogue computers are concrete materials used in the cause of abstraction. Related to this, there is a world of teaching possibilities in the construction of simple calculators and a study of their logic.

A long time ago Cayley used arrow-graphs to represent relations. It is possible, thanks to them, to introduce young children gently and easily to the formal properties of relations and functions in the way popularised by G. Papy. The effectiveness of these coloured graphs is undoubtedly due in considerable measure to the way in which the configuration of the finished graph acts as a reminder of the mental actions which the pupil made explicit in drawing it, arrow by arrow.

Flow-charts give another example of the dynamic which can be materialised into the form of a schema. This device, used to record the succession of operations in an algorithm, can find a considerable place early on in fixing the steps of a calculation or a construction in the pupil's minds.

Again, a rough arrow-diagram can serve to illustrate a problem and show how the data and the unknowns are related. The overall view of the relations which link them gives a rational method for discovering paths from what is known to what is to be found.

At the end of this short survey of materials and auxiliary devices used in teaching, it seems appropriate to underline again the role these aids play in the induction to mathematical thinking.

Some teachers are against the use of concrete situations as a basis for acquiring abstract procedures. They want logical rigour, complete rigour, and will not permit any promiscuous compromise with a crude empiricism. Against them are those who favour the concrete for its own sake, replacing proofs with 'showing', believing that the immediacy of the concrete has a magic power and contains all of mathematics.

In fact, it is when we are engaged in a dialogue with concrete material that the principal mathematical ideas emerge: every perception or action derived from the concrete duplicates itself in mental imagery; this becomes structured and can then be recalled in its own right. The first objects for mathematical study are the relations between perceptions and actions made virtual in this way.

In our concrete experience we pay attention to the more or less satisfactory material consequences of our actions. In our virtual mathematical experience the objects are stylized and have no imperfections. That is why when we support our abstract experience with rough sketches or tangible models we disregard their imperfections compared with the mathematical entities for which they are substitutes. Mathematical experience and the objects on which it operates belong to the second order. They cannot be confused with the physical objects and experiences which belong to a lower order. Seemingly it is impossible to slip straight away into the second order without having been through the first. Most people, if not all, need a concrete trace of their mental activity; this is the function of languages, from the vehicular language to schematic representations and mathematical symbolism. The symbols and schemas are concrete models obedient to the rules of precise manipulation and are, basically, a means of achieving rigour.

All concrete materials that are isomorphic from our way of acting with them,[1] fulfil the same function from a mathematical point of view, even though one or other of them may be better adapted psychologically to our way of thinking, due to its colour, or its ease of handling, or its capacity to release intuition. Once this isomorphism has been recognised we can appoint a concrete material to play the role of supporting a mathematical activity which it can reproduce automatically. It is the job of mathematical machines in a contrary sense to make abstraction concrete. Thus the word 'model' is used in two complementary ways corresponding to the two aspects of the interaction between physics and mathematics:

> the physical material is a concrete model of the mathematical relation which it illustrates, the mathematical structure is an abstract model of the physical situation which it explains.

The greatest pedagogical value of concrete material is in allowing the pupil to gather his mental experience at his own pace without the authority of the teacher. There are conscientious teachers who wish to help by telling everything and then repeating it; they do not see that their zeal is

---

[1] Servais, W. 'Concret-abstract' in *Le matériel pour l'enseignement des mathématiques.* Delachaux et Niestlé, Neuchatel, 1958.

useless as long as it fails to engage the deeper intellectual activity of their pupils. They are teachers who are not sufficiently aware of what they have to contribute to learning.

To a certain extent, material, if it is well thought out, can protect a pupil from his teacher and shelter the creative freshness of youth from adult knowledge which is a little threadbare through being used too much.

For a mathematical teaching aid to fulfil its function it must be handled by the pupils, helping them to work out, co-ordinate and organise their ideas. The contemplation of a complex ready-made model, for this reason, produces a very small return.

The most useful thing that manufacturers of materials could do for teachers is to put at their disposal all the constructional games—geometrical, mechanical, electrical, algebraic or logical—which will stimulate children's activity and free the time of the teachers.

In those countries where the difficulty of recruiting good teachers, at all levels, adds another burden to those in charge of education, we should hopefully consider the effect of a supply of materials and auxiliary teaching aids.

The ideal would be to bring to fruition the development of a range of pedagogical equipment which could, in the best possible way, help pupils to become students; that is, people who accept responsibility for achieving knowledge through their own activity.

# AN EXPLORATION IN REFLECTION GEOMETRY

*by* W. O. STORER

At the A.T.M. course at Winchester in July 1964 Sillitto gave a lecture on symmetry, with his characteristic virtuosity affording both enjoyment and enlightenment. Among his many examples and illustrations he referred incidentally to the proposition that if two angle-bisectors of a triangle, measured to their intersections with the opposite sides, are equal in length then the triangle is isosceles, and in particular he spoke forcefully and disparagingly of the ugliness of a proof of this which I had used in *Some Lessons in Mathematics*.[1] He expressed his conviction that a geometrical configuration that contained so many angle bisectors and therefore possible axes of reflection would yield an elegant proof based on this principle; but he had to admit that he did not himself know of such a proof.

This proposition has, of course, long been recognised as a converse of an easy proposition that is unexpectedly difficult to prove. Discussion and proofs of it go back for more than a century; for example, Sylvester[2] developed an interesting analytic argument from which he claimed that no direct proof was possible, but only one by *reductio ad absurdum*. A convenient reference for a number of different proofs is the *Mathematical Gazette*,[3] and other proofs are to be found elsewhere. Known proofs vary considerably in method and complexity, and most leave much to be desired in economy of construction and argument. The least ungainly I know is that ascribed[4] to Descube,[5] which (in essence) I chose to use in *Some Lessons in Mathematics* not so much for its own sake as to illustrate the logic of an inverse proof. It is reproduced here for reference, the diagram in fig. 1 having been given the additional line $QR$, with mid-point $G$, for later use.

It is given that $BQ$ bisects $\angle ABC$, $CR$ bisects $\angle ACB$, and $BQ = CR$. It is required to prove that $\angle ABC = \angle ACB$.

[1] Fletcher, T. J. (Ed.), *Some Lessons in Mathematics*, Cambridge University Press, 1964, p. 178.
[2] *Phil. Mag.* IV, 1852, pp. 366–9.
[3] *Math. Gazette*, XVI, 1932, pp. 200–2 and XVII, 1933, pp. 122–6. I am indebted to Dr G. A. Garreau for these references.
[4] *Math. Gazette*, XVII, 1933, pp. 124–5.
[5] *Journal de Mathématique Elémentaire*, IV, 1880, p. 538.

W. O. STORER

Complete the parallelogram $QBRT$ and join $CT$. If $\angle ABC \neq \angle ACB$ assume (for definiteness) that $\angle ABC > \angle ACB$. Then, since also in triangles $QBC$ and $RCB$, $QB = RC$ and $BC$ is common, we have $CQ > BR$ and hence, in triangle $CQT$, $CQ > QT$,

so $$\angle CTQ > \angle QCT. \tag{1}$$

Further, in triangle $CRT$, $CR = BQ = RT$, therefore

$$\angle CTR = \angle RCT. \tag{2}$$

From (1) and (2), by subtraction, $\angle RTQ < \angle RCQ$, therefore

$$\angle RBQ < \angle RCQ, \quad \text{so} \quad \angle ABC < \angle ACB,$$

which contradicts the hypothesis $\angle ABC > \angle ACB$.

Hence $$\angle ABC = \angle ACB.$$

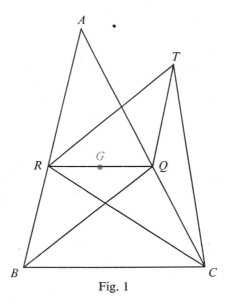

Fig. 1

This, then, is the proof which attracted Sillitto's displeasure, and we must all recognise and share his perfectionism which desired a proof limited to the bare essentials of the problem.

Let us therefore try constructions based on reflection. Fig. 2 shows the diagram obtained on reflection in $BQ$, where a suffix is used to indicate an image point and the axis of reflection (or centre of reflection in other diagrams) is shown in green. We observe that $C_1 R_1 = CR = BQ$, and are perhaps momentarily hopeful that $C_1 R_1$ and $BQ$ are images of each other in $CR$, but this is easily seen to be generally untrue. It is not easy

210

to see a simple extension of the argument in the direction we wish, and in any case the lack of symmetry in the treatment of $BQ$ and $CR$ is unwelcome.

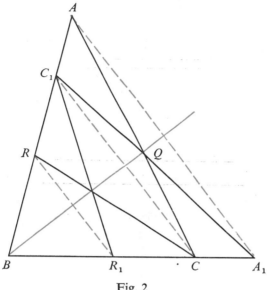

Fig. 2

If $I$ is the point of intersection of $BQ$ and $CR$, since $AI$ is the bisector of $\angle BAC$, reflection in $AI$ gives greater promise, because of its symmetrical treatment of $BQ$ and $CR$. The diagram is shown in fig. 3, with $BQ = CR = C_2R_2$, and for our desired purpose we need to prove that $BQ$ and $C_2R_2$ coincide.

The essentials of this problem are shown in fig. 4, in which are shown lines $SU$, $VW$, etc., through $I$ varying from the symmetrical position $YZ$ through the position $MN$ perpendicular to $AZ$ to the limiting position $IL$ parallel to $YA$. If we could prove that as $SU$ varies from $YZ$ to $IL$ its length varies strictly monotonically (increasing, in fact) then, in fig. 3, if $BQ = C_2R_2$ these segments must either coincide or be mirror images in $AI$ (this latter occurring only in a degenerate case of the original problem). To prove the monotonic variation in the length of $SU$ is easy for positions $VW$ lying between $MN$ and $IL$, when each of the two portions $VI$ and $IW$ is easily proved to be strictly increasing; but it is not obvious by simple argument for positions $SU$ between $YZ$ and $MN$, for which $SI$ increases and $IU$ decreases. It may be proved by trigonometry, since if $\angle IAZ = \alpha$ and $\angle ZIU = \theta$, $SU = IN\{\sec(\alpha-\theta)+\sec(\alpha+\theta)\}$; but this method is hardly acceptable to our present purpose.

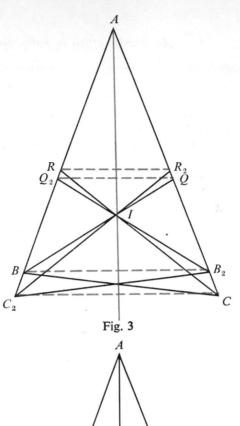

Fig. 3

Fig. 4

It is not easy to take this line of investigation further within our self-imposed limitations. However, although the diagram may not simplify the situation it has displayed the essential relevance of strictly monotonic variation in the length of $SU$. It may well be this fact that makes an indirect proof appropriate (though not essential) to this problem.

The other reflection which treats $BQ$ and $CR$ symmetrically is that in $BC$, though this is not an angle-bisector and therefore is not so natural to the problem. It would be sufficient to prove (in fig. 5) that $BQ$ and $R_3 C$

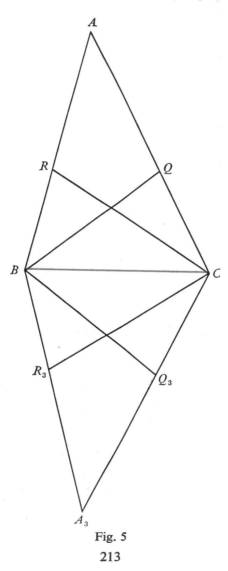

Fig. 5

are parallel, but there is no simple and obvious argument to accomplish this.

Since reflection in a bisector or some other line has not led us immediately to success, let us consider reflection in a point. The point most symmetrically placed for this diagram is the midpoint $D$ of $BC$, and the reflection is shown in fig. 6. Part of this figure, with $QR_4$ joined, as shown in fig. 7, yields one of the proofs given in the *Mathematical Gazette*,[1] the principle of which is similar to that of fig. 1. As there, the tentative hypothesis that $\angle ABC > \angle ACB$ leads to $CQ > BR = CR_4$ and hence, in triangle $CQR_4$, to

$$\angle CR_4Q > \angle CQR_4. \tag{3}$$

Further, $BQ = CR = BR_4$, therefore in triangle $BQR_4$

$$\angle BR_4Q = \angle BQR_4. \tag{4}$$

By addition of (3) and (4),

$$\angle BR_4C > \angle BQC. \tag{5}$$

However, in triangle $IQC$,

$$\left. \begin{aligned} \angle BQC = \angle BIC \quad &- \quad \angle ICQ, \\ > \angle BIC \quad &- \quad \angle IBR, \\ > \angle BRC, \quad &\quad = \angle BR_4C. \end{aligned} \right\} \tag{6}$$

Since (5) and (6) are inconsistent, we conclude that $\angle ABC = \angle ACB$.

This line of argument is essentially the same as that used with fig. 1, but is a little longer. We may indeed obtain fig. 1 not by 'completing the parallelogram $QBRT$' but by reflecting triangle $QBR$ in the midpoint $G$ of $QR$, so this proof may be regarded as being based on reflection, and thereby be more acceptable in the present context.

This possibility of using reflection to obtain fig. 1 leads to a further consideration. Among the varied proofs given in the *Mathematical Gazette* collection one[2] is singled out as of special interest in that it is independent of an axiom of parallels; and this aspect of the problem is investigated more thoroughly in Coxeter.[3]

Euclidean geometry is an interweaving of the two strands of affine geometry and absolute geometry. Both of these require axioms of order (which were virtually overlooked by Euclid himself through their being too obvious for attention); affine geometry arises from the addition of two axioms involving parallels, whereas absolute geometry arises from the alternative addition of axioms of congruence.

[1] *Math. Gazette*, XVII, 1933, pp. 123–4.
[2] Ibid., p. 125.
[3] Coxeter, H. S. M., *Introduction to Geometry*, Wiley, 1961, pp. 263–5.

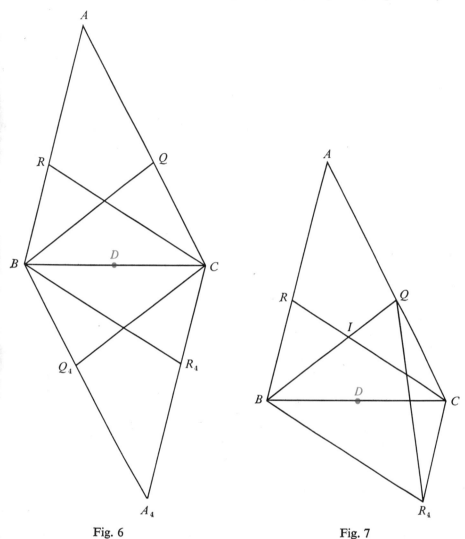

Fig. 6             Fig. 7

The proposition under discussion, although usually occurring within the context of Euclidean geometry, is in fact a proposition of absolute geometry, in that it does not depend on an axiom of parallels. This is shown by the proof just cited from the *Mathematical Gazette*, and also by one indicated by Coxeter,[1] which is reproduced here in our own notation. In fig. 8 we are given that $BQ = CR$.

[1] Ibid., p. 16, Ex. 4.

Assume $\angle ABC \neq \angle ACB$, and for definiteness that $\angle ABC > \angle ACB$. Then there is a point $H$ on $QA$ such that $\angle HBQ = \angle HCR$, and a point $J$ on $CH$ such that $CJ = BH$. Since the triangles $CRJ$, $BQH$ are congruent,

$$\angle RJC = \angle BHQ. \tag{7}$$

But $RJ$, $BH$ intersect at $K$ (say). For triangle $HJK$, ext. $\angle KJC >$ int. $\angle KHC$, or

$$\angle RJC > \angle BHQ. \tag{8}$$

But (7) and (8) are inconsistent; therefore the original assumption was false, so $\angle ABC = \angle ACB$.

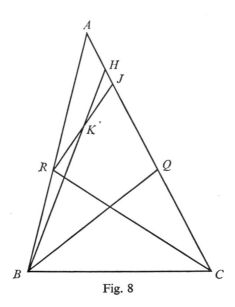

Fig. 8

The arguments used here are all valid in absolute geometry,[1,2] whereas most other proofs involve the properties either of parallels or of angles in the same segment of a circle, which are not valid in absolute geometry. It is of particular significance to our investigation, however, that reflection can be defined in absolute geometry,[3] and conversely Bachmann[4] has developed absolute geometry from the concept of reflection in a line. Does it follow, then, that our first proof, with the point $T$ obtained by reflection of triangle $BQR$ in the midpoint of $QR$, is valid in absolute geometry?

[1] Ibid., pp. 264, 428.
[2] Kerékjártó, B., *Les Fondements de la Géométrie*. Budapest, 1955, vol. 1, pp. 161–3.
[3] Coxeter, *op. cit.* p. 264.
[4] Bachmann, F., *Aufbau der Geometrie aus dem Spiegelungsbegriff*, ch. 2. Berlin, 1959.

An essential step in this proof was 'From (1) and (2), by subtraction, $\angle RTQ < \angle RCQ$', and the correctness of the subtraction is justified by the tacit assumption that $T$ lies to the right of $AC$. But our intuitive acceptance of this fact (or our more deliberate proof) arises from our experience of Euclidean geometry and not simply of absolute geometry. This assumption is certainly not intuitively obvious for a spherical triangle, as fig. 9 shows, in which triangle $TRQ$ is obtained by the reflection of $BQR$ in the midpoint $G$ of $QR$. It might yet be true, of course (but is not obviously so), in the special cases when the angle bisectors $BQ$ and $CR$ are equal, and if so the argument of the first proof would be valid in its entirety.

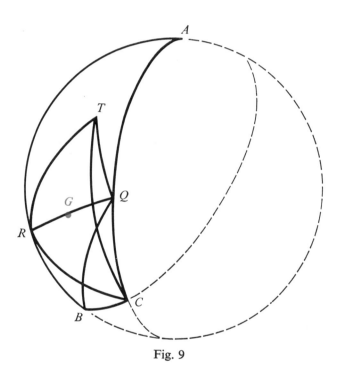

Fig. 9

Our search for a simple, intuitively clear proof of the proposition by means of reflection has not been successful. The conclusions of the last paragraph, however, will make us in any further search be more explicit whether we are thinking within the broader framework of Euclidean geometry or the narrower one of absolute geometry. Even without the restriction to reflection methods it may be that a direct proof is possible only within the broader system, and that within the narrower system of absolute geometry only an indirect proof is possible.

Without wholly accepting the view that it is better to travel hopefully than to arrive, we can draw satisfaction from the fact that this journey and search, though unsuccessful, have yielded a wider perspective over the territory. It was Sillitto's forthright desire for perfection in the field he made characteristically his own that prompted this particular journey, and that may yet inspire its successful completion.

# ANY MUST GO

## by E.B.C. THORNTON

### I  INTRODUCTION

In a simple-minded approach to learning and teaching one might group the aspects to be considered under two headings, positive and negative. The positive are to do with teaching. Does the teacher know and/or believe in what he is teaching? Can he communicate his ideas and/or enthusiasm? Can he by natural talent or pedagogical wiles inspire maximum growth on the part of the learner? What are these pedagogical wiles? The negative are mostly concerned with learning. Many things can stunt the mathematical growth of a child and we need to investigate each one and remove the cause if we can. Best known of these, and most vicious, is early failure to form the complicated concept of number before going on to later stages. A similar difficulty, less disastrous, arises from lack of spatial 'intuitions'. Both of these are well enough recognised today, though it remains to be seen how effectively they can be disposed of. Then at a later stage great differences exist in the individual's natural power of abstraction: the child, or student, who is hurried through his slow but necessary processes of concept formation has to rely more and more on the rote learning of tricks. Understanding and the growth of mathematical ability gradually cease under the intolerable burden of mumbo-jumbo. This difficulty is not so well recognised.

A fourth difficulty that needs to be removed is the widespread ambiguity of language which exists at most levels of mathematical instruction. Even if the teacher is quite clear about what he means, the words and symbols that he uses may have connotations for him which they do not have for the learner: and the learner hears only what the teacher appears to be saying. Often the teacher is not really clear himself. It may be that an imprecise notation has misled him: mathematics is full of such notations, convenient for communication between the cognoscenti, but dangerous for others. Or it may be that an important underlying concept has received necessary refinement since the teacher's student days. There is no difficulty in supplying examples of this from school mathematics.

Or it may be the use of the vernacular that causes trouble. Obvious examples spring to mind from all departments of elementary mathematics. It is one particular example, namely the use of the word 'any', which

219

forms the subject of this discussion. Unfortunately this example is not confined to elementary mathematics. Any idea that it is can be discounted by the same means that any false generalisation can be disproved: if any counterexample can be found the proposition cannot be true. But let us first make a survey of the logic that is or might be taught in schools.

## 2   LOGIC IN SCHOOLS

Perhaps the most famous of the many facets of mathematics is the inter-connectedness of its results. Chains of *deductive* reasoning link theorem to theorem, and theorem to axiom, so that mathematics has a good claim to be called the most logical of man's activities. From another point of view, since everyone uses deductive thinking at times, mathematics has a claim to be called one of the most universal of human activities. But in real mathematics, mostly confined to the postgraduate and primary stages, there is also a good deal of *inductive* thinking, putting two and two together (in the common phrase) to make an inductive inference. It is this mode of thinking, based on experience together with ideas of pattern and probability, that is the important one in everyday life. As for proof in everyday life, 'The proof of the pudding is in the eating'.

In mathematics there is no need for testing to destruction: the proof is deductive. Implication, logical equivalence and indirect proof are the basic ingredients. When angry voices are raised in defence of the traditional geometry—'It teaches you to think'—it usually turns out to be this deductive thinking that the speakers have in mind. In reality, of course, the effect of traditional school geometry is usually little more than an introduction to the idea of implication, e.g. 'If the triangle $ABC$ has $AB = AC$ then angle $C$ = angle $B$'. It is not even a very good introduction. There may be some difficulty in appreciating an essential feature of implication, namely the difference between such a statement and its converse, 'The triangle $ABC$ has $AB = AC$ if angle $C$ = angle $B$'.

For all but the small minority with a natural bent for deductive reasoning that is about as far as it goes. It seems extraordinary that so much fuss could be made of so small a content. Is this really all that comes out of those hours of struggling with 'riders'? Perhaps the subject matter of the traditional geometry is at fault: few of the arguments involved are simple enough to make the use of the one way implication sign '$\Rightarrow$' appropriate. Nearly all the theorems have true converses, too, so that the distinction between a theorem and its converse—just the moving of an 'if'—seems rather artificial and pedantic to the pupil. Also relevant, perhaps, is the cavalier treatment that this distinction receives in most textbooks about algebra, trigonometry and co-ordinate geometry.

Evidently for the majority of school pupils the three basic ingredients of simple two valued logic just do not come across, unless they are explicitly taught and carefully attended to. Modern textbooks are beginning to face up to this situation, but there is still little idea how the ideas may be, or should be presented. The syllogistic approach of classical logic is virtually dead, and not before its time. The 'All $X$ is $Y$' approach, with Venn diagrams and/or Boolean algebra is another dead end from the point of view of deductive logic. And the truth table treatment of the propositional calculus seems too abstract for school children: there is a real danger of submerging the ideas under a welter of notation and terminology. As with so many important aspects of the body of mathematics, the needs of the learner are in conflict with the conscience and convenience of the teacher. Which of the subtleties and refinements can be deferred until later, without actually misleading, in order to make the broad ideas accessible to beginners? Let us consider these broad ideas in turn.

## Implication

Ordinary mathematics abounds in '*If*...*then*...' assertions, such as 'If $x = 3$, then $x^2 = 9$'. Such a sentence is an *implication* which can be symbolised

$$p(x) \text{ is true} \Rightarrow q(x) \text{ is true, or more shortly}$$

$$p(x) \Rightarrow q(x) \qquad \text{or, shorter still,}$$

$$p \Rightarrow q.$$

It tells us nothing about $q(x)$ if $p(x)$ is not true. It is a restricted form of the more general type of implication called *material implication*: in material implication, if $p$ is true (whatever that means) then $q$ is true, and if $p$ is false then $q$ may be either true or false. The distinction between these two types of implication can also be made by calling the second a *conditional*, and using a different symbol for it. And there are other subtleties which can be considered, such as the idea of a necessary connection between $p$ and $q$. This gives a 'strict' implication that has its own more complicated calculus, and of course excludes many of the examples that one might use for illustration.

But such examples are best avoided anyway. In the usual developments of the basic ideas of the propositional calculus using truth tables, $p$ and $q$ are taken to be *propositional variables*, replaceable by statements that are *true* or *false*. Thus if $p$ is replaced by 'the sun is hot' and $q$ by 'the earth is flat', then $p \Rightarrow q$ is false; whereas if $p$ is replaced by 'the oceans are dry' then $p \Rightarrow q$ is true. Such examples are either irrelevant and confusing, or else if they are relevant their meaning distracts attention from the form of the logic which is being illustrated. For illustrative purposes it is more

221

convenient, and probably essential with beginners, to use replacements for $p$ and $q$ which are *open sentences*, neither true nor false until further information is available. Thus 'Sam is human' might be used for $p$, 'Sam is mortal' for $q$. Whether either or both of these is true depends on Sam: man, dog, or Teddy bear?

## Logical equivalence

If $p \Rightarrow q$ and also, conversely, $q \Rightarrow p$, then they are both 'true' or both 'false'. The two propositions are said to be logically equivalent, and the notation '$p \Leftrightarrow q$' is used. This can be read '$p$ if and only if $q$', or '$p$ is a necessary and sufficient condition for $q$'. Sometimes it is written '$p$ iff $q$', 'iff' being an abbreviation for 'if and only if'. It is interesting to note that in each of these cases, providing we read from left to right, the arrowhead on the left corresponds to 'if' and 'necessary'. As a simple example of logical equivalence consider '$P$ lies on the locus if and only if its co-ordinates satisfy the equation of the locus': sampling the proofs in co-ordinate geometry textbooks may suggest that logical equivalence is not widely taught in schools...

## Indirect proof

Many widely accepted parts of mathematics depend for their proof on the *two valued* nature of our ordinary logic. If $p$ is a meaningful statement, for example an open sentence in which permissible replacements for the variables have been made, then *either $p$ is true or $p$ is false*. No other possibility is admitted. This is the famous law of the excluded middle.

The statement '$p$ is false', or more fully, 'It is false that $p$ is true' is called the *negation* of $p$, and can be symbolised 'not-$p$'. To prove a statement $p$ to be true, the indirect method is to show that the negation of $p$ is false. In the most famous example of this type of proof, $p$ is the statement '$\sqrt{2}$ is irrational': not-$p$ is then the statement '$\sqrt{2}$ is rational'. Using the accepted fact that a rational number can be expressed as $m/n$ with $m, n$ coprime integers the proof then shows that not-$p$ implies

$m, n$ have no common factor *and* $m, n$ have a common factor.

This last sentence is false for all permissible replacements of the variables. (Such a sentence is called a *contradiction*: compare with sentences which are true for all replacements of the variables, called *tautologies* e.g. $p \Rightarrow p$.) From the definition of implication it follows that not-$p$ is false, and thus that $p$ is true.

Despite the great importance of this method of proof it seems to be little regarded by the writers of school textbooks. The Mathematical

Association reports on Geometry of 1923, 1937 and 1953 gave less than one page to it out of total of 380. On the whole the tendency has been to regard it as suitable for the best classes only. Is this because the structure of the proof was not broken down sufficiently to make the segments acceptable to the pupil? There still seems to be little idea how the break down should be arranged. One promising line of approach is to introduce the idea of the *contrapositive*. Let us look again at

$$p \Rightarrow q. \tag{1}$$

We have seen that this means that $q$ is 'at least as true' as $p$, or more precisely that it is not possible for $p$ to be true and $q$ false. Thus given that $p \Rightarrow q$,

$$q \text{ is false} \Rightarrow p \text{ is false.} \tag{2}$$

In other words the statement (2) follows from the statement (1): it is called the contrapositive of (1). We wish to establish that it is in fact logically equivalent to (1). Thus we must show that (1) follows from (2). (1) is equivalent to

$$p \text{ is true} \Rightarrow q \text{ is true}$$

i.e. to 
$$\text{not-}p \text{ is false} \Rightarrow \text{not-}q \text{ is false} \tag{1'}$$

and (2) is simply 
$$\text{not-}q \Rightarrow \text{not-}p. \tag{2'}$$

Comparing these last two with (2) and (1) it is evident that (1') follows from (2') in exactly the same way that (2) follows from (1). The reader who is not convinced is invited to think through the argument using '$x$ is a parallelogram' for $p$, '$x$ is a quadrilateral' for $q$.

What we have shown is that each of the sentences

$$p \text{ is true} \Rightarrow q \text{ is true,}$$

$$q \text{ is false} \Rightarrow p \text{ is false}$$

follows from the other, i.e. that they are logically equivalent. Each is the contrapositive of the other. Clearly an abstract argument like the above may not be suitable for pupils; but the conclusion of the argument is suitable, and can be established convincingly by the use of everyday 'If...then...' statements and their contrapositives. The idea can then be used, at a not very rigorous level, to establish converses of $p \Rightarrow q$ by showing not-$p \Rightarrow$ not-$q$. For example the alternate segment theorem, the ratio theorem (Thales), and the various theorems about concyclic points have suitable converses of this kind. In the words of Sillitto 'we use vividly apprehended geometrical situations to clarify and vitalise the logical abstractions...The form of the argument is powerful and important; ...we should show pupils its power even before they can formulate it explicitly in the abstract'.

As an example of a proof by contrapositive consider the following:

*Example:* If $\pi$ and $\pi'$ are parallel planes and a line $l$ is perpendicular to $\pi$, then $l$ is perpendicular to $\pi'$.

Here $p$ is '$\pi$ and $\pi'$ are planes with no common point, *and l* is perpendicular to $\pi$'

q is '$l$ is perpendicular to $\pi'$'.

Then not-$q$ $\Rightarrow$ there is a line $m$ in $\pi'$ making an acute angle with $l$

$\Rightarrow$ $m$ and $\pi$ have a common point $P$

$\Rightarrow$ $\pi'$ and $\pi$ have a common point $P \Rightarrow$ not-$p$.

This proof can also be put in the form of an indirect proof. But if one starts from a negative definition of parallel planes there is no hope of a direct proof. Theorems such as 'There is no greatest integer' also require indirect proofs; but in this case the theorem cannot be put in the form of an implication, so that no contrapositive proof is available. There are also avoidable difficulties which can arise when there is more than one (partial) contrapositive; but there are very many examples where the contrapositive proof is simple and helpful, and it may prove the bridge to indirect proof.

Perhaps in the not too distant future it will be possible to introduce these three basic ideas of deductive thinking to a wide section of the ability range. It certainly should be so, if mathematical *education* is to mean anything. It seems likely that the methods to be used will involve some of the symbolism of the propositional calculus, and copious illustrations, but no truth tables. The idea of propositional variables $p$ and $q$ is almost certainly unsuitable, as explained above, so that *open sentences* must be used instead. Such sentences, already mentioned, and known also as propositional functions, statement forms or predicates, contain variables, e.g. '$x$ is $\sqrt{2}$', 'He likes jam', and the truth value remains in doubt until each variable is replaced by some particular element from its domain. In the previous example on page 222, the 'Sam' in 'Sam is human' is a variable on the set of things called 'Sam': on the whole it seems more honest to use 'he', which is quite obviously a variable, despite the euphonious attractions of 'Sam likes jam'.

## 3   VARIABLES AND QUANTIFIERS

The fact is that, as the previous section has shown, it is not really feasible to discuss the basic logic of elementary mathematics at all without introducing the idea of an open sentence, and this in turn requires the idea of a *variable*. To simplify the discussion let us consider open sentences which involve one variable only. Then given an open sentence $p$ there is a set $P$

called the *truth set*, or solution set, of $p$ which consists of all the possible replacements for the variable that make the proposition $p$ true. Denoting the truth set of $q$ in the same way by $Q$ ,we then see that '$p \Rightarrow q$' is logically equivalent to 'All members of the set $P$ are members of the set $Q$', or, in symbols '$P \subset Q$' (see fig. 1).

For example, if $p$ is the sentence 'He is a man' and $q$ is the sentence 'He is mortal', then $P$ is the set of all men, and $Q$ is the set of all mortals. '$p \Rightarrow q$' can be read as 'If he is a man then he is mortal', and '$P \subset Q$' says 'All members of the set of men belong to the set of all mortals', or, more briefly, 'All men are mortal'.

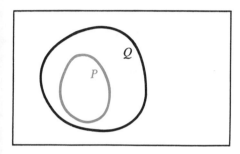

Fig. 1                                        Fig. 2

The solution set for the sentence not-$p$, which means '$p$ is not true', is the set $P'$, see fig. 2, called the complement of $P$: and similarly $Q'$, the complement of $Q$, corresponds to not-$q$. The contrapositive 'not-$q$ $\Rightarrow$ not-$p$' is logically equivalent to '$Q' \subset P'$': in words 'If he is not a mortal then he is not a man' corresponds to 'All immortals are not men', or, more briefly, 'No immortals are men'.

Thus we have the following four common ways of saying the same thing:

(i)   If he is a man, then he is mortal;
(ii)  If he is immortal, then he is not a man;
(iii) All men are mortal;
(iv) No immortals are men;

Four other usual forms of words are illustrated by:

(v)   He is mortal if he is human;
(vi)  He is human only if he is mortal;
(vii) Being mortal is a necessary condition for being human;
(viii) Being human is a sufficient condition for being mortal.

Each of the last four can also be found in contrapositive form. It is quite an amusing exercise to derive these contrapositives with the minimum

225

change of words and/or word order. Note that all the eight (or twelve) statements assert the same thing. Whether or not what they say is (empirically) true is not a question of logic. The question of empirical truth is another matter altogether. With the literal use of the word 'immortal' they are all (as far as anyone knows) true. But other meanings can be given to this word, and then since all the statements are equivalent, if one is false they all are. Thus when an Englishman refers to 'the immortal bard' he is exhibiting a counterexample which shows that (for his use of the word 'immortal') they are all false. If *some* man is immortal then it is not true that *all* men are mortal.

This last example shows that

It is not true that *all* men are mortal

is equivalent to

*Some* men are not mortal.

In the same way the negation of

*Some* immortals are men

is

*All* immortals are not men.

This close connection between the words 'some' and 'all' is basic and fundamental.

In all the above discussion it is doubtful whether the Venn diagrams really help very much. As mentioned before, the nineteenth century approach has served its purpose in leading to the development of twentieth century ideas about logic, and is no longer in the main stream of mathematics. It would be a pity if it were to be resurrected just to provide problems after the style of Lewis Carroll for children to be examined on.

But the two words 'All' and 'Some' are right in the main stream of mathematics. As soon as the basic and unavoidable ideas of open sentences and variables come under consideration these two words are equally unavoidable. There is really nothing modern or startling about this remark. The following words appear on page 8 of a well known and easily available book by Whitehead (*An Introduction to Mathematics*, Oxford University Press): '...it was not till the last few years that it has been realised how fundamental *any* and *some* are to the very nature of mathematics...' That was written 69 years ago.

## 4  ANY

In the years since 1911 there has been a refinement of ideas and language in this connection. It is no longer good enough to talk about 'any' instead of 'all', as Whitehead did. Corresponding to the universal quantifier ∀ we have in the vernacular 'For all...', 'For every...', 'For each...'; and corresponding to the existential quantifier ∃ we have 'For some...', 'For at least one...', 'There exists... such that...' Unfortunately the English language also provides the word 'any' which can do duty for both these, under suitable circumstances, as well as having other meanings. The reader who has a Shorter Oxford English Dictionary by his elbow is invited at this point to study the entry under 'any', in conjunction with the uses of the word above. Three of its uses are exemplified in a sentence at the end of the introductory section. This will doubtless convince him of the extreme unhelpfulness of using the word when it is desired to communicate clear thought.

Why do we still do it? The French don't: nor do the Russians, and lest this might make the answer appear too obvious, it is worth pointing out that many Americans don't either. Possibly it is something to do with our supposed characteristic national dislike of reason. Perhaps a clue can be found by considering the basic idea of generalisation. Over and over again in mathematics one takes a typical element $m$ of a set $M$ and proves something about it. Suppose one has proved that it belongs to the set $N$, whose typical element is $n$, i.e. that $M \subset N$. Then one says 'An $m$ is an $n$', which implies the word 'necessarily' after 'is'; or alternatively one says 'Every $m$ is an $n$'. For example 'A number that is divisible by six is divisible by three', or 'Every number that is divisible by six is divisible by three'. Here $M$ is the set of multiples of six, $N$ is the set of multiples of three.

In advanced work the first form of words seems more usual, and accords well with an axiomatic approach. But at school level we are usually working at a low level of abstraction, and the step from a particular, albeit typical, element to the totality of members of an infinite aggregate is no mean step. In order to do it for a denumerable infinity, even in cases where we are quite convinced, we are obliged to appeal to the unprovable Principle of Mathematical Induction.[1]

Yet to extend to a *non-denumerable* infinity of real numbers a result which has been proved for a single real number, for example $f'(a) = \frac{1}{2}a^{-\frac{1}{2}}$, is easily done! Just start by considering 'any number $x$', then with the result established for that number, point out that it is therefore true for *ANY* number $x$. The emphasis and/or arm waving indicates that 'any' has now stopped meaning '*some* arbitrary' and started meaning '*all*'. Of course, if it is possible to find one or more replacements for $x$ for which this result does not hold (as here) the generalisation is invalid unless qualified; but the procedure described avoids such tedious difficulties by

---

[1] 'A statement $P(n)$ is true for every natural number $n$, if the set of natural numbers for which $P(n)$ is true forms an inductive set.' An inductive set $I$ satisfies the conditions (*a*) $I$ contains 1, and (*b*) if $I$ contains $k$ then it contains $k+1$.

This principle can be 'proved' only by making even wider assumptions.

avoiding the whole issue. It is very convenient to the teacher, who does not have to analyse his own meaning too carefully. Whether it is helpful to the learner is another matter.

There is an entertaining example of the confusion caused by 'any' which can be found in many textbooks that deal with the equilibrium of forces in a plane. On the assumption $V$ that the vector sum of the forces is zero, we then have

$$S \Rightarrow E \Rightarrow A,$$

where $S$ stands for 'For some point $P$ the sum of the moments about $P$ is zero', $A$ stands for 'For all points $P$ the sum of the moments about $P$ is zero', and $E$ stands for 'The forces are in equilibrium'. Thus $V$-and-$S$ gives a set of sufficient conditions for $E$, which are also trivially necessary: and $V$-and-$A$ gives a set of necessary conditions which are grossly over-sufficient. But let $N$ stand for 'For *any* point $P$, the sum of moments about $P$ is zero', and consider $V$-and-$N$. When used as a necessary condition the 'any' in this will mean 'all'; when being used for sufficiency the 'hypothetical, interrogatory or conditional' form of the first part of the implication gives 'any' the meaning 'some'. Thus $V$-and-$N$ gives a single (?) splendid set of necessary and sufficient conditions...The enjoyment of this joke is somewhat spoilt if one knows that it is still standard bookwork for A-level candidates, and asked for in exams.

But to return to the difficulties which stand in the way of the learner, here clearly is a prime source of imprecision, even confusion, and an obstacle to the communication of ideas. Without doubt it is time that the use of the two quantifiers should become much more widely known, and that the use of 'any' should be wholly abandoned. 'Any' must go!

## NOTE

A classroom presentation somewhat on the lines of Section 2 above can now be found in:

SCOTTISH MATHEMATICS GROUP *Modern Mathematics for Schools*, Books 5 and 9. Blackie-Chambers, 1967, 1969.

## FURTHER READING

KNEEBONE, G. T. *Mathematical Logic and the Foundation of Mathematics*, Van Nostrand, 1965.

BASSON, A. N. & O'CONNOR, D. J. *Introduction to Symbolic Logic* (3rd ed.). Univ. Tutorial Press, 1965.

WILDER, R. L. *Introduction to the Foundations of Mathematics* (2nd ed.). Wiley, 1965.

ALLENDOERFER, C. B. & OAKLEY, C. O. *Principles of Mathematics*. McGraw Hill, 1955.

FANG, JOONG. *Abstract Algebra*. Schaum, 1963.

# DRAWINGS AND REPRESENTATION

*by* D. H. WHEELER

1   A class of top infants (7-year-olds): a group of children were making patterns with coloured wooden cubes and recording their patterns on paper. Without exception, the children in this group produced drawings, with their rulers, of strings of squares.

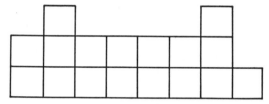

Fig. 1

The teacher talked to them about their drawings and, holding up a cube in her hand, asked if they could show that the cubes were 'solid'.

Billy said he could, and drew:

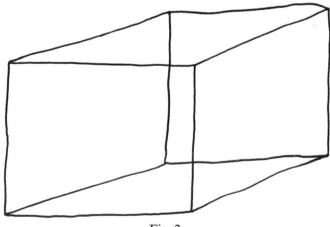

Fig. 2

This was drawn freehand slowly and carefully: first a square then a second square, above and to the right of the first, and finally the lines joining the corresponding corners.

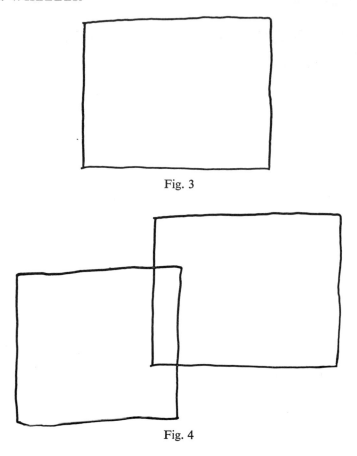

Fig. 3

Fig. 4

Two other boys in the group became animated and said that now they saw how to do it. Timothy covered a sheet of paper with differently coloured versions of fig. 5 (the outer square drawn first, then the two central verticals, and then the short horizontals).

Terry also produced a page of drawings superficially like Timothy's. But he began with the outside square (fig. 6) and then drew the inside line (fig. 7: starting at the top), finishing with three additional strokes (fig. 8).

All three boys seemed pleased with their work and did not question their results or make any further direct comparisons between them.

2   I find that I have a stereotyped method of drawing a cube. Unless there is a particular reason for including them, I omit the edges that 'cannot be seen'. If I do need them, I normally draw them last, probably with dashed lines.

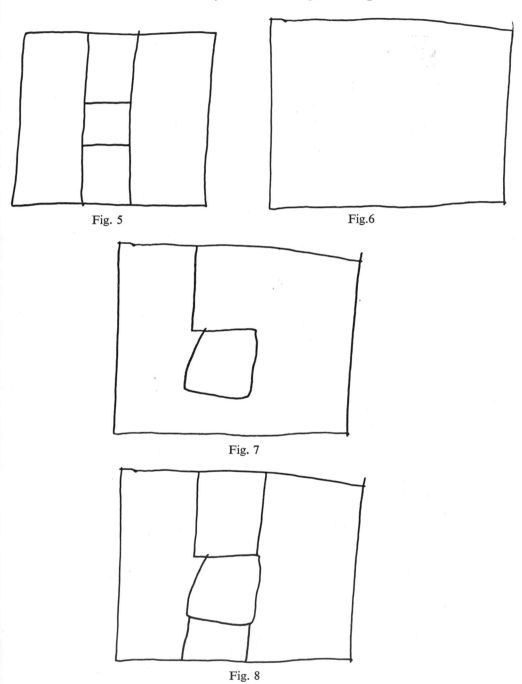

Fig. 5

Fig.6

Fig. 7

Fig. 8

There is a fixed procedure, too, by which the lines are drawn. I draw them in the order and the direction indicated (fig. 9).

I wonder if I developed this order rationally? The procedure follows the dimensional structure very closely. I do not draw the outline first and then fill in the other lines. But perhaps I draw it this way because I am good at drawing parallelograms—simpler elements from which I can build up this more complex picture.

I notice that drawing *line 1* first enables me to place the figure as far to the left as I want it to go, and it gives me a good indication of the overall size of the finished diagram—which will be about as wide as *line 1* is long, and will extend the same amount above the top and below the bottom of *line 1*.

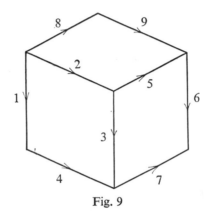

Fig. 9

I am certainly not conscious of all this while drawing. Nevertheless, although I have developed over the years a graphic algorithm which requires very little attention to set it going, if I introspect and watch myself doing it, I can find traces of half-conscious thoughts and feelings.

*Line 1* is 'about half-way back'. I can feel myself coming forward from it, and moving back behind it as I draw other lines of the figure. There is some resistance to drawing *line 1* downwards 'too far'. I have to force it down as far as it will go against this resistance. (Is this 'resistance' my estimate of the amount of room available, or the size I want my diagram to be? I cannot rationally account for it.) In spite of what I said above, I do not feel that *line 1* on its own is enough to determine the figure, and I only feel safe when *line 2* is drawn as well. *Line 2* also meets resistance, but I think the only source of this is the already-drawn length of *line 1*.

When *lines 1* and *2* are drawn, I am sure I will be able to finish the diagram without needing to make any further judgments. At a logical level this seems odd, as I ought to need *line 5*, for example, as well.

232

Having said all this (and I have no great confidence that it is very significant), I can as least assert that my drawing is not a copy of any cube I have ever seen. If I *do* sit down and try to sketch a cube 'as I see it', the algorithm disintegrates entirely and I am involved in making judgments and decisions of a quite different order.

3   Paul Klee says, 'The cube is a balanced synthesis of three definite dimensions and as such the normative symbol of corporeality.'[1]

4   A group of six 6-year-old children could recognise a cube and name it. Asked to draw it, four of them drew:

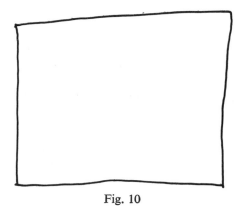

Fig. 10

But Sally drew:

Fig. 11

[1] Klee, P., *The thinking eye*. Lund Humphries, 1961.

233

and James drew:

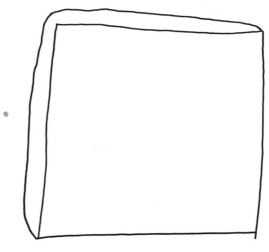

Fig. 12

Asked to 'show' what a cube was like without using words or drawing, four of them described the outline of a vertical square with a finger. Two of them placed their hands apart, palms parallel and facing each other; then shifted their hands to show top and bottom, then back and front. James was one of these, but Sally was not the other.

The four children who had drawn a square when asked what their drawing 'looked like', said it looked like a square.

5  Some rearrangements of three parallelograms (fig. 13).

The contextual pressure is very powerful. At least two of the diagrams give me no sense of three-dimensionality if I look at them drawn on separate sheets of paper. I have to exert some effort to make the third dimension appear. But here, with them all together, I cannot escape the illusion of three planes, perpendicular in pairs, in each case. An even greater effort is required to make them go flat now.

I notice, too, how crude an approximation I will accept as a perspective rendering. The first figure is 'a cube seen in perspective'. And yet, of course, I could not have played my game with the component quadrilaterals if it had really obeyed the rules.

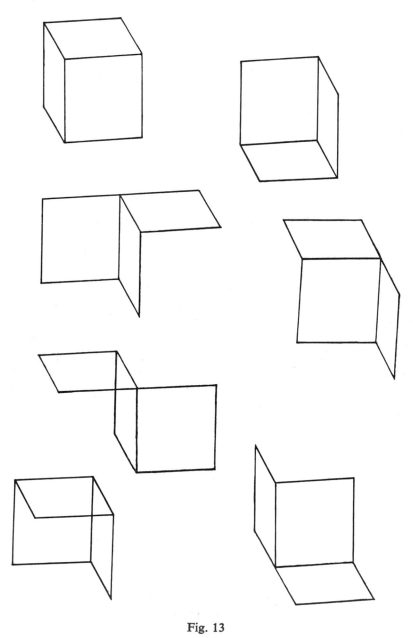

Fig. 13

6   Another top infants class; again a group of children were working with cubes and recording their patterns. James produced a drawing:

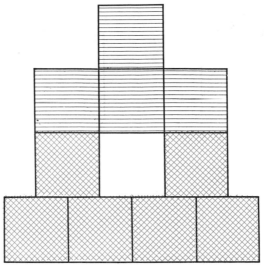

Fig. 14

Above it he wrote: 'I used 19 bricks' and underneath it he wrote: '6 greens and 4 whites'.

His teacher, glancing at it hastily, suggested that he count again.

James then added the words 'in the front', and also wrote: 'there are really 12 bricks that are green. There are really 7 white bricks.' On the back of his sheet of paper he drew:

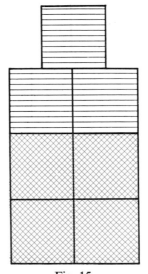

Fig. 15

and wrote: 'This is the side of my casel. This is why there are 19 bricks. There are 6 green and 3 whites at the back.'

7   Some 9-year-old children were asked to draw a cube and then to colour its faces fig. 16. Linda and Simon have both drawn a 'good' representation of a cube, but their paintings show more than the three colours which one would be able to 'see'. Wendy and Catrina know that only three colours will be visible, although their schemas are unconventional in other ways.

Being set to copy or represent a cuboid with each face coloured differently seems, in some cases, to displace the schema that is otherwise well under control. Roberta (11) asked to copy such a cuboid produced:

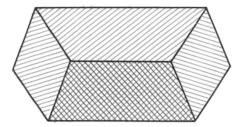

Fig. 17

It is not perhaps surprising that a child may feel it necessary in these circumstances to give more information. When you know there are six colours, and you know what they are, it is frustrating to feel that one is only supposed to show half of them.

Some 5-year-olds were set the same task and given a set of crayons including the appropriate colours. Their drawings are shown in figure 18. Alison seems to be the only one who has made no response to the shape of the object. Several of them already approach the selectivity and sophistication of the conventional representation. But it would seem to be presumptuous to make comparisons between them and say of some that they are 'better' or 'more accurate' or 'more advanced' representations than the others. The overwhelming impression is of a richness of response that can only be wondered at, leaving me with a feeling of regret that the openness of the situation for these children will soon enough become closed and stereotyped.

8   The six children mentioned in 4 were shown a cardboard model of an octahedron. Gary said immediately, 'It looks like a pyramid reflected in the river.' They handled it and talked about the ways in which it differed from the cardboard model of a cube. They did not have the language of

237

'faces', 'edges' and 'corners', but they knew 'triangle' and this was mentioned. With prompting they counted the number of triangles. The octahedron was said by one of them to be 'sharper' than a cube.

After this they each drew the octahedron.

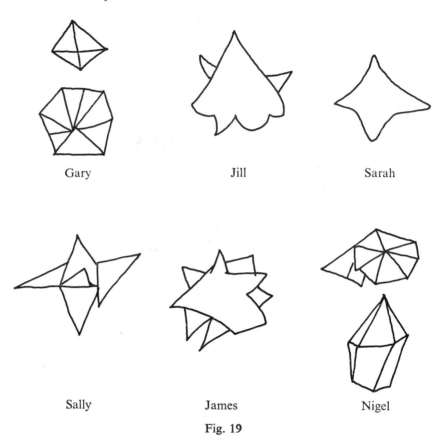

Gary         Jill         Sarah

Sally         James         Nigel

Fig. 19

I can risk saying that there is no chance that these children had previously been taught how to draw an octahedron. It looks as if they had probably drawn, or seen drawn, other diagrams involving triangles; but this is not certain. What emerges from the attempts—and it is particularly clear just because all the results are, in a sense, failures—is that the conventional organisation of graphic elements to produce a recognisable picture of an octahedron is extraordinarily sophisticated and complex. More striking still is the evident ability of these children to set about this almost impossible task in a thoughtful and controlled way. None of the drawings could be described as a guess or a shot in the dark. The more

238

mysterious drawings convince me that the children have created representations that say something about the octahedron which the conventional representation fails to transmit.

How silly of us to suppose that there is a right way, or even a best way, of drawing a cube or an octahedron, or whatever. It is an error comparable to that of thinking that there are uniquely virtuous algorithms for computing a difference or a product.

And yet...The analogy only holds to a limited extent. Making a representation is one thing. Flexibility in handling graphic elements and the rules of connection, juxtaposition and superposition, may produce more vivid and suggestive representations than conventional diagrams. But the

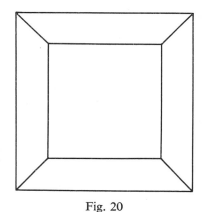

Fig. 20

conventional diagrams, especially of certain solids like the cube, cuboid and tetrahedron, are also required to act as symbols or icons. So although a drawing like fig. 20 is in some ways a 'better' representation of a cuboid for some purposes than the familiar version (it displays all eight vertices, and five faces rather than three), in its iconic form it has been schematised into a standardised substitute for a cuboid. Not only can we readily reproduce it by applying our learned sequence of graphic strokes, but we can instantly recognise it. We do not have to puzzle out what it stands for, or consciously construct a translation of it into visual imagery. For the vast majority of purposes we can say of it that it *is* a cuboid.

*In either case—making a representation or reproducing an icon—we have constructed a mapping from the object to the diagram, and we are able to say, of an element of the diagram, that it corresponds to a certain element of the object. (The mapping is not normally reversible.) But this is only a formulation of the operational characteristics of the completed diagram. It says nothing about our state of mind, or the focus of our attention, while we are in the act of drawing.*

9   A 7-year-old boy shown a tilted disc drew an ellipse and said: 'It goes like this; it looks as if it wasn't round, but it is round all the same.'[1]

10   It has frequently been said that a child does not draw what he sees but what he knows. This is supposed to account, for example, for the way in which a young child will draw a circle when he is shown a tilted dinner plate and asked to draw that. Maybe the dictum serves to rescue us from taking too naively realist a position on this, but it doesn't manage to suggest the real complexity inherent in acts of representation.

Any developed theory of representation will prove to be a function of several dependent variables. We shall have to draw a good deal from the work of the Gestalt psychologists about the kind of graphic configurations that are stable and unambiguous. (Arnheim's *Art and Visual Perception*[2] draws almost exclusively from this tradition.) We shall also need to take something from Piaget on the developing mental structurations involved in the experience of representation. But neither the Gestaltists, nor the Geneva school, give much attention to the power of cultural factors, and particularly language, in determining what is seen and how it is represented. Gombrich in *Art and Illusion*[3] comes nearest to giving due weight to these factors. A theory need not be an eclectic jumble if it subsumes these various sources. A very slight attempt to move towards a simple description of the complexity of graphic representation is given in *Notes on Mathematics in Primary Schools* (pp. 125–8).[4] This could be clarified and extended.

And the theory, if it is ever developed, will have as its first major postulate that man is an image-producing symbol-inventing metaphor-creating language-maker. All his intellectual activity is rooted in signs and symbols—replacements and substitutes and encapsulations organised by, and organising, his experience into an operational kitbag. The very young child, long before he has learned which particular signs and symbols are meaningful in his society, proves by his assiduity in seeking them that it is no surprise to him that human beings operate in the world in this way.

Making representations by drawing seems to involve three things: a set of symbols, a set of procedural rules of composition and substitution, and a set of criteria for matching and checking constructions against experience.

[1] Piaget, J. and Inhelder, B., *The child's conception of space*, Routledge, 1956.
[2] Arnheim, R., *Art and visual perception*. Faber, 1967.
[3] Gombrich, E. H., *Art and illusion*. Phaidon, 1962.
[4] A.T.M., *Notes on mathematics in primary schools*. Cambridge University Press, 1967.

(Catrina)

(Simon)

(Wendy)

(Linda)

Fig. 16

(Christine)

(Nicola)

(Katherine)

(Sarah)

Fig. 18

(Jane)

(Tim)

(Iain)

(Iain)

Fig. 18 (*continued*)

(Alison)

(Paul)

(Glyn)

(Shirley)

Fig. 18 (*continued*)

(I could almost be talking of mathematics itself.) Given an understanding of how cultural and social forces present them to the child, it is not difficult to appreciate the way the child comes to master the first two. But the third, the acquisition and application of reality checks, seems unutterably mysterious. I think of some of M. C. Escher's drawings,[1] and how they employ the conventional graphic symbols and the conventional rules of composing graphic symbols to produce drawings which fail to meet some of the criteria of experience. Escher is, I suppose, merely playing a game to show that strict adherence to the right procedural rules will not necessarily guarantee a successful representation. When someone else—say Picasso—breaks the rules and produces something which immediately seems a valid extension of the notion of representation I am baffled to know why the criteria have been shifted. If I analyse the Escher drawing in terms of the logical incompatibility of its component presentations, why should it not be equally to the point to assert that it is logically impossible to see two eyes in a head shown in profile? I am not yet sure whether I have asked a serious or a silly question.

More probably it is the wrong question....

## ACKNOWLEDGEMENT

I would like to thank the teachers and children who gave me the examples I have used.   D.W.

[1] Escher, M. C., *The drawings of M. C. Escher*. Oldbourne Press, 1967.

# INDEX

# INDEX